THE EMERGING SELF

THE EMERGING SELF

IN SCHOOL AND HOME

By L. Thomas Hopkins

Professor of Education, Teachers College, Columbia University

HARPER & BROTHERS

Publishers, New York

Contents

Contents

Preface

This book was conceived many years ago and has developed slowly since that time. It was one of the unwritten outcomes of my project for an advanced degree at Harvard University on *The Intelligence of Continuation School Children,* a study of young people who had left high school on job permits immediately upon reaching their fourteenth birthday. While working with three thousand pupils, their many teachers, and parents, I was impressed by three factors: the dislike of pupils for their schools, the belief of parents that their children were learning little of value to them, the testimony of teachers that they worked so hard trying to teach these pupils subject matter with such meager learning results.

As a superintendent of schools, I had heard these criticisms before from all three sources and I had tried some of the accepted practices for meeting them. For the first time, I realized that these superficial rearrangements of the existing program of education were inadequate, for the underlying causes went deeper into the culture, even to the foundation of our basic institutions. I extended my researches to study pupils who on external evidence were succeeding, only to discover that they, their parents, and their teachers had similar feelings toward what the school taught and the results achieved. And each person placed the cause of the unsatisfactory condition on the others, never admitting that he as a member of the team should assume any responsibility.

I then searched further to find out why present homes and

schools rear children with such unacceptable results. The answer of course is in the people themselves; for they tend to perpetuate the psychological environment in which they were reared, unless by some means they raise their self-maturity to the level where they can discriminate more intelligently among the factors in their development. Since this accidental method is too slow ever to develop enough people with the insight and courage to change their basic ways of life, I began to search with the students in my college classes for better means of helping more people to become conscious of the situation more rapidly and to study more hopeful directions of action.

This book is the result of that inquiry. I deal here with the theory and practice of the basic biological growth potential with which babies are born and by which they can become adults who continue to raise their self-maturity to heights heretofore unknown. Since many attitudes and patterns of behavior are formed in childhood years, I describe life in homes and schools, appraise its effects upon children and adults, and suggest how to improve conduct through better utilization of the growth process on higher deliberative levels of action.

The material has had the benefit of criticism of thousands of students in college classes in this and other countries; hundreds of parents in study and discussion groups; members of other professions, such as medicine, psychiatry, nursing, law, and social work; thousands of laymen to whom I have lectured; and hundreds of persons who have come to me voluntarily to find out how they can become the better selves toward which they strive. They helped me sharpen my perspective and focus my thinking.

The audience for this book is everyone interested in becoming a better self or in helping others to do so. More especially it is for students preparing to become teachers or administrators, for those in active educational service on all levels, for leaders of youth or adult groups, for parents and citizens consciously concerned for a more intelligent and effective direction of education for children, youth, and young adults.

The manuscript was read in part by high school and college students, preservice teachers, nurses, parents, college professors, teachers and administrators in service. Their suggestions are deeply appreciated. I am especially grateful to Professor Emeritus of Education William H. Kilpatrick, who as a colleague at Teachers College, Columbia University, inspired me to explore more fully this biological view of life and learning. To my wife, Hester Rich Hopkins, I am deeply indebted for constant encouragement throughout the years and for critical reading of the entire manuscript. With deep appreciation to everyone, I assume responsibility for the ideas included and the form in which they are presented.

L. Thomas Hopkins

Hophill
Truro, Cape Cod
Massachusetts

THE EMERGING SELF

Chapter **I**

WHAT MAY YOU EXPECT?

This book is addressed to the pressing problem of how to help people develop the mature forms of behavior necessary for integrated living in the modern world.

Man has constantly improved his efficiency in those areas of life that have produced his material comforts as well as the monsters that can destroy him. He has not yet developed his emotional and social stability, his creative functional intelligence, that basic process of learning necessary to make his gadgets as well as his other activities work to his own good. His institutions are attuned to the conditions of earlier days when life had a simpler rhythm, the stresses and strains were less numerous and profound, the demands upon him were fewer, and his decisions affected only persons in a limited area. Now his life is complex, the tempo is increased, the upsets are many and deep, and the consequences of his decisions affect people everywhere. Man must now face himself as the great problem in his world.

Man has the capacity to become a more mature self, but he lacks the environment in which to develop it. His inherited concepts of what culture is, how it should be transmitted, the ways it can be improved, how his institutions can serve him, are disabilities rather than tools. These external conditions groove his actions, restrict his growth, limit his thinking to accepted areas, suppress his attempts to improve his behavior, deny him the opportunity to develop creatively the potential ability with which he was born. He faces the dilemma that he can either continue to allow his past experiences to restrict his development, or utilize them to release his ability to create the new forms of behavior necessary to bring the good life to everyone.

Man makes the quality of his life out of the materials of his world—himself and his external environment. Any improvement must come through him. Each person is the center of his life; man is the center of his world. His concept of his world becomes, through his experiences, the agent of his maturation. The qualitative expression of his perception is his behavior here and now—what he does to himself and how he treats others. He must improve his knowledge of himself, of the way in which the conditions in his external world are affecting his growth, and of his competence to use both to his good. He must discover himself.

To improve himself and his world man must improve the quality of his experiences. The only things man has ever studied or thought about are the experiences of others alive or dead, and his own present efforts to become himself. The problems which he now faces are an outgrowth of years of concentration upon the experiences of his ancestors to the neglect of his own. He has been misled into believing that he should pattern his life after that of some relatively great geniuses of the past while disparaging his own ability to create ways of making his life better in the present. Yet his only capital for learning is his own experience.

The quickest and best approach to this problem is through the education of young people in homes and schools. Three aspects of this task must be considered. The first is to help today's adults to keep the world stable until a more mature younger generation can grow up. The second is to educate children in a period of eighteen to twenty-five years through a natural learning process which they can and will use to continue their later development. The third is to help today's youth in secondary schools and colleges to understand so clearly the real meaning and purpose of home and family life that they will give their children the advantage of a better learning process and expect it to be continued in the schools.

The quality of living is the quality of people managing their experiences together toward common purposes. This is a continuous relationship, a dynamic, ongoing activity. In the succeeding pages I describe this vital person-to-person interaction through words which are not the happening, the thing-in-itself, the face-to-face association, the movement which is life. I write about the inner feelings, thoughts, and overt behaviors of people searching for ways of making their experiences better. I can picture their struggle to free themselves from the early behavior patterns that block their conscious desire to improve themselves. I cannot bring to you the thing, the situation, the life experience. I can only try to catch with words their onward movement to find themselves. The problem of becoming mature cannot be solved by a mathematical formula, for the center is people with many living variables. All anyone can do is to help others become more aware of it, to explore its limits, to locate its dominant center, and to suggest directions of action which show greater promise for a better life in the future.

This book is written around a few basic principles. Some of these will be stated in different chapters with a varied approach and a specialized emphasis but with a consistent point of view. To accept them as guides for action, a reader must view them broadly and intimately, for he must take them into himself in an emotional context within his experience which makes assimilation possible. The simple statement for initial perusal which leads only to superficial acquaintance and the studied approach resulting in only academic knowledge are both valueless. As the view of a mountain is different from the four cardinal points of the compass so a principle of behavior must be examined from different approaches better to comprehend its significance. These principles are stated positively for emphasis to promote reflection, not as dogmatic affirmations of universal truths.

1. *The essence of all life is change.* Every living organism exists in constant interaction with its environment. This relationship is so close that some biologists assert the organism and its environment are one and inseparable. At least they are interdependent, for through interaction the organism alters itself in whole or in part and modifies in some way the external conditions. And the changing external conditions in turn affect the alterations which the organism makes in itself. This constant dynamic, interrelated movement is called change. Without it life as we know it ceases to exist. But change of itself is not concerned with quality. It carries no prediction for better or worse. Everyone must face it as the essence of life, and guide the immanent organic energy into actions for the benefit of the growing individual and for the good of mankind. This is our unique opportunity to affect the development of self and others.

2. *The continuity of all life is process.* The term "process" refers to the succession of interrelated movements of an organism which produces the changes in itself and its environment. Some persons hold that process, like change, implies no quality. Others believe that the biological life process does imply quality since the change is emergent, bringing into being something which was not there before. When the change lacks quality either the life process does not function normally owing to external controls or the change emergent in such process is not favorably accepted by the organism's environment.

I assume that the biological life process is qualitative, that quality of living is a function of the quality of the process.

High-quality learning develops in and through an enhancement of the life process, while low-quality learning accompanies its restriction or regimentation. Those who wish to
improve learning in school or home must better understand
in action this life or biological growth process. For it is ever
present, it operates continuously, and it cannot be denied if
the life is to continue.

3. *All life has direction.* Every life activity has direction,
for it begins and ends somewhere. The beginning may sometimes be lost, but some locus or end in view always prevails
until the activity ceases. Such direction is immanent in the
interactive, organism–environment relationship. Changes in
the organism or its environment are always moving toward
life-fulfillment. All life is composed of cells which are a mass
of circumscribed protoplasm containing a nucleus. All cells
have common characteristics such as metabolism, motion,
change in shape or size, sensitivity to the external environment, ability to reproduce themselves or the organism of
which they are a part. Man is a specialized embodiment of the
life process of a single cell. He moves to fulfill himself by
striving toward the highest conscious integrative action possible within his inherited capacity. The child has to learn
how to achieve this directive existence by qualitative learning
through the use of higher brain centers. Our great opportunity as adults is to help him better understand himself in
the conscious realities of his life process of which direction is
an important aspect.

4. *All growing, behaving, learning are differentiated
aspects of or are creative emergents from the same biological
life process.* Every aspect of growing up to life-fulfillment or
self-enhancement stems from or is an integral part of the same
basic process. Adults break this down into growth areas such
as physical, emotional, social, moral, mental. Almost universally they accept the basic biological process of physical
growth but ignore its crucial importance to all other aspects

of self-development. They reflect the cultural myth that mental development with its emotional and social concomitants is controlled, directed, and evaluated by forces outside the individual. This theory was accepted and transmitted long before people knew much about biology. It is based upon a priori reasoning rather than experimental evidence or experiential insight.

The child is born into a world of conflict. He *must* grow up according to his inherited biological process, extended into the realms of conscious understanding and acceptance of himself and others. Yet adults in his environment constantly reverse the process by insisting upon specific behaviors. This places the child in a serious dilemma which blocks his own self-development. School and home are important forces in maintaining this great dichotomy. The urgent educational problem is how to change homes and schools quickly and effectively so that their beliefs and practices harmonize with the known facts of the biological growth or life process. The child may then discover his inherited capacities and develop them by normal energy release in all life activities.

5. *Self-enhancement or self-maturity or self-fulfillment has no fixed upper limit.* The whole man does not stop growing when his body does. The self includes more than the mere physical aspect. It is a living, unique, becoming person—accepted inwardly as "I" and observed by outsiders as a complex of behaviors that distinguishes one individual organism from all others. Maturity of self is not reached at an early age, to remain more or less fixed throughout life. Any person can go on maturing or becoming so long as the heart can supply enough oxygen and other nutrients in the blood stream to keep the brain active.

Physical handicaps need not check such maturing. Those limitations that are placed upon it by the individual are because of demands of the regressive cultural environment. Many children inwardly and outwardly comply with these demands while others reject and rebel against them. These ways of reacting are external evidence of abnormal internal self-development. Every child arrests his maturity at some point to save as much as possible of himself. Outside persons are so interested in protecting these external regressive forces that they have neither time nor desire to help him. The home and school as major social institutions have a definite responsibility for the existing immaturity of people and a great opportunity to furnish the conditions through which the younger generation may reach higher levels of self-development.

6. *Maturity is developed or hindered by all life activities in or out of the school or the home.* Changes in some form and in some direction take place in every individual at all times, however slight or violent they may seem to him or to others. Life experiences are never neutral. They move the individual upward toward higher functional behavior, arrest his development temporarily at or near the existing level, or push him backward to more immature actions. The school has the unique opportunity and purpose of maintaining at all times an environment in which each individual may find the best conditions for continuous upward movement toward self-fulfillment. This means that in all of his activities he is learning, first, how to release, conceptualize, and focus his past experience, and second, how to select and incorporate new experience by positive creative assimilation. Under such conditions each person is consciously active and alert, his ego-structure is in fluid organization, his learning process is creatively improved, and his direction of action is thoughtfully self-enhancing. The school more than any other institution can help all children develop their creative growth process so that they can and will use it in all life activities.

7. *Every individual constantly strives for the good life or the better life as he sees it.* This effort is so universal with all individuals that it suggests a strong biological base. Cultural variations are the results of such common strivings in different

environments. Behavior at all times is an individual's best under his immediate circumstances. Persons with different perceptions of the same situation arrive at different actions. All are moving toward the good or better life, but they disagree as to the existing conditions and what they mean for the future. People must learn how to live together by cooperative interaction better to examine common situations realistically and take action which shows promise of achieving the better life. To help people live on the higher levels of deliberative group action is an important function of the school.

8. *To move progressively toward a better life each person must continuously improve the quality of the meanings which constitute himself.* All behavior of every individual is an attempt to satisfy his needs so as to enhance himself. Some of these needs are superficial, some penetrate deeply into the center of the self. Whether they be shallow or deep he always meets them at the outset with perceptions, meanings, and values derived from his past experience. When unforeseen conditions prevent them from operating to bring need-satisfaction, he creates around the novel situation new meanings which he uses to reorganize his experience and his concept of self. Under normal life conditions each individual continuously modifies his perceptions of internal and external influences, while maintaining with his environment a fluid but organized interdependence. These new meanings cannot be given to him ready made by some older person or institution. Such hand-me-down meanings restrict his process of creative assimilation and eventually arrest his self-development. Each person must learn how to create his new meanings with others in common life situations.

9. *The school program must be built around basic conditions which foster self-maturity.* Every school program is composed of two interrelated and interdependent parts, activity and direction. The two have to be in harmony. The activity must flow into the direction or the direction must be possible

within the activity. Every school must furnish the conditions, promote the kinds of activities to lead in the direction of their better self-development. Every educator, parent, taxpayer, citizen should look at his school system to see whether it can fulfill such promise. Every parent should examine his home life to see if the activities and direction encourage meaningful behaviors which children can thoughtfully modify toward mature adult actions. Parents and educators interested in improving the behavior of children and adults must encourage organized institutions or social groups to examine their beliefs, activities, and directions better to furnish the conditions which promote maturity. Adults can then cooperate toward a common end, with the school as the vital center, concentrating on the development and spread of the process through which normal growth is fostered and maintained.

10. *The professional competence of teachers lies in their understanding and use of the unitary biological growth process.* Such competence has two interrelated and variable aspects. First, teachers must know how to use this process in meeting their own needs. They must see how they create in their experiences the new meanings through which they continuously enhance themselves. Any person who is not improving himself tends to arrest at a lower level the development of others with whom he associates. While this condition may prevail in life, it cannot be tolerated in teachers from nursery school through university. Second, teachers must be proficient in helping others to develop their life experiences by this process. A teacher cannot help another use his biological growth process adequately until he first sees how it functions in his own life. He must respect it in everyone, even though he may not agree with the result. As he helps children understand and use it, their behaviors will emerge into new and better actions based upon more refined meanings. They will have no guilt, fear, or stigma attached to earlier performances supported by their best perceptions at that time. The

elementary teacher or college professor examines his own behavior in order to assess the status of his continuing effort to improve his ability to guide children or students in making their own self-assessments. How to do this should be given major emphasis in professional education.

11. *The perception of a situation by the behaver is more important in determining his behavior than the perception of an observer.* A life situation usually includes a number of people, each behaving according to his perceptions and each observing the behavior of others according to his perceptions. Not having the perceptions of the behaver, the observer frequently disagrees with his actions. Not having the perceptions of the observer, the behaver cannot act accordingly. Each sees the situation as colored by the many variables that constitute his unique self. Each must allow the other to do just that, for neither should expect his behaviors from another who lacks his perceptions. This book is written from the standpoint of the behaver: the child facing the life situations of his experience, the adolescent meeting his accumulating problems in his expanding world, the graduate student facing demands which may enhance or wreck his life purposes within a few hours. Parents, teachers, college professors— each with different levels of maturity—are also a vital part of these situations which the growing behaver faces. The persistent problem is whose perceptions shall prevail in determining what is desirable behavior. The judgments of older, powerful observers which still dominate group behavior are largely responsible for existing unsatisfactory world conditions. Examining behavior from the point of view of the behaver has many possibilities for improving living which the older viewpoint lacks.

The control of education through the perceptions and behaviors of adults began in Alexandria more than twenty-two centuries ago. After the decline of Athens as a center of the ancient world the scholars moved to Alexandria where, with the help of local rulers, they established a school to teach the wisdom of the great Greek scholars as recorded in books. This was the perception of their situation by the scholars who founded the schools. It was not the peception of Socrates, Plato, or Aristotle, who uttered the words or brought together the materials recorded in the books. These three spoke and wrote from a vantage point of recognition of a unitary biological process—as does everyone who creatively assimilates his environment. But the Alexandrians did not recognize this. They faced their needs with their perceptions within their knowledge of their biological process, but reached conclusions which denied this same process to their students and to future generations. These scholars took the results of the normal biological process of Plato and Aristotle and taught them as end behaviors, minus the process used to create them. Since they eliminated the original creativeness, they impressed these fixed end behaviors or truths in the minds of others by different means.

The Alexandrians began the reverse teaching procedures which are now standard educational practice not only in schools but in almost all aspects of western culture. Their action was the most deliberative of which they were capable. In the light of modern knowledge their perceptions were limited and inadequate. The result is the inability of present generations everywhere to face their problems of living and learning realistically.

12. *The normal biological unit of growing, behaving, learning is a child facing and acting in his own need-situation with his own perceptions by his own process.* The abnormal or teaching unit of learning is a child trying to face or meet a need-situation of an adult whose perceptions he (the child) is unable to understand. This dichotomy between a learner trying—within his perceptions—to face and act in his own situations as intelligently as he can and the demand of adults that he face and act in their situations with their

perceptions and behaviors results in an enormous loss and misdirected use of learning energy. Any individual who tries to understand his own behavior better to make empathic contact with other behavers must rethink the traditional concepts of learning. Usually he finds emotional difficulty in reconverting his teaching methods—for which he expended so much energy—even when he recognizes their ineffectiveness.

The evidence to support these few basic principles comes from experience, which is the only material anyone ever can or does study. Every individual justifies his behavior by his own experience, for he has no other source upon which to support it. The quality of his behavior and the quality of the evidence to sustain it are therefore the quality of his experience. But the quality of the experience is a function of the quality of the process by which it was derived. Experience thoughtfully and critically appraised, verified by emotional and conceptual consequences to the self and to others, is better experience than that accepted by emotional contagion or by authority without the benefit of such constructive evaluation. Such appraisal does not mean that people will judge the behavior alike, but they should be able to agree on the basic characteristics of the process towards its improvement. Each person, therefore, improves his experience by helping others improve theirs, for in the interaction both constructively evaluate themselves.

Since every individual supports his behavior by his experience each must respect and accept his experiences in order to improve his actions and himself. Respecting and accepting do not mean crystallizing or formalizing. Every individual has to establish certain behavior patterns to give order, consistency, and predictability to his actions for his own inner security and for better interaction with others. These behaviors should be established by the self as a fluid unity, constantly and thoughtfully modified through new experience. Respecting and accepting mean facing the fact that all behavior emanates from and is validated in experience, and using every intelligent way to improve its quality. Many students, educators, and laymen are afraid to justify their own behavior through their own experience. They search for some source outside themselves in books, the culture, stronger individuals, or higher authorities. They do not realize that they are supporting their actions through their own experience but that their dependence upon outside sources keeps the quality low.

The source of evidence to support these principles is my own experience. I have consciously and deliberately derived them by thinking about it with the help of learners on all levels from nursery school through graduate schools. From my earliest reactions to teachers manipulating me and others in classes, from my reflections on my own teaching, from my observations of other teachers as their supervisor or administrator, one perception is outstanding. Teachers work hard applying all the methods which they were taught, always with the same two predictable results. First, the amount and quality of subject matter learned by the pupil is small; second, the effort, both internal and external, expended by pupil and teacher in achieving this meager result is high. In existing traditional schools teachers and pupils may expect little learning from great effort when there should be much learning from great effort or meager learning from slight effort.

Fortunately I discovered early in my career—while teaching to high school seniors the United States history required by state law for a diploma—the effects of misdirected energy due to reverse methods. I used the textbook, state syllabus, and other outlines but at the end of two months I realized that all was not well. I expended increasing effort, the pupils read with decreasing meaning, the general atmosphere was unwholesome and explosive.

On Monday morning I said, "You are not happy and neither am I. This is an unwholesome feeling for all of us.

Yet we must continue since this subject is required by law and you all want to obtain your high school diplomas. Let us forget about history today and talk about what is wrong, why things are not going right, what we can do together to make them better. Let us begin with what is wrong as you see it." During that period there was more or less good-natured sparring for an opening which I sensed would come when pupils felt sure of themselves. The next day the oldest boy (much older than I) said, "Do you *really* want to know what is wrong here?" "Of course I do," said I. "If you are sure you really want to know then I will tell you. The trouble is that you are a rotten teacher." Catching my breath, I said to the group, "I can see by your faces that you all agree with Dick. And I think you are right. But I do not want to be a rotten teacher. I want to be a good teacher. If you can spot a rotten teacher you must also know what makes a good teacher. So will you take over the job, with my help, of making me this year into the good teacher that you would like to have?"

After recovering from their shock they agreed to do this, and for the next three weeks we discussed teachers from their point of view. I learned more from them on what constitutes good teaching or why the gap between teaching and learning exists than I did from all of the subject matter or education courses that I paid for in college to obtain my teaching certificate. We discarded the textbook, syllabus, and outlines. As we planned together, I saw for the first time why they were disturbed. They wanted to develop their own purposes within their own need-experiences, which is the normal way of learning.

While their immediate interests were far removed from conventional history, they were within the area of their cultural heritage. I went along with them, supporting my position by recalling the meaning of the frontier in American life so ably stated by Frederick Jackson Turner. After helping them see how they grew up in their local environment, we studied how other people grow in their cultures and eventually how the early inhabitants of the United States laid the foundation for the democracy which they expected and accepted as their birthright. By developing the experience cooperatively each pupil increased the range and clarity of his meanings. At the end of the year there was consensus on two points. They now liked history and I was a better teacher.

Every teacher is a better teacher, every parent is a better parent, every member of any group is a better member, when he helps others respect their experience and themselves. Since direction of behavior should be constantly toward maturity, all school subjects and all other life activities should contribute toward that end. Each individual should constantly examine through interaction the experiences of others to judge their worth to him in improving his. He should have some consciously formulated simple tests which can be generally applied. One such test is easy to use and gives immediate results.

How and in what spirit does the observer offer his experience? Does he offer it as the best, the final word, the highest authority, which others should accept with little or no modification? If so, it is safe to assume that he has inadequately appraised and verified it. He has overlooked pertinent factors; he has derived it by a deficient process; he is not interested in improving himself or helping others to do likewise. Or does the person share his experience with others as a resource for them to modify in order to meet their individual needs? If so, it is safe to assume that he has thoughtfully appraised and verified it in action. He is interested in helping others improve themselves, and he has developed his experience by a process which permits them to do so. Any child or adult can tell who is the better teacher or parent by the way he uses his experience in interaction with others.

Many adults believe that individual experience should never be accepted as evidence to support a principle, rule, or truth. They maintain that it must be quantified or verified through experiences of others. His perceptions of his experience by a witness is accepted as evidence in a jury trial. They are generally supported by other witnesses, but theirs are not the perceptions of the first, even though they fall within the same area. Some items in every experience can always be verified quantitatively. I am writing on a pad of paper which contains forty-eight sheets and I have just had them counted by another person who agrees. But this pronouncement is a minor detail in determining the quality of what I write, for my meanings are value judgments derived from sources broader and deeper than this mathematical fact or any other quantitative knowledge. No individual ever acts on facts or any externally quantified data. He acts on the personalized meaning or relationship of such data to his developing purposes. He wants to know whether others agree or disagree with certain small parts of experience, but he must appraise such knowledge as part of the experience as a whole in order to achieve his need-fulfillment. While I believe that I have derived these principles by critically appraising my experience in interaction with others, readers will judge its quality by the way I place it before them.

A source of evidence used to support these principles is the experience of others now living and engaged in creative endeavors in many areas of life. I have exchanged mind-picking with anyone on every possible occasion anywhere. Regardless of his economic or social status every person who approaches his life activities creatively has been a great stimulation not only in broadening and deepening my experiences but in giving interpretative testimony to my principles.

There was the boot polisher in the London hotel who read the lives of people through their shoes, the cab driver in Paris who in snatches of German, French, and English gave a penetrating analysis of world conditions and his relationship thereto, the waiter in the hotel in Venice who had been a prisoner of war of Fascists and Communists and who in fault-less English described the effects of these systems upon a personality. I recall the carriage driver in Interlaken who was noncommunicative until I told him the age of his horse by looking at his teeth, whereupon he released both a friend-liness and a penetrating insight into Swiss life. Then there was the Canadian World War II veteran engineer who came over to the car to talk with an outsider about his personal problems while keeping a watchful eye on the construction workers. The lumberman in the Ozark mountains was cutting the last big oaks in that area and trying to figure out what might have been "if people only had sense enough to use the land different." I must not forget the specialists in various fields whose opinions carry weight with some people: leading thinker-researchers in medicine, psychiatry, psychotherapy, psychobiology, biology in its many branches, sociology, biochemistry, anthropology, dynamic logic, and the new religion. There are also artists, professional writers in many areas, businessmen, fathers, mothers, and children. All of these many people trying to appraise critically their own experiences have shared their feelings and thoughts with me and I in turn have contributed my best to them.

Many persons believe that a viewpoint, a group of principles, or a position which deviates from traditional practice is acceptable only in so far as it is supported by scholars who write their need-satisfaction in books. I assume that some readers have the same feeling. I am appending a list of selected references[1] which I hope will help you reflect on some of the underlying researches in other fields. These references are not in conventional subjects required for college degrees or considered to be the essence of a liberal education, for these older disciplines approach learning from the standpoint of the adult observer. I have listed only titles that present

[1] See pages 357-360 ff.

learning from the point of view of the behaver. These books are in the newer and more vigorous frontier areas where materials are not yet crystallized into traditional compartments. There is, however, an occasional reference to a traditional field in which some author has shifted toward a behaver outlook.

Parents, teachers, students, and laymen are always impressed with the fact that subject teaching based upon external control by adults is the reverse of the normal biological process based upon the need-experiences of the learner. They want to know if, today, there are teachers who approach education through the eyes of the learner. There are some. Every teacher who is rated high by students approaches learning in terms of his pupils' experiences regardless of what he teaches. But such teachers are the exception. The institution known as the school, whether public or private, elementary or graduate, is based upon and organized around the reverse cultural teaching method. The problem is how to extend the recognition of the principle of biological learning so that it is the basic process in all schools.

Parents, teachers, and students also ask me to give them in a few words specific directions for using their biological life process in home, school, church, hospital, or business. They want a procedure, formula, or specific-response method for quickly improving the quality of experience. No such formula or quick method exists or is likely to be found in the future. A dynamic, creative interaction of live individuals with a modifiable environment cannot be established. Rather, one must study all variables in ongoing life situations to locate the novel, crucial aspects around which new meanings must be created. The behaver does this through a few fluid principles verified in action. He learns a better process for improving his experiences by using intelligently the process in experience.

The only formula anyone can recommend is to begin using

the biological growth process at birth and to continue with it until death. Since adults have selves organized through a reverse process, they should begin to study themselves through their behavior in their psychological fields, relying on their improved experience to verify their actions. This is sometimes called "functional thinking" or "acting on thinking" as distinguished from acquiring static organization of academic knowledge or learning fixed procedures, practices, or behaviors. This strikes deeply into persons who believe they improve the experience of others by giving them increasing quantities of information taken from books on an ascending scale of academic difficulty. They confuse quantity of second-hand information with quality of behavior. This is a valid conclusion from their perception of their experience, which has not yet been creatively appraised in action.

All learning has three relationships or aspects or effects which operate simultaneously. One is to the self, a second is to others in the immediate environment, and the third is to the larger world or universe of which the interacting individuals are members. What one believes or does toward others, and what one conceives is his place in the great universe are dependent upon what he is to himself. And what he accepts himself to be is a function of the quality of his interaction from infancy to majority. If his relationships to others and to his world are taught as specific responses under authoritarian control, his self never matures so that he can deal intelligently with the larger issues of his total existence. And a proposed remedy of teaching him more specifics in international relations or the brotherhood of man is of no avail, since the original disparagement of the self and his experiences cannot be overcome by further manipulation of the external environment. The condition can only be corrected at its source through normal learning in the early years.

In common with others, I want to make this world a better place for a child to be born, to grow into maturity, to contribute wisely to his fellow men, and to leave to younger generations a greater opportunity to clarify their biological growth process through which they may achieve the better life. Students say that this is too idealistic. They want something more practical, which to them means specific behaviors for specific situations following the life pattern in which they were reared. They have not yet understood that the most practical value in life for layman or educator is a theory of behavior tested in interpersonal situations. Ideals which exist outside a pragmatic process for improving experience lack adequate quality in all three behavior relationships. They are derived by the self and are as meaningful in action as the maturity of the idealist.

People have the inherited capacity to develop a better life. They have ample need but they lack knowledge of the process through which to release and direct their energy toward this end. In this book you may expect to find out how to locate better your needs, how to study them by a normal biological process to fulfillment by higher levels of deliberative action, how to help others—children and adults—understand their need processes so as to become better selves. Thus may all people, impelled by their creative power and guided by their emerging intelligence, become united in spirit, process, and performance. The chapters which follow are designed to make such an ideal a reality in daily living.

Chapter **II**

WHY HAVE SCHOOLS?

The schools are people, young and old, living and working together. They are teachers and children in kindergarten and elementary grades; adolescents in various classes in high school; students with their professors in college and graduate groups. They are adults and their leaders in workshops trying to find better ways of solving their pressing problems. But that is not all. Schools are parents who conceive, nurture, rear children into adulthood. They are professional persons who read, study, discuss, think, plan how to help each other and younger people improve their living together. They are adults who pay taxes even though they have no children. Schools are really all the people in the communities which they serve. They are not buildings or equipment, textbooks or courses of study, supplies or teaching materials. And this is as it should be. For people, young or old, change, develop, grow year by year. They live so as to help each become a normal wholesome person. They have schools so that each may reach higher maturity, develop better interpersonal relations, become the ever more adequate self which is the operating center of their personality.

WHY ARE PEOPLE SO IMPORTANT TO EACH OTHER?

People are the most important continuous influence in the lives of everyone—children, adolescents, young adults, older

persons. They determine whether or not a child is wellborn.
They lay the early emotional foundation of his personality.
They define the attitudes and values which he must accept or
reject. They teach him a psychology of learning or a basic
way of meeting new and unforeseen problems of life. They
affect deeply and permanently his working relationships with
his agemates and with adults. And their influence is continuous in every life situation. The doll, the blocks, the sand, the
toys, the picture books, the food, the bed are important inter-
mittently to the young child, but the psychological effect of
people is active on and in him at all times whether he be
awake or asleep. During the early years in school people affect
the ways a child learns to read, write, and spell. Even an
adolescent doing his homework in algebra in his own room
feels the human situation out of which the assignment was
made and anticipates the effects of his labors on the pupils
and teacher tomorrow. Only he knows how encouraging or
depressing his class may be. Human factors are a powerful
influence on each child in learning every school subject,
whether in the first grade or the secondary school.

What has been said about children and adolescents is
equally true of young adults. The high school graduate who
applies for a job finds that employers evaluate the self within
him as well as his competence in a specific skill. After being
employed he must be able to get along with his associates
in order to continue in the job. As he assumes more and more
adult roles and responsibilities, he finds that people are a
crucial factor in every kind of activity in which he engages.
And what he becomes in later life is affected by how they have
helped him shape his behavior through all the preceding
years. In the twilight period people seem to be even more
dependent upon each other. They develop yearnings for
companionship similar to the emotional cravings of children
for social warmth and belongingness. Thus people have a
profound effect upon the personalities of each other. There

seems to be no way of eliminating such effect, not even through psychoses.

Emphasis upon people in the maturation of personality does not deny other influences. Every individual must have food, shelter, clothing. He is surrounded by a physical universe of trees, rocks, air, water, sunshine, and storms. He is born within a culture which has its written and unwritten records of past achievements, present demands, future expectations. He is a member of many institutions—home, school, church, intimate group, gang—all with traditions and a body of developing practices over which he may have little influence. He may live in the country or the city, on a farm or in a slum, in a hot or a cold climate, no one of which may have been of his own choosing. His family may have wealth, position, power, or it may have a marginal income, low social status, general insecurity.

But the external conditions which appear to be physical or nonhuman are really people in their relationships to him. For people create the situations that become the powerful psychological needs which he must resolve to develop normally. Not even siblings or identical twins at home or in the same school find the same psychological situations or develop the same ways of meeting their life problems. The nonhuman environment thus facilitates or retards maturity through the way people interact in its presence while taking it into account as one of many factors in a situation.

Schools exist primarily to facilitate the living and learning of children and young people or older persons who wish to increase their competence in certain areas. Children are required by law to attend a school or to receive equivalent instruction for a certain number of years or until they acquire a designated educational competence. After that period attendance is voluntary for those who can qualify for admission. Whether compulsory or voluntary, schools are organized on the theory that some older and more mature people will help younger or less mature people improve the quality of their learning. The teaching or learning relationship is that of a person with a broader experience who knows more, instructing another with a limited experience who knows less. This traditional theory is founded on two principles. One is that the older and more experienced person knows what he is to teach to the less experienced person prior to the teaching situation. The other is that the child or less mature person needs and wants to learn what the older person is competent to teach him. The teacher does not enlarge his experience or learn much of what he is to teach in the teaching situation. He is not a learner in it in the same sense that the pupil is a learner in the same experience. He will necessarily learn something that he never knew before, but his position is primarily that of a teacher who knows, while that of the pupil is primarily that of a learner who is to be informed.

Regardless of the functions of adults and children, living and learning situations are never static. They change constantly from day to day and from year to year. They move in some direction determined by someone before, during, or after the learning situation or perhaps in all three positions at different times. All life situations are people interacting through common or individual purposes which guide their activities and efforts. Direction is always present whether it is recognized and consciously formulated by those within or without the learning experience or whether it is an unconscious compulsion laid down in the immature years of childhood. Schools organized by adults to improve the living and learning of their children have direction whether or not it is thoughtfully defined and deliberately followed. The program, traditional or modern, involves activity regardless of how it is named. The activity begins somewhere and goes to someplace which defines its direction. The quality of the activity is a function of the quality of the direction, for neither blind adherence to tradition nor impulsive acceptance of everything new can make better schools. Every activity must be thoughtfully chosen to contribute to a direction consciously formulated and accepted.

Since schools exist to help young people develop into mature adults, questions immediately arise. First, what is the direction which adults want in the education of their children through the schools? Second, is such direction a desirable one for children? Third, if such direction is desirable, is the present program of education effective in helping children achieve it? Fourth, if the present program is ineffective, what changes will make it more valuable to children and more satisfactory to adults?

WHAT DIRECTION DO ADULTS WANT IN THE EDUCATION OF CHILDREN?

During the past hundred years many studies have been made on this question. For the last twenty-five years they have increased both in number and in accuracy of methods. They have been made with parents, citizens at large, and special groups and organizations such as businessmen, farmers, labor unions, newspaper and magazine editors, religious groups. From them certain conclusions are drawn.

1. Adults want the direction of education to be expressed in behavior. They judge the quality of education through the behavior of their own and other children in the various roles they play in adult life—in the home, on the job, in the community. They judge the behavior after the child leaves school, whatever the number of years attended. They make such judgments as external observers of the actions of the younger people, and the judgments are based upon established social norms, customs, or the acceptable behavior for the community. These observations are generally modified to fit the class to which the individual belongs, the position he holds in community life, and the number of years he has been in

school. Rarely are judgments of the behavior of young people by adults based upon the point of view of the younger person who is behaving. Adults are less concerned with understanding the behavior of a person to discover why and how he acts than they are with evaluating his behavior by existing standards. So adults think the direction of education is expressed by behavior from their vantage point as external observers, not from the internal point of view of the behaver.

Adults want schools to prepare children to meet adequately future roles in life according to adult standards of behavior. They rightly believe that behaviors of children in early years have an important relation to their behavior in adult years. So they evaluate the behavior of a six-year-old not only by what is acceptable for his age in his environment, but also by its relationship to what will be expected later of him. Frequently the requirement of a six-year-old is a miniature version of the adult standard.

2. The forms of behavior which adults expect their children to develop fall into two large groups. The first is general behaviors. The second is specific behaviors. This order has been constant in this country for the past hundred years. The general forms of behavior are described by adults under such headings as character traits, moral responsibilities, and personality characteristics. More specifically they use such terms as dependability, reliability, honesty, initiative, enterprise, creativeness, ability to size up a situation, willingness to accept responsibility, reasonableness, good working relations with others. They expect younger people to exhibit the behaviors which they as external observers call thoughtful, deliberative, intelligent ways of meeting everyday problems with due regard for and consideration of the rights of others. In modern terminology they expect children to develop mature personalities.

Adults also expect children to learn specific behaviors in certain fields of knowledge such as reading, writing, arithmetic, geography, and history. These behaviors are generally classified as the expanded three R's, but new streamlined terms are being introduced such as the core curriculum, general education, and persistent problems of living. Adults insist that schools teach children not only the basic facts in the development of our country, but also information about present world movements—their antecedents, the existing forces which keep them alive, their probable future developments. Adults accept the proposition that the greater the amount of such specific knowledge, the better the behavior of the individual. This is a powerful reason why they want the three R's, essentials for the acquisition of adult knowledge-behavior, taught to children in their early school years.

3. Adults believe that achievement of proficiency in these general and specific behaviors is inadequate, not only while children are in school but after they leave, regardless of number of years of education or degrees granted. There is ample evidence to justify such a conclusion. Any school or school system can show by its usual methods of external measurement and evaluation that the quality of learning by children in these two groups of behaviors is unsatisfactory both for present living and for later adult roles. Educators are more concerned about this condition than are adults, for it offers a profound challenge to their professional competence. In many communities professional and lay groups are working cooperatively to study and remedy this condition.

4. Adults agree that the general and specific behaviors are learned simultaneously through the school's educational program. This is a sound observation since the entire organism is involved in all learning, even though there are different degrees of activation of the various organs. When an individual learns, he learns all over. Psychologists say that he learns many things simultaneously. While he is learning a specific skill he is also learning working relations with people in that situation. If he is studying general working relations

with people, he is extending and refining his knowledge about some topic, event, or concrete situation since he cannot improve his interpersonal relàtions in a vacuum. The evidence supports the view that general and specific behaviors develop concurrently in each life situation.

5. Adults disagree as to what relationship between the general and specific behaviors should direct the program of education offered their children in school. The difference is one of means and ends. Shall the governing direction be toward personality maturity with the expanded three R's taught as a means toward that end? Shall the program be organized to teach the fixed knowledges and skills in the various subjects, with personality development as concomitant to such teaching?

Because adults differ on this relationship, they also disagree on the activities and methods for achieving the desired behaviors. Some assert that inadequate learning or behavior in the three R's or general education stems from poor teaching. They believe that improved teaching of these specifics will naturally bring better personality and sounder character. They advocate greater stress on knowledge fundamentals as a reliable method of improving both types of behavior. Other adults are equally committed to the belief that self and personality development must be the controlling direction in education. They see the self as the source of behavior, using subjects as variable data for its growth. To them both general and specific behaviors vary with individual needs. Neither group would eliminate or lessen the value of either type of behavior. The argument is over which comes first.

While such disagreement exists, the general tendency of adults is to make the specific behaviors or three R's the operating center of the education program and thus the chief directional factor in it. They believe, first, in the direct action value of objective knowledge, second, in the direct teaching of such information under external controls, and third, in the use of more rigorous external controls to overcome deficiencies in learning. Adults further tend to believe that general personality behaviors are learned as concomitants of such direct teaching of specific knowledge and skills. When general behaviors are inadequate or unsatisfactory, the remedy lies in more emphasis upon or improved teaching of the specifics. There are many reasons why adults hold this belief. It will be examined at various points throughout the book.

6. Educators also disagree on the relative value of general and specific behaviors as directives for the education program. Most of them accept the position held by adults. They want more stress on the three R's in the elementary school, a core program of common knowledges and skills in the secondary school, and general education in the colleges and universities. A growing minority—composed more of teachers than of administrators—believes that the general behaviors leading toward the best possible maturity at each age is not only the better of the two educational objectives, but also the only one that has any reasonable probability of improving the behavior of pupils in both. There are two definite results of such disagreement, one within and the other without the school. Internally, the program of education moves in the direction of the specific behaviors as it has for hundreds of years. Changes called improvements are merely minor refinements. Externally, educators have no unified policy and give inadequate educational leadership to the public. Lay members of a community do not have the benefit of competent professional guidance in improving their educational outlook. They want better education for their children, but they do not know how to achieve it.

Students are usually quick in pointing out fundamental difference between the direction desired and the educational program to achieve it. Adults expect functional, integrated behavior in all life situations, whereas the schools teach the three R's as isolated, independently organized bodies of knowledge. While teaching and learning such knowledge is behavior, it is not what adults desire. They want behavior in meeting life situations outside the school and view the school as a preparation for such performance. To them English, mathematics, science, and the arts are a way of behaving, not subject matter to be taught and learned. There is ample evidence to indicate that when such specific knowledge is learned as subject matter, it cannot be used in or transferred to actual life situations. Its value lies in learning more subject matter by the same detached-from-life process. So students conclude that since adults expect life behavior, life behavior must be the basic program of the schools. If they continue to emphasize isolated subject matter, mature life behavior cannot be expected as a result. The pivot in direction is the meaning of the word behavior, which will now be examined.

WHAT IS BEHAVIOR?

Behavior has many different meanings, depending upon whether it is viewed by the observer or by the behaver. The demands or expectations of the adult as an observer of the actions of the child are related to how he interprets his observations. The movements of the child as the behaver in the situation are related to his perception of himself or the way he sees himself as functioning in what he believes is his environment. A particular behavior never has the same meaning to an observer as it does to the behaver. This is one reason why problems of interpersonal relations arise among individuals everywhere in life.

Every individual is a self, operating in a psychological field. Some writers refer to the individual as a phenomenal self within a phenomenal field. Again he may be called a personal self living in a behavioral field. All of these terms convey approximately the same meaning. The *phenomenal self* is all aspects of the phenomenal field which are usually associated with the terms "I," "me," "Tom Hopkins," "Mary Brown,"

or whatever the name. It includes everything in the phenomenal field which the individual experiences as part of himself. The phenomenal self is known to and only to the individual. The phenomenal field is the area of the universe of
which the individual is aware at any particular moment in the
continuous movement of his experience. It has two parts: the
internal, which is the phenomenal self; the *external*, which is
the phenomenal environment or the area of awareness not
included in the self.

The phenomenal field has certain characteristics: (a) It is
in constant change. It is fluid, dynamic, emergent. (b) It is
always organized in meaningful relationship to the individual.
A meaningless object cannot exist in a phenomenal—a purposeful—field. (c) It is selective. What the self takes in from
the phenomenal environment and the way the self uses it
within the field is chosen by the self to meet its needs. (d) All
movements or all behaviors of each person in his field are his
attempts to satisfy his needs. (e) Each person is always expanding, differentiating, and integrating his field around
himself as the center, thus reorganizing it for ever better use
in subsequent experiences. Such changes are his struggle to
maintain and enhance himself through better need-satisfaction. They are his behavior whether they be overt or covert.
And his need as he experiences it is the determining factor in
his behavior. Thus the behavior of any individual lies completely within his phenomenal field as he sees it at the moment
of action. It depends upon the meaning which the moving
aspects of the field have to the self.

The psychological principles of the phenomenal self–field
relationship are the same for the adult as for the child, for
the mature as for the immature individual, for the genius as
for the moron. Neither the self nor its meaning of the field
relationships can be observed directly by an outsider. They
can be studied only by inference from observations of overt
behavior, and the inferences are reliable only when the

conditions are favorable for the individual to reveal himself
to the outside world. Theoretically there should be a one-to-
one correspondence between the self and the overt behavior,
but this rarely happens. External conditions have been or are
now a threat to the self, causing it to take protective action by
moving with, away from, or against them. Thus overt be-

CHILD   ADULT

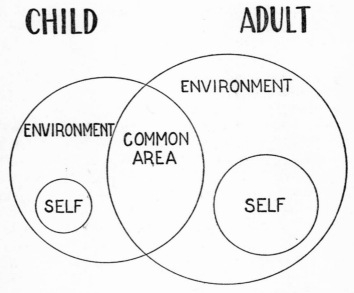

Chart I. Phenomenal Field Relationship of Child and Adult

havior does not reveal the real self either for the adult in his
field or for the child in his. Both draw inferences from distorted actions and never really know each other.

The distortions of the adult are serious since he expects
similar distortions from the child. This statement will be discussed from two angles: how the adult views the behavior of
the child, and how the child views his own behavior. Chart I
shows the relationship between the field of the child and that
of the adult.

The child is his phenomenal self operating in his phenomenal field and the adult holds a similar relationship to his field. There is a common overlapping area through which they communicate. To the adult this area is clear, definite, and meaningfully organized around himself. To the child this area is vague, indefinite, and relatively unknown. Over many years the adult has selected and differentiated in the common region those learnings which he has accepted to meet his needs. But he dims his memories and distorts his vision to assume the following:

1. This common area consists of a number of discrete objects or stimuli which exists independently of himself and the child or independently of either behaver or observer. They are static, unchanging, objective, and impersonal.

2. Behavior is caused by these external objects or stimuli lying outside the self over which the adult has little or no control and in which he can make little or no change. He ignores other aspects of the field or considers them insignificant.

3. These objects or stimuli can be broken down into individual units which can be measured quantitatively and objectively.

4. Behavior is directly related to the quantity of these fixed, discrete, and objective units. New behaviors result from new combinations of these unchangeable parts by association, integration, or synthesis.

5. The qualitative value of behaviors synthesized from these quantitative units can be judged by standards set up apart from the behaver and from the adult as observer. These qualitative standards are the average behavior of many people of appropriate ages when confronted with these objects or stimuli. Such average becomes the learning norm for the child or the accepted action for the adult.

Thus the adult so distorts his field as to demand for the child an educational program organized around discrete objects, called subjects, composed of units of static, unchanging, objective subject matter supposed to exist independently of both of them. The child is taught this discrete subject matter in the school under the title of the three R's or general education. Since these discrete objects are really units of organization of the field of the adult, and since the child has inadequate need and experience to understand or accept them, the common area becomes a demand for the child to distort his field as adults have distorted theirs. Thus no one has opportunity for normal communication or mutual interaction for the better development of all.

The child as a behaver or the adult with a more normal field sees the common area from a different viewpoint from the distorted one just described. They believe the normal area is the process of growth or development or learning by which each self emerges in its entire phenomenal field. They see all objects, human and nonhuman, in the phenomenal environment as resources upon which each individual draws whatever is of value to him in enhancing the emerging self. This growth process is a continuous, purposeful, and interrelated series of movements in the dynamic field. The basic characteristics are similar for all individuals, young and old, regardless of inherited capacity and the opportunity for its development.

This growth process is the only consistent and persistent basis for interaction among individuals throughout life. Since it will be discussed in detail in the next chapter only two points will be mentioned here. The first is that the self, disturbed by its own inner needs, selects from its external environment materials to make over into new materials with which to build and maintain its structure and develop the new behaviors necessary for complete living. The other is that direction of growth is always toward maturity of structure and behavior, both of which are relative to and functions of the phenomenal field. Maturity of structure is completed or ended at some fixed spot. Maturity of behavior is never fixed, completed, or defined in any constant or unchanging actions. It is always relative to need and the conditions for satisfying it. It is a continuous yet probable and variable tendency to action, occurring in a series of related situations which constitute a larger unit known as experience. There is no limit to maturity in learning or behaving if conditions are favorable.

I have discussed behavior from two sharply contrasting points of view. To the normal maturing child or adult, behavior represents the covert and overt aspects of the process by which each satisfies his needs in his phenomenal field as he views it. To an adult with a consciously or unconsciously distorted field, behavior is the overt evidence of the accumulation of new combinations of unchanging, discrete objects existing independently of him in his phenomenal environment by association, integration, or synthesis. In either case each behaver has his covert and overt actions evaluated by outside observers. These external evaluations are important to growing children, for the adult evaluator usually has a wider experience in a richer phenomenal field, a broader perspective of the future value of such behavior, a more detached analysis of the behavior without personal emotional involvement, and a better possibility of detecting distortions which to the behaver are realities. Thus an interchange of viewpoints is very desirable. The problem is how to introduce external observations into the field of the behaver. Shall they be presented as data to help the behaver refine his meanings in his growth and learning process better to differentiate himself on higher levels? Or shall they be used as demands to control his behavior in the direction of ends set by the adult evaluator? The meaning of behavior held by the evaluator will determine how he introduces his observations into the field of others.

The two aspects of behavior which adults expect of children when they leave school can now be reinterpreted. The general behavior is qualitative movement of the self in all life activities near the upper end of an immaturity–maturity scale defined in adult meaning of mature actions. The specific behaviors are also qualitative on a maturity scale but are shown only in specialized situations or quantitative parts of larger experiences. While they are taught in school as discrete environmental entities known as subjects, the learner must use them as self-selected values to meet his needs in appropriate life situations. Adults expect him to develop behaviors by the need process, whereas they teach and demand quantitative subject matter which distorts his field and prevents him from doing so.

WHAT IS THE CENTER OF BEHAVIOR?

All behavior lies within or is determined by the phenomenal field which is the individual in interaction with his environment. The self is the center of the field, is the focus around which it is organized, is the source of all behavior. The field moves dynamically on a focus–margin or figure–ground relationship. The figure or self is the center and is always more differentiated than the remote aspects of the environment which are the ground. Energy flows from the figure or self outward into the ground and back into the self. Aspects of the ground are clarified and returned while the self becomes more differentiated and unified. This flow is similar to the movement of energy in a single cell from the nucleus to the surrounding cytoplasm which is the basis of all life. The self is more complex and the environment is more intricate and involved, yet the direction of energy is unchanged.

Since the self is both the center of the field and the source of all action, locating the center of behavior is the same as finding what constitutes the self. This involves many questions. Would what constitutes one self be similar for all selves? Are certain aspects of the self more continuous than others? Are some more likely to be figure than ground? Do some have greater possibility of differentiation and refinement? Are these centers of the self so stable in overt behavior that an outside observer can infer the covert actions and the structure of the phenomenal field to help the behaver improve the process of his own growth? The best evidence indicates that there are such centers, they are similar for all individuals, they can be inferred from overt action, and they can be used by intelligent observers to help the behaver improve himself.

These continuing centers of behavior are personalized learnings which constitute the inner core of the self. They are his tendencies to action evaluated and accepted in his many life situations. While the learnings of each self differ from those of every other self, there are five broad areas into which they may be grouped: (1) Meanings, feelings, attitudes, and values, whether open or closed, modifiable or fixed; (2) dispositions toward people or working relationships with people or what is frequently called interpersonal relations; (3) processes of dealing with the dynamics of situations, or tendencies to action in meeting new and unforeseen conditions; (4) general adequacy of the self, the acceptance or rejection of the self, the integrative quality of the personality as the product of a long-time educational development; (5) particular feeling of adequacy of the self or the existing state of integrativeness of the personality at the beginning of or throughout the duration of any life situation. The individual does not act on external conditions, on so-called objective facts, or on abstract knowledge. These are data unknown to him in the external environment. They may be placed within situations which he faces by outside adults who prize them highly and demand that he learn them. But they have no behavior-stimulating quality for him until he translates them into the personalized learnings which are the source of his internal and external behaviors. What and how he accepts them to incorporate into himself is the value on which he acts.

The problem is how to help each child refine the meanings or achieve better quality in those learnings which he self-selects to become the inner core of himself and which are the center of his behavior. He learns his general and specific tendencies simultaneously as they are interwoven in the self. But the general behaviors represent the over-all quality of the self and affect greatly the selection and personalization of the specific learnings. Thus the educational direction of maturing the child's self is superior to teaching the three R's since the former is superior in promoting desirable behavior.

WHAT IS MATURING BEHAVIOR?

Maturing behavior can be defined for any individual at any age, time, or place only as *direction of growth*. It is not a series of specific acts or the way in which an individual works in a few specific situations. Rather it is a general tendency to action in meeting new experiences over a long period of time. While specific behaviors in particular situations are relative to age and experience of individuals, the direction of action which represents maturing is a continuing, operating characteristic that is similar for all people of all ages. Specific acts are considered normal or abnormal, depending upon their meaning to the individual who exhibits them. Specific behaviors of a six-year-old may be normal when observed in his field, whereas similar acts may be abnormal for some other child under different circumstances. Furthermore, maturity and adjustment are not synonymous even though the terms are sometimes used interchangeably. Adjustment means conforming to patterns or ends of action set by adults without allowing the individual to modify them to his personal needs. Maturity means thoughtfully and creatively reconstructing both the self and the external conditions which it has to meet. Progress toward maturity refers to continued refinement of the personalized learnings basic to one's behavior. Since variability in behavior is wide, maturing is a tendency toward a straightforward, realistic, creative, thoughtful, and enhancing relationship to the outer world. Abnormal or immature behavior is a tendency to escape from or failure to meet existing conditions through fear, anxiety, inferiority, or general inadequacy. Maturity does not represent a fixed concept. It has no definable limit, for there is no point at which growth ceases. It is the behavior of an adequate self dealing actively, deliberately, and realistically with the situations which it must face.

Since maturing is the direction of the behavior of the whole individual in the whole situation which he faces, it cannot be broken down into a number of separate and discrete aspects. However, for purposes of discussion, five overlapping tendencies may be distinguished. Operating together, they describe the direction accepted as maturing behavior in our culture.

1. *The maturing individual shows a unity of organization or integrating wholeness within himself.* His action indicates freedom from inner conflict. He is able to resolve opposed personality trends, such as the conflict between his selfish and social goals. He can concentrate his energy on a small group of harmonious and interrelated purposes. His behavior exhibits movement from an egocentric to a sociocentric direction. He enjoys this social movement because he realizes that his own personality develops well-being when it includes other selves. He spends his energy dealing with external conditions in situations rather than in overcoming internal conflicts. The maturing person sees himself not only as an organized unity in action but as a member of many groups in which he is willing to work on the principle of the Golden Rule.

2. *The maturing individual has a positive outgoingness or a dynamic relation to the environment in which he lives.* He is constantly searching for new kinds of experiences and is always alert for new insights within older areas. He realizes

that qualitative behavior emerges through new relations, new meanings, new ideas, all of which depend upon new experiences for their fertilization. He is flexible, plastic, malleable. He shuns emotional ties that limit his growth and development. While certain areas of his personality are organized and established, he maintains a wide margin for positive, creative, adaptive action.

3. *The maturing individual faces reality in all his life situations.* Reality has two major aspects, one internal and the other external. The maturing individual assesses his abilities and talents correctly, both as he thinks they are and as they affect others. He is free from excessive fantasy. He does not hunt for ways to compensate, but builds his limitations into strong supports to his greater abilities. He knows the areas in which he has emotional blocks and strives to release them normally. He expresses his feelings through a purposeful drive toward better experience. To face reality the individual must also be able to analyze the external aspects of situations. He looks for and examines all conditions and all data, whether he has emotional learnings for or against them. He searches for their relevance to the problem, whether they be central or marginal. He makes the decisions necessary to promote inquiry. He assumes responsibility for his acts, individually and collectively. He has self-control, self-direction, self-judgment, and self-responsibility. He never relinquishes these to outside authorities.

4. *The maturing individual works cooperatively with people to solve common needs by a process of deliberative action.* He likes people, believes in people, enjoys social contacts. He shares willingly and freely with others in mutual experiences. He values a person for what he is, rather than for his social status or position. He recognizes ability in other people, is willing to free it and encourage it at all times. He builds many permanent and lasting friendships while constantly extending the range of his contacts with new individuals. He

believes in and is a student of the process of deliberative action. He knows that impulsive, prejudiced, or unreasonable solutions to common problems leave emotional scars which prevent the continued growth of everyone concerned. He does not wish to participate in such action either for himself or for others. He recognizes that people develop quality of behavior through the quality of the process used in resolving their common problems. He is always ready to center his efforts on studying how to improve the ways in which people live and work together.

5. *The maturing person has a forward-looking view toward life.* He conceives of the world as a warm, friendly, hopeful, desirable place in which to live. He believes that reasonable people working together cooperatively can and will release the intelligence necessary to improve life for everyone. He accepts the past behaviors of people as antecedents to present difficulties which he and others individually and collectively must face in the present. He does not look to the past for answers to present problems, nor does he glorify or regret the decisions of people who have preceded him. Rather he studies their process of action in their situations to find clues for improving his process of action in his situations. He is consciously and continuously developing—toward himself, other people, the world in which he lives—a set of operating values which give a common yet flexible core of consistency to his actions.

These aspects of behavior functioning together in life situations define the direction of action of a maturing individual. The home and school should educate children in feeling, understanding, accepting, and practicing this direction. Even if the home does not, the school must do so if it expects to meet its responsibility for improving learning and achieving more qualitative results. Thus the program for any group must be evaluated on its merits for its contribution to this acceptable direction. Many parts which lack positive influence must be re-examined and modified or eliminated. Other practices with great possibilities but not now in schools must be included. The three R's must be taught so as to mature the behavior of children rather than give them specific items of objective knowledge or specialized skill. When the self in its phenomenal field satisfies its needs by a normal learning process, its behaviors will show to the external observer a movement upward on the immaturity–maturity scale.

WHAT CONDITIONS FACILITATE MATURING BEHAVIOR?

The conditions which facilitate maturing behavior are not now found generally in schools, neither do they appear in the history of public or private educational institutions and their practices. This statement is not made as a criticism but as a record of fact. Except in rare instances, schools were not organized and maintained to mature people. They were established to transmit to children and adults the unchanging, universal facts, objects, and stimuli supposed to exist independently of people in the common environment of all. As evidence of their independent existence, they could be recorded in books for everyone to read, accept, and interpret alike, for uniformity was the essence or good of life and deviation the error or evil in it.

For many centuries learning exact and uniform knowledge from books has been the basic activity of people in schools. Reading has been the universal standard of literacy and culture. Few people have dared to criticize this arrangement, for it seemed to represent the inevitable and ultimate relationship between schools and culture. About one hundred years ago certain inquisitive, creative, and experimental-minded individuals began to study people: their origin, structure, and internal functioning; how they affect their environment; how they learn; why they behave as they do. These innovators have developed many new life sciences to which one must go to find the conditions most favorable for the growth and development of people. A few of the more important fields are biology, child development, field-theory psychologies, embryology, genetics, neurology, experimental medicine, psychiatry, psychotherapy, cultural anthropology, sociology, and dynamic logic, together with their many and varied ramifications. Researchers in some areas have studied the basic process of growth and development, others have concentrated on internal and external conditions which cause the self and personality to disintegrate, a few have clarified the positive factors in the growth of mature people. Yet little of this wealth of available materials has entered schools, public or private, to change the direction away from a book curriculum to teach the three R's for literacy.

The conditions which tend to develop mature people as indicated by corroborative evidence from a number of these sources are summarized in Chart II, together with their relationship to existing school practices.

Column 1 of the chart shows the educational direction toward maturing people, the characteristics of which have already been described. In Column 2 are listed the conditions which *tend* to promote such maturing, although no one can guarantee the results. Because of factors of individual differences, some people may not develop normally under the best circumstances. But where these conditions prevail most people will not only reach higher levels but will also develop a desire to continue and a knowledge of how to do so. These conditions are that each individual should study his own needs by the exercise of his biological growth process in groups of similar individuals with similar problems. He should self-select his own learnings and evaluate their effects upon himself and others. He should understand, use, and accept the process of his own growth. From the point of view of the learner, the result is not rugged individualism or egocentric effort, since all behaviors are developed in organic groups as a cooperative social experience.

Column 3 indicates the conditions which now operate in

4. Resources for meeting the conditions which promote maturing	3. Conditions which now exist in schools	2. Conditions which tend to promote maturing	1. Educational Direction
1. People	1. Pupils study needs of others called subjects	1. Pupils study own *needs*	
2. Other forms of life	2. Reverse teaching methods are used	2. Biological *growth process* is used	
3. Physical universe	3. Aggregates, but not groups are formed	3. Organic *groups* are formed	Toward Maturing people
4. Buildings, books, equipment	4. Adults select and evaluate learnings	4. Pupils *self-select* and evaluate own learnings	
5. Subjects	5. Process is ignored	5. Process is used and accepted by pupils	
6. Other aspects of culture past and present			

The resources of column 4 are used in schools under conditions in column 3.
The resources of column 4 should operate in schools under conditions in column 2.

Chart II. Relationship of School Conditions and Maturing People

schools. Children study the needs of others, called subjects, by appropriate methods of teaching in aggregates or classes. The knowledge taught and the learnings expected are selected and evaluated by outside persons who generally ignore the biological concept of learning, except in instances where overt behavior challenges the authority of the teacher. Some children go through school under these conditions and appear to act normally. But behavior analyses indicate that, owing to partial understanding and use of the normal process of growth, they have internal stresses that tend to arrest development. Educators tend to locate children in one of two personality groups, depending upon the way children protect themselves under these conditions. One is called "apple polishers" and the other "troublemakers," neither of which represents normal behavior. A few who show normal growth fall between these two modes of a bimodal distribution.

Column 4 shows some of the environmental resources available to everyone for meeting the conditions necessary for his normal growth. These are not stated in order of importance, but people are always first since children experience the others through their interpretations. These resources are not mutually exclusive. Subjects are listed as one aspect of the culture since they are emphasized by adults for all learners in all types of schools. Other aspects of the culture are not given equal consideration.

The practical educational problem is how to reorganize programs from kindergarten through graduate school to incorporate the more favorable conditions which the public expects. Past attempts have been rearrangements of teaching and administrative procedures within the conditions of Column 3. These were in harmony with the uncritical beliefs of many laymen and educators that the ills of educations can be corrected by placing greater emphasis upon essential subject matters under the Column 3 conditions. Since available evidence shows that more emphasis upon knowledge existing independently in the common environment will not help learners release their abilities and redirect their behaviors except by accident, deeper and more functional changes must be made. And the time for making them is long overdue.

WHAT CONCEPT OF INTERPERSONAL RELATIONS SHOULD OPERATE IN SCHOOLS?

Schools that are organized around subjects emphasizing teaching and learning fixed, unchanging facts and skills under conditions noted in Column 3 of Chart II promote authoritarian reactive relationships among individuals, with the teacher as status master in every classroom. Here many people—children, students, learners—are controlled and managed by a few people to meet the needs of the few. Under conditions outlined in Column 2 of the chart, however, people have a cooperative interactive relationship, for they all work together purposefully and intelligently to resolve mutually determined needs. Both concepts are as old as the history of man. The authoritarian concept has dominated and still dominates all human institutions—home, school, government, churches, economic system. Instances of cooperative action in families, schools, churches, and industry are the exception rather than the rule. The antidote of the people for authoritarian control has always been revolt. Most revolts of history have not led to cooperative action, but have placed in power a new authoritarian group. It is a method by which the outs become the ins rather than a new way of dealing with human problems.

The techniques used under the two concepts of learning are very different. The authoritarian techniques are control, compulsion, exploitation, coercion, restriction, fear, propaganda, cold war, hot war, compromise, peace treaties which do not keep the peace. The loser, materially and psychologically, works within the compromise to recoup his power so as to again revolt, start another war, have another compromise treaty as a breathing period before repeating the same cycle.

The cooperative techniques are exploration, search, inquiry, respect for individuals, freedom of thought and action; discovering, releasing, upbuilding human intelligence; developing integrating personalities, promoting purposeful and deliberative social action. There are few occasions for revolt since hurtful impingements of people on each other can be readjusted without emotional bias and with positive personality effects.

Which concept of human relations should the schools of America promote? This is not an academic question. They will promote one or the other, for there seems to be no middle ground. There are degrees of humanity in authoritarian control which some people misinterpret as the cooperative technique. Educators not wanting to be classed as authoritarians, but lacking the emotional or intellectual stability to become genuinely cooperative, have refined and made more subtle such authoritarian controls. They mistake this action for a middle position where one does not exist.

Does it make a difference which concept of human relationships prevails in our schools? America is supposed to be a liberal democracy, founded by the early settlers as a revolt against authoritarian control. *We the people* has always meant cooperative action of the people, by the people, and for the good of all the people. So the schools of the people, public or private, should promote cooperative human relations. To learn democratic action children must understand, accept, and practice it in every life experience. Yet the schools have never been and are not now organized around cooperative human relations. So a democratic people defeat their own ends by maintaining authoritarian schools which are a potent antecedent of the growing immaturity of their children. No one can guarantee that cooperative interpersonal relations will cure all present ills in education. Yet the theoretical and practical evidence now available indicates that they are better than authoritarian relations for developing the mature persons with the general and specific behaviors necessary for maintaining and enriching our democracy.

A BACKWARD AND FORWARD LOOK

Some years ago in the library of an English professor I picked up an old and little-read book entitled *How to Write Essays*, in the last chapter of which the authors picked Emerson as the greatest essayist of all time. They asserted that he never summarized what he had said but at the end reinterpreted and focused it toward better thinking or action in the future. His reinterpretation of the past into a forward look for the future appealed to the authors. And it has always seemed reasonable to me. The chief purpose for studying past experience is to understand better a present situation in order to take more intelligent actions in the future. No one can relive the past of himself or anyone else. He does reinterpret its meaning in the light of his need-direction at the moment. Since need-directions vary, one expects and finds different reinterpretations of common past experience by those who have lived through them. So an individual's interpretation of what he has experienced should be respected by others.

Yet an outside observer may help another clarify his learnings if the observations are offered without pressure and he is free to assimilate them creatively, just as every reader of these words is free to accept, reject, or modify them. But there is a quality to this freedom which is frequently overlooked. Selection or rejection by impulsive or compulsive drives is not the qualitative freedom of the flexible, mutual, mature self using thoughtful inquiry. In succeeding chapters I shall show how homes and schools as important educational institutions can help each person—child or adult—discover, release, and use more of his potential capacity toward becoming a maturing self. And the next step is to examine in some detail the meaning of the basic biological process of growth.

Chapter ***III***

WHAT IS GROWING UP?

For years I have studied the hopes, desires, ambitions parents have for their children. In large gatherings, small discussion groups, or individual conferences, I have probed the direction of their thinking. Most of them start, "I want my child *to grow up*," or "I want my child *to become*," after which each describes the behaviors acceptable to him. When asked their hopes for children in school, educators generally use the words *to learn* or *to know*, after which they describe the knowledges and skills which to them are necessary for successful living. Since parents use biological terms and educators use psychological terms the meanings are not clear to either group. When I ask parents to explain the terms *grow up* and *become* they refer to *the results* of the growing or *the products* of the becoming rather than the process of growing and becoming. Rarely do they explain behaviors as emerging in experience, but generally define them as products of teaching. The same dichotomy exists with educators. They use the term learn when they mean teach and knowledge when they mean the subject matter taught in schools.

While parents and educators differ in the terms used to express their hopes or desires for children, they agree that the method of achieving them is authoritarian teaching. Both should have clearer meanings of the words growing up or becoming, learning or teaching, from the point of view of the child if homes and schools are to educate more mature people. I present here the information which I have discussed with hundreds of adult groups and thousands of students.

Since most adults and students have never studied biology or have forgotten what they were taught, I always start by reviewing the simple facts about living organisms necessary to interpret growth in more complex human beings.

All life comes from life. The new life is a smaller, simpler whole of the life from which it originated, with the potentialities of the larger life of which it is a new generation. All living things are composed of cells which are circumscribed masses of protoplasm containing a nucleus, although a few cells have more than one nucleus and some, such as red corpuscles, have no nucleus. Yet it is characteristic of a cell to have a nucleus surrounded by cytoplasm, which means the protoplasm outside the nuclear wall. Protoplasm has the characteristics usually attributed to or necessary for life, even though these are difficult to define. The new life behaves according to these characteristics, which distinguish it from nonliving matter.

This protoplasm or this cell has certain vital properties. First it has the power of motion. Action is always going on both internally and externally, directed toward its environment. The energy of a living cell is unlike that of nonliving objects which are also forms of energy. A living cell changes by regenerating itself, whereas nonliving matter changes through degeneration or expenditure of itself.

A second characteristic of protoplasm is sensitivity to or irritation from the surrounding environment. A cell can send out stimuli into its environment and receive stimuli from it. The cell can contract or expand according to its meaning of such stimuli. An amoeba generally moves by pushing its protoplasm out in front and pulling it in behind, but if a bright light is directed to it the amoeba always moves away from the light. An earthworm on the surface at night will dart into its hole when a boy intent upon fishing flashes his light upon it. This power of motion or dynamic change growing out of sensitivity to the environment is common to all living things, the single-celled amoeba or the complex cellular structure called man.

A third characteristic of a cell is the power to take from the environment other forms of energy which it converts or transfers into the form of energy necessary to maintain and regenerate itself, or to renew its own protoplasm, or to become the organism itself. This is sometimes called metabolism or creative assimilation. No living thing can maintain itself without the power to convert other forms of energy to its own uses. The conversion takes place in the presence of oxygen and is similar to the burning of fuel. The converted heat energy is retained, smoke in the form of carbon dioxide is given off in the air, and unusable solids and liquids are expelled. The more highly specialized the function of cells, the lower their power of regeneration. A scratch on the skin will be quickly repaired by surrounding cells. When the more specialized mature nerve cell is killed it is never replaced, and even when damaged it is more likely to die than skin cells which have suffered more serious injuries.

A fourth characteristic of living organisms is that they can and do increase the size and complexity of their structure. An amoeba increases in size until the nucleus attains a certain magnitude, when it divides by simple fission and forms two amoebas, each daughter cell repeating this performance at the proper time. While the amoeba does not increase in complexity, being only a single cell at all times, it has one quality not possessed by more complex structures. It grows old but it never dies, for at the point of maturity it becomes two new daughter amoebas. A human organism not only increases in size but differentiates its own complex structure. In the beginning two gametes—the egg and the sperm—fuse to form the fertilized egg, or zygote. The egg is the largest cell in the human body, containing a nucleus with a large amount of protoplasm, while the sperm is almost all nucleus. After fusing there is a period of about twenty hours in which cell division takes place without expansion or until the ratio of nucleus to protoplasm in each cell is characteristic of the human organism. Thereafter the zygote expands and differentiates the new cells in the order and arrangement which ultimately becomes the specialized organism functioning as an integrated unit. Expanding, differentiating, and integrating are characteristics of all complex living structures.

The fifth characteristic of all living organisms is the power to reproduce—not themselves but their kind, for no two individuals of any of the various kinds of living things are the same. This reproductive function has two aspects. One relates to a single cell within the organism and the other concerns the organism as a whole. In human beings single cells are reproduced by mitosis, which is different from simple fission in amoebas. The chromatin which carries the chromosomes and the gene pattern forms a thread which splits in half lengthwise so that an equal number of like chromosomes goes to each daughter cell. Thus each new cell maintains the same number of twenty-four pairs but more specifically it contains the genetic pattern or codescript with which it began life in the zygote. This codescript does not change throughout the entire life of the organism. Cells which contain the twenty-four pairs of chromosomes are called diploids. Sex or haploid cells produced by a particular group of diploids are an exception to this method of cell reproduction. The number of chromosomes in the egg and the sperm is reduced to twelve pairs each by a failure to split the chromosomes at some point in the maturation of each cell. Yet regardless of method, reproduction is a characteristic function of all living things.

The cell as the basic unit appears in almost every imaginable size and shape in the human body. Originally scientists thought that the structure of a cell determined its function.

Now they tend to hold that all cells have in common the dynamic property of being able to convert creatively the energy from outside into what they can use to carry on their own life process. The size and shape of cells and their organization into organs within the body have evolved because of the specialized nature of the work to be done in maintaining internal unity while the whole organism regenerates itself in interaction with the environment. However one views this relationship between structure and function or whatever his concept of the origin of life, he must face the fact that the highly specialized activities of the various organs of the human body and the dynamic movement of the organism as a whole are only specialized reflections of the life process of the individual cell.

WHAT DO WE MEAN BY GROWING?

Educators and laymen use the words "growing," "developing," "teaching," "learning" to describe a single life phenomenon in children and adults. While all of them relate to changes in individuals from conception to adulthood, they are not synonymous. There are three basic ingredients of growing or developing or learning which must be understood by the child and also by parents and teacher as they observe his behavior. These ingredients are: first, the capacity to learn or to become a unique personality, with which the child is born; second, the surrounding environment or culture which the child uses to develop his inherited capacity; and third, the process by which he uses environmental materials to develop his maturing behaviors.

Growing is the unique life process of all living things composed of protoplasm formed into cells. In this unique process the living organism selects and takes into itself from the outside environment energy materials which it converts within itself into new forms of energy for the purpose, first, of differentiating new structure and maintaining old structure

at a high level of operating efficiency, and second, of differentiating new behaviors and reorganizing old behaviors
necessary for effective living in the culture in which it is
born. While the structural and maintenance aspects relate to
internal physical and physiological conditions, both affect
behavioral development. Differentiating new behaviors refers
to the relationship of the whole organism to its outside
environment which has internal aspects. Thus the life process
goes on simultaneously inside and outside the organism,
affecting changes in it and its environment.

Wherever there is life there is always a product of such
action. But the product is not the process and the result of the
growing is not the growth. The product is one and only one
aspect of the total process. This can be readily observed in
structure, but is more difficult to recognize in behavior. A
mother takes her infant to a pediatrician, who finds him
longer and heavier than at the previous examination, stating
the amount in inches and ounces. This leads the mother to
believe that the growth is the increase in height and weight
when they are only evidences that the process is functioning
normally. The infant takes in material from outside, changes
it into something different inside, and uses the new material
to produce the height and weight. Without the entire process
there could be no increase in height or weight or perhaps no
infant. Anyone can see a product of the process by looking
at a tree, bird, animal, or any other form of life open to
normal observation. Yet laymen and educators confuse
product with process in the behavior of children. They watch
for fixed ends similar to the increase in height or weight, not
realizing the nature and value of the underlying process which
produced the observable behavior.

WHAT IS THE DIRECTION OF GROWING?

Growing always has purposeful direction even when the
grower is not conscious of it or when outside observers cannot detect it. Direction exists whether it be acceptable or

unacceptable to the behaver or to the observer. The direction of growth in structure is toward maturity of structure. The baby becomes taller and heavier, his internal organs increase both in size and in the performance of their particular functions. At some point determined by each individual such maturation ceases, for the time, height, weight, and size differ for each person. The conditions which promote, retard, or stop physical maturity are both internal and external since the observed result is a product of the interaction of the internal hereditary systems and the environment. Emotional disturbances or a deficient diet may arrest physical growth. A favorable emotional environment or an adequate diet may prolong it. After physical growth ceases, the organism maintains its structure at the highest operating efficiency possible with the existing internal and external factors. While the body is maturing, the organs are learning how to work together and the whole organism is learning how to live in its environment. So structure and behavior grow up together or mature simultaneously. The ability of the child to behave in a specific way at any given time is directly related to his stage of structural development. After he is physically mature, he can under favorable conditions behave on a higher level than at any prior period.

The direction of growth in behavior is toward maturity of behavior. As in structure, this is relative to inherited capacity and the opportunities in the environment for developing it. They differ in one important aspect. Maturity of behavior has no limit. Any individual can continue to raise his level of action so long as the normal growth process operates. Yet he may arrest his self-development at any time because of internal or external conditions. The mother who wants her only son always to be her baby furnishes an environment which causes him to arrest his behavior at an adolescent level. An adult may become so obsessed with the rightness of certain behaviors that he closes his growth at that point. Anyone may live in an environment offering inadequate material to convert into new forms of energy, thereby limiting behavioral growth. The grass sown on barren soil, the tree planted in dead sand, the baby born in a home where he is not wanted, the child in a school where he is taught the three R's, the college student required to take subjects of no value to him— all of these are instances of how a sterile environment may and does impair the process and arrest maturity. I have used the term arrest rather than complete, for a child with arrested behavior may be placed in a new and fertile environment where he can so reactivate his normal process as to raise his level of action.

The control of growth toward life-fulfillment from conception to birth is maintained by interaction of the genes laid down in the original zygote and carried as a codescript in every diploid cell. Whether the gene is a hereditary unit of separate existence or merely a chemical point of reference on a complex chain molecule called a chromosome is not a point for discussion here. By expanding, differentiating, and integrating in a sympathetic environment containing necessary nutrients, the new life under the interactive direction of its genes moves to become a normal integrated organism.

Immediately after birth, control of growth starts to shift gradually from the genes to the autonomic nervous system, which is composed of two parts, the parasympathetic which restricts, and the sympathetic which dilates. Smooth muscles and visceral organs, such as heart or stomach, have a branch of each part which regulates their action. At birth the brain and central nervous system are to a great extent too undeveloped and immature to function although the autonomic or life system is ready for action. This autonomic system is closely related to the endocrine glands secreting chemical stimulants called hormones which are very important for internal balance and cell activity. In interaction with the endocrine glands, it regulates temperature; carbohydrate, water, fat, and protein metabolism; sexual behavior; sleeping and waking states; general visceral functions; and emotional behavior. While the genes furnish the pattern of continued growth in structure, the autonomic system regulates the internal environment, in which such structure develops. But what is more important, it adjusts the infant's movements to his outside environment, giving selective direction to his behaviors in his new world. Since he is also growing physically, these behaviors are built into the growing nerve structure, becoming powerful autonomic tendencies to action and repeating themselves in a modified form whenever the infant faces similar situations. Thus an infant has strong autonomic direction to learning and personality before the cerebrospinal cells are mature enough to affect his actions to an important degree.

Gradually the central nervous system takes over the direction of behavior. Being more flexible than the autonomic system it has greater potential for learning, but takes more time to develop than the primitive life system. Its influence is toward deliberative or thoughtful, mutual or cooperative, social action. Thus the control of growth begins with the genes and moves through the autonomic system into the higher nerve center of the cortex of the brain. Until an individual behaves most of the time on this highest level his development is arrested, for he has never reached the potential maturity with which the zygote was endowed.

The meaning of the term "growing up" can now be further explained. "Growing" is the process and "up" is the direction. "Up" has two related aspects. One is increase in the size and operating efficiency of the internal organs. The other is shift in the control of behavior internally and externally. Internally, "up" is the change of operating center from the genes through the autonomic to the cerebrospinal nervous system. Externally, "up" is toward behaviors accepted by others as thoughtful, deliberative, reasonable actions. Parents want

their children to show behaviors which they believe represent these high-level cerebral responses. Yet they know little
about how to help them develop such intelligent actions.

For emphasis I have distinguished between growth in structure and growth in behavior, even though no such difference
exists. In actual life all physical and psychological change is
psychosomatic, for what happens anywhere in the organism
affects it as a whole. Over a period of time, a person may
become so upset about what was some minor psychological
difficulty as to disarrange the normal operation of the entire
organism or show structural damage to a particular organ.
Sedatives, biotics, or surgery will not effect a cure since the
individual operates as a unit. The basic causes of the unitary
breakdown, of which the damaged organ is only a symptom,
must be located and relieved. Mental or psychological breakdown and physical or structural disease are evidence that a
normal person has impaired his normal growth process as a
result of abnormal conditions in his environment.

WHAT ARE THE IMPORTANT ASPECTS OF THE LIFE PROCESS?

The life process is usually described by such words as continuous, dynamic, purposeful, integrative. It is a molar movement in that the organism operates in its phenomenal
environment, searching for that unity of relationship which
will enhance its wholeness. The life began as a simple whole
and struggles to maintain its unity even with its complex
structure, its high potential capacity for learning, its wide
range of motility in its environment, and its highly developed
mechanisms for utilizing its experiences. Under such circumstances the important aspects of the biological process
should be described in molar terms, but no such terms are
available. Books on biology and psychology are full of words
that analyze and dissect the structure or behavior but are
short on words that describe unitary action. So here I must

break the unitary process down into simple functional aspects, each of which operates simultaneously in the moving dynamic of life.

1. *The process originates internally.* It begins with some need, upset, tension, or irritation in the organism, ranging from the unconscious tension of the week-old infant who cries for food to relieve his stomach pain to the conscious need of the adult to remove the butterflies from his stomach brought on by his inability to decide among possible courses of action in a life situation. In either case, the irritation, tension, or need arises out of interaction with the environment. The individual must feel the tension in order to select something from the environment to release it. The better he understands it the better he can select among many possibilities. Building and releasing tension is an integral aspect of the normal rhythm of life. The individual feels his tension but an outside person can never observe it. He sees only the behaviors which indicate its presence. He can only approximate a realization of the nature of the upset, as the behaver rarely discloses his real need and the observer lacks insight and empathy to trace it from the overt action. The observer cannot feel or see the changes inside the behaver as he converts selected outside materials into new energy. The outside person must accept and respect the internal origin, direction, and control of the creative actions of another person, young or old, to relieve his stress. Yet any outside person, if he so desires, can help any other individual understand his process better in order to use it in resolving his needs.

2. *The process is creative.* The organism cannot use directly for its purposes the materials which it takes in from the outside. It changes them into something else with different energy properties which are not always predictable from those of the original materials. This ability of all living organisms to make such change is accepted in biology as the principle of creative emergence or creative assimilation. The only con-

stant or predictable or continuous aspect is the creativeness. At each level of development the individual possesses unique properties of structure and behavior which depend upon the properties of the constituent elements, but appear only when these elements are creatively assimilated in new emergent properties or systems. While the process of growth is constant from birth to adolescence, in the latter stage there are unique features of structure and behavior not found at birth or in any other individual at any time. One person becomes a giant while another is a dwarf or one is a genius while the other is schizophrenic. Each is an emergent of creative assimilation.

Both in structure and in behavior previous emergents affect subsequent emergents. The tree builds new structure upon old structure. The adult develops new behavior out of old behavior. At no point in the development of structure or behavior does an organism begin *de novo*, disregarding completely the products of prior growth. Some writers refer to creative emergence as the whole process, for it includes the need, the materials taken in, the way they are changed, the new result. Its significance cannot be overestimated.

3. *The process is self-selective.* The individual selects from outside himself what he believes will relieve his need as he sees or feels it. Since the need grows out of previous experiences in which tendencies to action are already built, the individual is disposed to select materials which are compatible with previous behaviors. The clearer he perceives the need and the better he understands the functional value of outside materials, the more he tends to select things which modify or reconstruct previous behaviors rather than continue them. But self-selection goes on regardless of the clarity of the need or the understanding of the external environment. And it takes place on both the autonomic and conscious levels.

Animals show a wide range and high quality of self-selection to meet internal needs which they have never before experienced. A rat with a total resection of thyroid glands will build a nest to conserve body temperature and will modify it as the external temperature is raised or lowered. A rat with a damaged cortex of the adrenal glands will increase his intake of salt to compensate for the greater amount now eliminated in the urine and thus keep the same internal balance which existed prior to the damage. Cannon called this the wisdom of the body, or the tendency of the organism through self-selection to maintain internal homeostasis when the necessary materials are available in the external environment. Such autonomic wisdom has extreme limitations because of the small area within which it can operate with selective effectiveness. Yet such wisdom is inherent in protoplasm or in the inherited biological equipment of everyone. Conscious self-selection in man has unlimited possibilities for improvement through qualitative learning in an adequate environment. But regardless of conditions, self-selection will always occur and will always be towards what at that moment to the behaver is self-enhancement.

A high quality of self-selection can take place only in a high quality of environment. The shrub which finds in the soil few materials for its growth will self-select what is present and strive valiantly to live, but it gives outward signs of an inner struggle. The intelligent gardener interprets these signs and supplies proper materials to the soil. The protoplasmic process of the plant cannot distinguish between favorable and harmful materials. It will select potassium permanganate which destroys it as well as nitrogen which develops it. Sheep will feed on poisonous laurel along with nonpoisonous shrubs without being aware of the inevitable outcome. Like the sheep, a child must have some materials removed from his radius of self-selection until he is capable of appraising the effects of their creative assimilation. Feeding experiments show that infants autonomically distinguish among formulas, selecting the one best for their growth, as verified by external evidence. While self-selection exists on the conscious level, environmental restrictions tend to submerge, conceal, or disparage it. No individual could long exist as an integrated self if he operated on internal self-selection autonomically and externally controlled selection consciously. When conflict arises between the autonomic and cerebrospinal systems the autonomic or life system tends to dominate so that self-selection always prevails but on a lower level.

4. *The process is differentiative*. One evidence of the process called growth is increase in size of the organism, but not all increase in size is growth. To be called growth, increase in size must have two characteristics. First, it must be developmental, or move progressively in the direction of maturity of structure and behavior characteristic of the organism. Second, it must be differentiative: that is, in both number and diversity of function the parts which compose the complex structure must be developed from within by the organism while the latter maintains its integrative wholeness. The progressive diversification, the keynote of development, is easy to recognize, for any developed body differs from its own earlier stages not only in size but in changed proportions and in different general consistency. The emergent development or differentiation of its parts at the various stages from conception to physical maturity is controlled by the growing organism. Adults in the environment may arrest or facilitate such differentiation, but they cannot demand and produce one cell in a growing fetus; neither can they determine the differentiative function of a heart or a lung. The gardener cannot produce one leaf or flower bud on a tree. Yet the mother can help the fetus and the gardener can help the tree by supplying an environment rich in materials which each can self-select for its differentiation.

The principle of differentiation, or progressive diversification, also applies to behavior. The child is constantly expanding his area of experience, is differentiating or increasing the diversity yet clarity of experience, and is integrating the emerging action into a better unity of the self. Observations of behavior confirm such aspects of growth when a child is relatively free to explore his environment with the guidance but not the coercive restriction of adults.

The child can expand his environment so as not to result in growth. Under outside demands he can take into himself temporarily and superficially materials which he cannot assimilate by differentiatioin. He appears to absorb them, but expels them when the outside pressure subsides. Only what he selects and accepts by differentiation can he convert into the self-energy necessary for his progressive development.

5. *The process is interactive, cooperative, social.* Each individual life begins as a simple yet integrated whole which develops into a complex, highly differentiated structure while maintaining its basic wholeness, although at a higher level. Although through the years it differentiates its parts into maturity of structure, the dominance of the whole is apparent. Each part makes a special contribution to such wholeness, and the needs of the whole affect or regulate the operating efficiency of the parts. During the years of expanding, differentiating, and integrating structure the whole maintains communication among the various parts on a free and active two-way basis while developing many kinds of media for rapid and effective interaction. When one part is overloaded or has its function temporarily impaired, messengers notify other organs, which cooperate to maintain the wholeness. When the demands of the whole upon any organ exceed the limit of its performance, structural and functional breakdowns occur.

The accumulating evidence both on the maintenance of unity and on the antecedents of disunity shows that each normal individual represents internally the highest form of cooperative interaction in existence. While energy drains into the centers carrying the load at the movement, no organ attempts to become a dictator and dominate the internal universe. Neither do the cells above the diaphragm assume membership in an elite group which should produce the leaders that rule the cells below it. Each organ has sufficient wisdom of the body to know that its responsibility can be adequately discharged only in the highest mutuality with others.

Thus the biological growth process is based on a respect of each part of the organism for the worth of others, a working relationship which best promotes the integrity of the whole, a willingness of any part to accelerate or retard its operation temporarily without assuming superior status, a marshaling of all forces to combat destructive germs or wild cancer cells, a tendency for the organism to develop integrative wholeness on higher levels by raising the quality of the cooperative inter-active process which is its biological inheritance.

For every child, growing is a two-way activity—within himself and with his external environment. Coming into the new world from the warmth, protection, and security of his intrauterine environment, he gives and expects to receive from others cooperative interaction, the only functional relationship which his organic structure knows. But people have a different concept of this relationship. Through igno-rance of or unwillingness to accept his life process, they assume superiority, acting as if they were his operating center and demanding that he reverse his biological development. They assert that he is too immature to take responsibility for his own growth, even though he discharged it so well in the prenatal life. Adults do not want him to mature through his cooperative interactive process; they want him to arrest his development through their authoritarian control. So he tries to operate on a dual system, with his structure developing and maturing according to his biological process and his external behaviors being conditioned by outside demands. He

is born into a world where adults are in conflict with each
other and with him, from which he cannot escape and in
which he may never emerge as a mature self.

The difference in the two viewpoints was sharpened for me
recently while on a train from Chicago to New York. At
Cleveland the porter in the lounge car brought in newspapers
giving an account of educational meetings being held in that
city. Two men opposite me—one a judge and the other a
counselor—began to discuss the educational news. The conversation turned on whether a child should be sent to a
private or a public school. The counselor, who sent his boy
to a private school, was needling the judge, who sent his son
to a public school. Finally the judge could stand it no longer
and said, "Counselor, what is the *real* reason why you sent
your boy to ——— School?" Said the counselor, "I sent my
boy to ——— School because it made him into exactly what
I want him to be." After a thoughtful pause the judge replied,
"Counselor, I sent my boy to a public school because it gave
him the opportunity to become exactly what he wants to be."
Whereupon the judge politely excused himself and left the
car. But I pondered for a long time the difference in the concept of growth which these two expressions implied.

The process of cooperative interaction always operates in
some form even when denied by powerful outside forces. The
child gives back behaviors which adults will use to modify
their relationship to him. Even an autocratic parent or
teacher will examine these behaviors in relation to his plan
of development for the child. Frequently a tree in its fixed
environment has less restriction on its growth than the child.
The tree self-selects both through the leaves and the roots.
It manufactures its own plant food and returns oxygen to
the air to replace the carbon dioxide which it took in. The
gardener does not restrict or deny its inherent right to do so.
The child who has both mobility and capacity to learn how
to use his cooperative process on higher conceptual levels

is given so little help by adults that he uses it on the lower autonomic levels. A great educational problem is how to provide an environment in which the cooperative interactive process may become the basic learning process in all home and school activities.

WHERE IS QUALITY IN THE PROCESS?

This question usually raises in students, educators, and parents an upset or irritation of the protoplasm that goes deeply into the self. At the outset few see how there can be quality in a process, for they have been educated to believe that it lies outside the individual in objects and stimuli whose energy he cannot convert into the organic energy necessary for his growth. The quality in these objects is fixed by persons better than he and perhaps by powers over which even his superiors have no control. Many students perceive the process as a new method of teaching these fixed objects and ends. Now they realize that no objects, knowledges, or skills are fixed and unchanging for all time. Each is only a form of energy which individuals convert into the self-energy necessary for their growth.

There are three important aspects of this conversion. First, the conscious process is common to all people yet is unique in each. What a child converts outside objects into is unique to him, for no other person has it, not even his identical twin. Second, conversion is really the heart of the process. Without it the child does not grow; with it he may grow but not grow up, depending upon what he converts the outside energy into within himself. What takes place inside of him, rather than what he gives back to the environment, is what counts in growing. Third, the child has little use for the so-called correct values placed by outside persons upon objects, knowledges, or behaviors. Through his own sensory, visceral, and conceptual energy he experiences what is satisfying and self-enhancing. He places his confidence in his process rather than in an externally organized system of objects with their energy values. When individuals satisfy intelligently their common needs by a mutually cooperative process, based on the reality and integrity of their own experiences, a genuine socialized living results for all.

The quality of the process is found in the kind of self which the individual becomes. All life is purposive in that it moves in the direction of survival, regeneration, and reproduction of its kind. While a human being has this tendency in common with an amoeba, the operating level is different. The direction of the amoeba is autonomic and subceptive; that of an adult can and should become conscious and perceptive. The individual develops a conscious self which is the center or the nucleus of his personality. His self selects outside objects, regulates their conversion, determines the amount and direction of energy expended, and enhances itself during these activities. What an individual perceives himself to be and how he accepts what he sees and feels are exceedingly important in determining his direction of action. Since the self is built gradually by a biological process immediately following conception, the process is definitive in determining what the self will be. When outside persons wish to modify behaviors emanating from an individual, they should help him study and improve his process rather than criticize or repair his specific actions, for these are only symptoms of his underlying energy organization. Thus the way each individual sees and accepts himself, and the way others see and accept his actions are the internal and external aspects of the quality of the self. And the freer the individual is to use thoughtfully his biological growth process in a sympathetic environment, the higher will be his resulting maturity and that of others associated with him.

Direction and quality of the process are inextricably interwoven for they are aspects of the movement of the total life to regenerate, enrich, and enhance itself. When the self is damaged beyond the possibility of organic regeneration the life ceases to function for death is the disintegration of the self. There is no mind distinct and separate from the body, neither is there a physical body that operates by itself alone. Each person is a self with different operating levels ranging from the autonomic, subceptive, to the most deliberative perceptive action. If any individual is to improve his biological process, he must understand his developing self and the behaviors which he is externalizing. Adults in home and schools should help children understand their growing selves. More important is the help adults give each other in understanding and reorienting their own selves toward higher levels. For the limit to self-maturity is infinity. And only adults who continue to improve themselves will allow children to do likewise.

HOW ARE GROWING AND LEARNING RELATED?

Since growing and learning take place simultaneously in the same organism, they must be related to each other. And since the self is the operating center of the life, each must affect the quality of the self. There is no agreement among educators or laymen on what the relationship is or should be. Yet there are two major groups and positions which can be identified without damage to the personal beliefs of anyone.

One group, a small but increasing number of persons, holds to only one process for growing up both in physical structure and in deliberative action. They assert that behavior is the total organism operating in some unified focused relationship to its world. Unity of relationship can exist to enhance the self only when the whole organism operates through or functions by a common process. What the outside observer calls physical and psychological growth are two aspects of the self, so defined for purposes of discussion. In reality there is only one person, who matures by one biological growth-learning process or is arrested en route at some low level by conflicting processes.

The other and larger group accept the biological growth process for physical development and physiological functioning but reject most of it for self-development and psychological behavior. They hold that the process of maturing the self in a culture is different from the process of growing up into physical maturity. They accept concepts of learning drawn from cultural sources centuries before the biological process of growing was understood. This dualism between growing and learning controls both educational practices and general living in all countries of the world today, including the United States.

The differences between the two groups are not so sharp that one rejects the total position of the other, yet there seems to be no middle ground. Those who believe in one life process for all aspects of growth reject the dualism and explain growing and learning by unitary or molar dynamics. Those who believe in the dualism use, under certain conditions, some aspects of the biological process as a method of teaching their fixed and unchanging behaviors. But the general tendency of action of each falls into one or the other position. I shall polarize these positions regarding learning by setting out in sharp contrast the concept held by each group, drawing the basic ideas from their expressed theories and their educational practices. Since I am unable at the moment to find more definitive terms, I will refer to biological learning as the need-experience process and to nonbiological learning as subject-teaching method.

The chief aspects of the need-experience process both in theory and in practice may be stated thus:

1. The learner has a felt need or tension or upset which he wishes to resolve or release.

2. He moves in his surrounding environment, both internal and external, to investigate the conditions which affect such need.

3. He self-selects from the external environment materials

to convert into others that will enable him to deal adequately with the internal need.

4. He creatively changes these self-selected materials into new emergent meanings, concepts, or values.

5. He uses these new meanings to reconstruct or reshape the dynamic conditions in the situation which caused the need to arise by (a) changing himself internally as a person, thereby viewing his environment differently, and/or (b) modifying his external behaviors so as to alter the external dynamics of the situation.

6. He continues to investigate the need both in its internal and external aspects through the cooperative interactive process. He self-selects, creatively assimilates, reconstructs himself and his environment until the tension is released in the direction of his better self-realization.

7. He desires, selects, and uses through creative conversion the advice of others. He expects such advice to be focused on cooperatively showing him how to use his external behavior to determine more exactly what is his internal self in order that he may improve the total need-experience process.

The majority of educators and laymen who hold that the learning process differs from the biological growth process generally believe in a subject-teaching method of education, the chief characteristics of which are these:

1. There is a need or tension in some person outside the child but within his psychological field, such as a parent or an educator.

2. The outside person predicates or imputes a similar upset or need inside the child.

3. The outside person selects from his environment the materials which he believes he can use to satisfy his needs. He attaches similar value to them for the child in satisfying his predicated need. Thus the child has selected for him materials to satisfy a need which he does not now and never can have, because of marked differences between him and the adult

both in biological inheritance and in experiential structure.

4. The adult denies or restricts creative assimilation by the child of the materials selected for him to learn. He expects the child to give back to him on demand in the form in which they were presented the materials which he (the adult) selected to satisfy his needs. The opportunity for creative conversion is so limited that the child develops few new meanings or values useful in reconstructing himself or his environment.

5. The adult uses every authoritarian means to "guide" the child into giving back to him the external behaviors which he demands. Rarely does he relinquish his control to the child, except in minor details where he can afford to be generous.

Some pertinent conclusions from this polarized analysis can now be drawn. First, under the need-experience process both the child and the adult use the same process. The child works on his need while the adult works on his, which is to help the child identify and study his need. Under subject teaching the adult uses the need process for himself, but denies it to the child.

Second, under the need process both the adult and the child concentrate on better understanding and using the process in order to improve the direction and quality of the expended energy. In subject teaching the child concentrates upon learning fixed knowledge as an end in itself, while this same knowledge may be functional energy to the adult who demands it.

Third, both agree that knowledge is action but disagree as to its origin and effect. In the need-experience approach knowledge is created by the individual in resolving his need. It involves the whole individual in relation to the whole situation. For some persons it is a shorthand word for the entire need-experience process. It takes place both inside and outside the individual, so it is both covert and overt action. It is as emergent and dynamic as life itself. Every individual seeks knowledge, not merely to understand himself and his world but to change both intelligently. The quality of the change is tested by the relatively dependable consequences upon himself and others.

Advocates of subject teaching think of knowing as eliciting fixed overt responses taught so as to control action in one direction toward one and only one preconceived end. Covert responses are secondary and immaterial, unless they impede or reconvert the controlled overt demands, whereupon external adjustments are sometimes made in the methods but not in the desired ends. Medieval scholars held that knowledge existed independently prior to the individual and was acquired and used for internal mental action only, never to change either the individual or his world. Modern subject teaching accepts the independent existence of knowledge but believes it to be an instrument for specific and unchanging overt action. The medieval and modern subject concepts of knowledge are similar in that neither contemplates change in the individual or in his world, since both are instruments to resist change. Thus the disagreement on the meaning of knowledge is deep and significant.

Fourth, the chief difference between the two approaches to learning is that the need-experience process is circular action, while the subject-teaching method is linear action. The former begins with the learner, goes out into his environment, returns to him for conversion, appears again to the observer. Since these unitary movements take place rapidly, they are difficult to observe. The latter moves from the outside adult to the child and directly back to the adult without external evidence of internal conversion. Yet conversion actually takes place unknown to the adult, for the child releases the converted energy outside at times and places unknown to adults who try to control him.

The differences between circular and linear learning are shown in Charts III and IV. I have indicated the self as composed of two parts. The inner ring is the true or real self. The outer ring is the protective or acting or seeming self, sometimes called the ego. The purpose of the protective coating is to shield the real or genuine self from disruptive external demands, by absorbing or diverting such blows before they become dangerous to the operating nucleus of the individual.

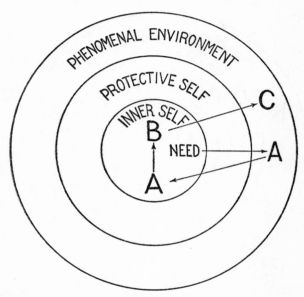

Chart III. The Circular Need-Experience Process

Chart III shows how, impelled by its own need, the self reaches out into the environment to self-select *A*, which it believes is desirable raw material to satisfy its need. *A* is converted or creatively assimilated into *B*, part of which is retained and the remainder given out into the environment as *C*. Thus the process is circular from the child into the environment and back again, with the control in the child. This is similar to the flow of energy in living cells from the nucleus into the cytoplasm and back to the nucleus, with the control in the nucleus.

As shown in Chart IV, teaching begins with Teacher X, who is outside the self of the child but within his environment. Teacher X teaches the child subject Y, which lies outside the child's field but is in the teacher's. The child takes it into his protective self and gives it back to X when neces-

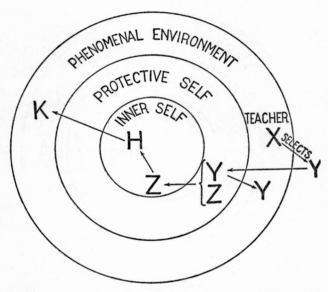

Chart IV.   The Linear Subject-Teaching Method

sary. But Y is only a part of the situation in which the subject is taught. It occurs with other field factors, such as Z. The child self-selects some Z factors which he changes into H, keeping part in himself and releasing the residue K where the teacher is not dominating the external environment. The child partially learns Y but adequately learns H. If he learns Y adequately, he must reverse the teaching into a need-experience process. Some children have ability to do this even under most difficult external conditions. They learn the three R's reasonably well while keeping themselves intact and maturing as persons.

WHAT DIFFERENCE DOES IT MAKE?

Many students ask what difference it makes whether a child is reared by the need-experience process or by subject-teaching method. The difference is in whether he will have an opportunity to become a mature or an immature self. From conception to birth the child develops by his growth process. Shortly thereafter, adults introduce him to the culture by reverse teaching methods. He struggles to creatively assimilate their demands by his need-experience process. Not understanding himself and his growth process and being unable to reconvert the adult requests, he faces each unintelligently, thus arresting his development. His normal growth process must become his cultural learning process, accepted by him and his elders, if he is to become a continuously maturing person.

Students now ask rapidly and directly a multitude of specific questions: "How can you give a child toilet training? How can you make him eat the right foods? How can you see that he gets enough sleep? How can you teach him what belongs to him and what belongs to others?" These behaviors are necessary to life in our culture and must be learned, but under conditions which permit the circular response. (1) They must be emotionally accepted by the child at the time and they must not block his normal circular, internal conversion. (2) They must be introduced into his experience when such emotional reaction can be favorably achieved. Up to that time adults must protect him from such demands or actions. (3) They must be presented by parents or teachers without emotionally preferred direction and control so that the tension of everyone will be on an even, normal learning level. (4) Later, they should be raised to the level of conceptual examination for re-evaluation, with the acceptance or rejection which accompanies all deliberative action. Under these conditions the child emotionally accepts toilet training, food habits, and many other responses. Later he reconstructs them by the need process on higher levels of unitary action. Thus they enhance rather than impede his growing self.

Students invariably ask what happens to children or college students who are under great pressure for linear responses, either in the home or in the school. Throughout his life everyone is subjected to external pressure, but it does not operate in the same way or have the same effect on each. When each knows autonomically that the pressure hurts him, he emotionally rejects it and tries to protect himself, for his biological drive for self-preservation is greater than his learning energy for derived cultural patterns. The child or the college student protects himself in one or more of the following ways.

1. He admits into the protective sheath surrounding his inner self or self-concept enough of the pressure or material to satisfy the outside demand. He gives it back in the form in which it was received at such times and places as the external control expects. He "polishes the apple" whenever necessary, to release the pressure. Eventually he develops ego involvements with his dominator, gradually accepts it as desirable, and thus prevents his inner self from maturing. He becomes a dependent person the rest of his life.

2. A child may follow the other extreme and fight against the external demands which hurt him. He becomes a troublemaker, a problem child, a difficult person to the outside authorities. They may change the nature or direction of the pressure to make it more palatable; they may use more pressure to break him or to make him more tractable; they may isolate him from his agemates by placing him in a special class. The methods which he takes to save himself may lead to rugged individualism, egocentric thinking, domination of other people, or compulsive independence.

3. A third child may withdraw from the pressure entirely by creating his own world of fantasy or by concentrating upon some activity approved by adults. Both of these may be simple beginnings of later mental breakdowns. An English professor put pressure upon his two elementary school children to become academic scholars. The boy, the younger of the two, rebelled and thus eased it. The girl engrossed herself in the books which her father approved. She came immediately home from school, went to his study to read according to his planned schedule, rarely played with other children, showed a marked precocity in literary criticism. When she was fourteen years of age, the father boasted that she had read more classics than he had at his college graduation. The next year his daughter attempted suicide. Only then did he realize the effect upon her of his pressure for academic achievement.

4. A child may take the outside demands in his stride. He does what he is asked to do without involving his ego or his self favorably or unfavorably. He realizes autonomically or consciously the low value of the goods which he is asked to receive, so he tosses them back with slight penetration and little emotional effect. He uses every opportunity outside the home and school to satisfy his needs by a normal learning process. Thus he releases and develops more potential capacity to higher levels than do persons with other protective mechanisms. But opportunities for such development, in spite of home or school, are decreasing each year. The child must live in parallel competing worlds until he has sufficient experience creatively to unify them.

All four of these protective directions of action are abnormal, since neither the child nor the adult releases, understands, and develops his potential capacity to live and learn. They do not prevent creative assimilation, however, even though the child rejects the goods selected for him to learn. He changes some aspects of the total experience into new meanings or concomitant learnings which he uses to build himself. He does not release these emergent learnings into the existing environment since he knows they will be disapproved, but he does liberate them where the authority has no control. A friend from a city moved his family into the country so that his two children, seven and five, could grow up in a more favorable environment. The next year the younger child, Richard, entered the first grade in the consolidated rural school, traveling eight miles a day in the school bus. He said he liked school, seemed happy, and showed other outward signs of a profitable experience, but when I asked him at the end of the year what he liked best about school, he quickly replied, "The ride in the bus."

The second year things were not going so well, for his behaviors indicated a marked change in his inner development. In a casual conversation in early November, while showing him how to saw a dead limb from a tree, I asked him how he liked school. He replied, "I don't like it!" "But," I said, "you liked it last year, why don't you like it this year?" "I got a new teacher." "And why don't you like the new teacher?" I continued. After some thought he said, "She looks like a witch." A long pause, and then, "Sometimes she acts like a witch." Then after a still longer pause, he blurted out, "You know I believe she is a witch."

This teacher was trying her best to teach Richard subject matter, but he was really learning how to identify witches. He was creatively changing some aspects of the total situation into his acceptable circular emergent, which he did not dare release in the school environment. His subject responses were unsatisfactory to the teacher but acceptable to him, for his real learnings that became part of himself were in a different area of meaning and value.

One great difference between circular and linear learning is that in the former the child learns his process openly, directly, and sympathetically, while in the latter neither he nor his elders know what his process is. One October day I received a telephone call from a parent asking to see me about his boy, who on many occasions had run away from school and now had run away from home. The father, a professional man, had his office in the front room of a first-floor apartment with living quarters in the rear. When the boy, an only child, was able to creep, the father placed a gate across the long corridor leading from the living room to the office waiting room. Soon Bobby mastered this barrier, much to the annoyance of the patients. Various coercive measures were applied to keep him where he belonged. The mother, who was socially active, gave little time to educating but much time to correcting him, leaving his general care to the maid. When old enough to play in the large open backyard on the apartment grounds, Bobby soon devised ways of getting through the fence or gate into the alley. Since both mother and maid were too busy to care for him, they harnessed him to an overhead wire so he could move a limited distance. Through other restrictive devices applied during these early years the boy became very quiet, docile, or what is generally called a good child. Enrolled in a private kindergarten at five, his teacher later reported that he was quiet and inactive, never showed much energy, never tried anything new, never gave her any trouble, always doing what he was told to do. She thought Bobby was a little peculiar, but since he was entered in the first grade of a public school, she did not report her observations.

In the first grade of a formal subject matter school, Bobby exhibited the same docile, inactive relationship to his environment. He began to read reasonably well but soon dropped to a middle and finally to a slow group in all of his work. But his teacher promoted him, believing he was a slow starter who would later show normal progress. Bobby entered the second grade hopefully after a summer in the country. Immediately he was placed in the slowest group in reading and arithmetic, and shortly thereafter in the new subject of spelling. This new teacher would take none of his lazy nonsense, so she put on extra pressure by withholding favors, giving him addi-

tional drill, and using many other devices. In the spring
Bobby knew autonomically that the school was damaging
him seriously, so he took direct relief by running away from
school. Brought back without an adequate understanding of
his situation, he worried through the year and was promoted
largely because of his father's position and the feeling of the
teacher that it was unfair to her to have him two years to mar
her successful record. The disturbed parents were too busy
to give much thought to the boy.

At the end of the first month in the third grade Bobby was
again in the lowest group in everything. With his past record
before her, his new teacher decided to take matters in hand
immediately. When he began to show his "lazy" behaviors,
she insisted that the mother come to school to hear her report and make firsthand observation of her difficulties. Up to
that time Bobby had felt that his hurt came from the school,
but when he saw his mother consulting with the teacher and
principal he knew subconsciously that his mother was also
against him, otherwise she would not be there. The next
night he ran away from home and was picked up by the police
two days later.

In the opening telephone conversation with me the father
made one of the most inaccurate observations of the century
when he said there was something wrong with the boy. Bobby
is now an active, alert young man, saved by a need-experience
process of learning in a new environment. His parents are
wiser and more mature people, after a terrific struggle to remake their arrested selves. Surely the concept of learning does
make a difference, as millions of children and adults testify
to every day by their actions.

A BACKWARD AND FORWARD LOOK

I shall comment on only one aspect of the biological growth
process—self-selection. Every individual self-selects from
every experience what he believes will help him better satisfy

his needs. I shall indicate here the range and types of self-selections made by students.

One person out of one thousand students challenges the soundness of the basic biology I have been outlining. He is usually a teacher of the subject in high school or college. He says that he was not taught such materials in his biology classes and cannot find them in any of the major college textbooks. The doctors, psychologists, psychiatrists, psychotherapists, nurses, and others in the class immediately help him broaden his concept of biology. One college biology teacher followed my suggestion to make an analysis of textbooks in biology and those in other areas dealing more directly with the process of growth. Later he reported in class the results of his study, defending the soundness of the class material and interpreting his new insight to the group.

Some students admit the soundness of the point of view but say they cannot accept it because of conflict with existing cultural patterns. Well do I remember the discussions with a group of third-year medical students in a European university. They were long on knowledge of anatomical structure but short on insight into the functional operation of the organism. These relationships between structure and function were more or less satisfactorily communicated. Yet by subconscious empathy I know deeper issues were involved. Finally, one member said, "This seems reasonable and I am sure that we as students are inclined to accept it. But as practicing physicians we will have to reject it. This approach places responsibility for the origin, direction, and quality of growth largely upon the individual, of course, in interaction with others. We operate on the theory that control of growth rests with certain dominant groups or with the cultural tradition or with forces outside the individual. And if we are to succeed in our profession, we must recognize and work within this cultural framework." I knew that he was accurately stating the philosophy of his as well as of all other authoritarian cultures. So we went back to the medieval concept of knowledge as thinking about thought to produce more thinking, but not to develop action to change the world into a better place in which to live.

A few students assert that they accept the biological process for both physical and educational growth, but say they are unable to use it in their particular positions. So we discuss why a person says he believes or accepts something mentally but does not use it in overt action. If growing is really the conversion of outside energy into new forms of energy within the self, the outward behavior should in some way reconstruct the environment. But if change takes place only in the protective self, the individual asserts his partial acceptance to please the outside persons, while the inner self rejects it and prevents overt action. Occasionally some person says he believes in need-experience learning so thoroughly that he will immediately put it into practice. A superintendent of schools who generally resisted this point of view during the summer session came to me on Wednesday of the last week wreathed in smiles. He said that now he understood and accepted this approach and that he would use it in his school system the coming school year. He proposed to return home and send out a bulletin stating that immediately all teachers in all schools should abandon the subject-teaching method and replace it by the need-experience process. It took a few hours of discussion for him to see that his method of introducing the need process violated the very process itself.

Many of the married members of classes explain how they can use this process effectively with their children, but they are unable to see how they can use it in their classroom teaching. They give excellent illustrations of cooperative living in the home and show how beneficial are the results when the group as a whole assumes responsibility for the growth of everyone. But the school has so many different rules and regulations defining what shall be taught and how the results shall be measured that they are afraid to use in school a process which they admit has been so successful in their homes. And their final response always seems to be, "If we were free in school to manage learning ourselves cooperatively with the children, we would work this way. But we are not free and we cannot change the conditions, so it is better to give the administrators or supervisors what they want."

Each person who takes any of the above positions is honest and realistic with himself, for he states his action as he perceives it in his own phenomenal field. But to an outside observer the fields of these students show distortions due to the prolonged effects of subject-teaching methods of education which prevented them from understanding themselves. A more realistic position from a less distorted field is taken by those who in private conference admit they cannot accept the need-experience process of learning because they are unable to change their inner selves, built on a set of meanings, values, and perceptions so different as to cause a violent and fearful conflict which they are unable to resolve. And so by nondirective or need-process therapy I try to help them face themselves.

But the majority of students say they can verify the viewpoints in their own experiences. They want to understand the biological process better in order to find out how they can use it to improve themselves as persons, and how they can apply it in existing school situations or in any life work in which they are engaged. In the following chapter I shall indicate some implications for what is now called the school curriculum.

Chapter **IV**

WHO MAKES THE CURRICULUM?

The people who make the school make the curriculum, for every school has a program of activities which it calls a curriculum. While these people argue as to what it is, where it came from, how it should be changed, what its essentials are, they do agree that the curriculum is made by people. Disagreements arise not so frequently in purpose or direction as in the means by which such direction shall be achieved. Since people make the curriculum, the most important question to ask is, What relationship shall exist among the people who make this curriculum? Shall it be authoritarian or cooperative? What difference does it make? This relationship among people makes a profound difference on many crucial points, for it determines whether the curriculum shall be defined from the point of view of the adult observer or from that of the child behaver.

WHAT IS THE CURRICULUM?

From the traditional authoritarian point of view the curriculum is a body of knowledge arranged systematically for progressive acquisition by the child, adolescent, or college student. This is consistent with the belief that changes in behavior result from association or synthesis of discrete objects existing independently of the learner in his environment.

This requisite knowledge is organized in a logical yet separate order or system called subjects.

In this country an early definition of the curriculum was "all the subjects offered by the school." At that time only a few subjects were studied by every pupil. The knowledge to be learned was written in books or presented orally by the teacher. Education was a race in which every pupil began each subject at scratch, and tried to beat his classmates to the end. The course was laid out in parallel lines to prevent fouling of the race by unfair tactics. In this way subjects, book learning, teaching, schooling, were all related, since they were the only source of the knowledge necessary for getting ahead of one's fellow men.

As life outside the school changed, new occupations opened, and new subjects were developed, more adults wanted their children to have an education. School enrollments increased in numbers and new subjects were added to the point where no person could study all of those offered. Preferences had to be made, so the authorities spoke. The curriculum became "All the subjects required for promotion, graduation, or a degree." Subjects of lesser value were called electives, while experiences too disorganized to be called subjects were labeled extracurricular activities, tolerated but not officially accepted by educators. This arrangement soon developed difficulties, and a new organization had to be found.

Many pupils now came to school with definite goals and they wanted a special arrangement of subjects more or less guaranteed to help them reach it. So the word "curriculum" was changed to have a third meaning: "Subjects selected and organized for a definite goal," such as college preparatory, vocational, commercial, agricultural. One city school system had its four-year secondary schools organized around nineteen such specialized groups of subjects called curriculums, one of which was selected by each pupil when admitted.

If he wished to change later, many complications arose because of this discreteness, for the content of a common subject such as English differed in each curriculum and one could not be substituted for another. In one school a boy who was a good pupil took five years to obtain his high school diploma because he changed his curriculum twice in order to obtain subjects which he thought would better satisfy his needs. The subjects offered by the school comprised what was called the program of studies. A course of study meant the material selected and organized in advance for a particular subject.

These definitions all show a difference of opinion among parents and educators as to which materials existing independently in the environment were really important in their concept of education for children.

About one hundred years ago this authoritarian viewpoint was seriously questioned. By the turn of the century many educators and laymen felt that these definitions of curriculum limited education to book learning within the four walls of a school. While secondhand experiences from books were important, their value was greatly overemphasized. The real test of the quality of learning was not in what the child gave back to the teacher in school, but in how he acted in all of his life experiences outside the school. These educators proposed that the curriculum represents "All the life experiences of children which are in any way affected by the school." This shifted the emphasis from subjects to life experiences or from the fragments of experiences of others to the ongoing activities of the child.

For a time this concept was favorably received by the traditionalists, for they naively thought that subject matter taught in schools affected favorably the behavior of children outside the school. They became alarmed when they realized, first, that their control over the curriculum would be decreased if not eliminated, second, that they must assume much responsibility for the life behavior of the child, whether it be good or bad from their point of view, and finally, that the accumulating evidence indicated that children made little use of the material taught in school in their outside life activities. They decided against releasing their control or assuming responsibility for outside behaviors. Instead, in the twenties they launched a counterattack to prove through objective studies the life behavior value of their respective subjects. They failed, for their own results from elementary school to college showed that pupils made little use in life activities of the subject matter taught to them. Its chief value was in learning more of the same material in the school.

As subsequent studies continued to verify these findings, subject specialists working with conservative general educators proposed a middle ground—that the curiculum be defined as "All the experiences (meaning subjects) which children undergo (meaning are taught) under the guidance (meaning control) of the school." This keeps the center of control with adults and the test of learning in the school. Adults can still select, organize, and rearrange fragments of the experiences of others for children to learn under new names, such as activities, units, cores, general education, or life-adjustment education. The psychology of the subject-teaching method remains. The human relations are still authoritarian. Education at all levels is still considered from the viewpoint of the observer. And neither the child nor the university student is better equipped to develop himself within his own psychological field. All of this is evidence of the compulsive drive in people to preserve reverse cultural traditions.

The advocates of cooperative human relations take the view of the behaver struggling to meet adequately his needs in his environment by a normal process. To them the curriculum is composed, first, of "Those learnings which each individual self-selects, accepts, incorporates into his inner self to act with, on, and upon in subsequent experiences." Since the accepted learnings are conversions of energy objects taken from the phenomenal environment, they sometimes define the curriculum as "All the available outside resources from which each learner may select and convert into the new meanings necessary to meet his needs." The resources are people, the physical universe, the cultural heritage, the learner's overt behaviors, and the interactions of others with him, all of which are dynamic, flexible, variable, and continuous. These definitions place control with the learner, where it has always been regardless of how a curriculum is defined or how much adults think they control it. No person can ever force another to select what he wants him to select, but he can make self-selection easy or difficult, impulsive or intelligent.

Traditionalists assert that children are too young and immature to control their own selections. They must be told when to study, what to learn, what to think, how to behave. The fact is that children now control what they learn and how they behave, even in the most authoritarian homes and schools. And this is a basic reason for the cooperative process through which they learn to select deliberately and intelligently with the help of others.

WHEN IS THE CURRICULUM MADE?

From the authoritarian point of view the curriculum is made for children by adults in advance of the teaching situation or even long before the children who study it were born. A visit for only one day in a curriculum laboratory or in a good traditional school will furnish ample evidence to support this statement. From the cooperative point of view the curriculum is made during the process of living it by those who participate in it. The nearer one is to the center of such living, the more actively is he engaged and the more responsibility does he assume for learning how to make it successful.

From this point of view a group of first-grade children with their teacher will assume more responsibility for their curriculum than their parents or the superintendent of schools, no one of whom is engaged in the living situation. The authoritarian point of view reverses these positions. The superintendent, who is farthest removed, will have the most responsibility for making the curriculum and the children will have the least, if any at all. But what difference, then, does it make? It depends on whether one believes that living should be directed from without or within, or whether adults or children should learn how to manage it. Shall children learn how to manage it cooperatively or how to meet individually the external demands? The result is not only a different kind of curriculum but a marked difference in the resulting maturity of behavior of both children and adults.

Students understand these differences better when I explain that the authoritarian approach results in the curriculum that *was*, while the cooperative approach results in the curriculum that *is*. Adults who sift, evaluate, select from the surrounding culture the materials which they want taught to children experience the *is* curriculum through an active, outgoing, purposeful, and convertive relationship to their environment. On paper these selections become their *was* experiences. Teachers take these *was* curriculum materials and try to teach them so that they become the dynamic *is* experience for children. It is more difficult for the best teachers to make these dead need-satisfactions of adults into learning resources for live children than it is for the college professor to have his subject matter become the need-selections of students. By the cooperative approach the curriculum is always made as an *is* or ongoing or becoming experience. However one views the curriculum the fact remains that the present life process of the learner is the source of his behaviors whether they be considered adequate or undesirable.

The two concepts are shown in these flow charts:

Line 1: Authoritarian human relations→ subjects→ subject matter→ teaching methods→ subject matter essentials→ results in arrested development of people who believe in and use authoritarian human relations.

Line 2: Cooperative human relations→ people→ needs→ learn-
ing→ human essentials→ organization and administra-
tion→ results in people high on the maturity scale who
believe in and use cooperative human relations.

A curriculum for children based upon authoritarian relations, if well done, results in adults who live by authoritarian
techniques. The curriculum developed with children through
cooperative relations, if well done, results in adults who live
by the cooperative process. The two are not interchangeable.
The authoritarian curriculum can result in cooperative adults
only in rare instances, for cooperative action is a higher form
of social relationship which takes a long time to learn. The
cooperative curriculum may develop some adults who live by
authoritarian controls, for they are a less complex form of
social relationship which can be quickly learned. Regressing
is always easier than ascending on the maturity scale.

There are no adequate single words to designate these
two approaches to the curriculum or the kinds of curriculum.
The terms authoritarian and cooperative, which emphasize
the human relations, are little known and rarely discussed
in curriculum classes or in educational literature. In earlier
books on *Integration* and *Interaction,* I used "subject curriculum" for the authoritarian approach and "experience
curriculum" for the cooperative approach. This confused
some students, since subject matter is an aspect of experience
and experience includes subject matter in some form. Recently students suggested "the teaching curriculum" for the
authoritarian approach and "the learning curriculum" for
the cooperative approach. These terms will be used throughout this book.

People who sponsor the teaching curriculum are concerned
about subjects, subject matter, teaching methods, the minimum essentials in subject matter. Those who support the
learning curriculum are interested in the behavior of all
people, but more especially that of children. By improving

the process by which children satisfy their needs, they help them recognize and direct the dynamics of their behavior. Essentials are the basic aspects of the cooperative process, together with such individual learnings as each child selects to incorporate into himself. Advocates of the teaching curriculum also give much attention to pupils, but in their own authoritarian way. They study, test, and guide individual children, but always within the framework of their traditional controls, which they vigorously support. Advocates of the learning curriculum help children to study the surrounding culture, past, present, and future, but not through the systematic organization called subjects. They help pupils to make intelligent selections from the culture which preselected subject matter of the teaching curriculum denies.

Thus each group considers the pupils and the culture, since both are necessary for a school and a curriculum. They differ sharply in the way the child and the culture should affect each other. The way they grow up together—authoritarian or cooperative—determines the kind of self each individual will develop into. And the kind of person he becomes affects the direction and amount of change he will advocate for the culture in the future. Most adults reared as children in an authoritarian environment perpetuate it through their offspring. Most adults reared in a freer, more cooperative environment provide it for their children. For various reasons there are always some persons who want the opposite relationship for their children. Yet more people now realize that the process of making the curriculum which continues in the selves of adults is their best asset in changing the culture toward the better life.

SOME BASIC DIFFERENCES BETWEEN THE TWO CONCEPTS

A few of the many basic differences in point of view and practice between the teaching and learning curriculums will be explained here. Others will follow in succeeding chapters.

The teaching curriculum operates on the principles that follow.

1. It is controlled by adults. Aims, materials, organization, teaching aids, standards, criteria for success or failure are all selected and managed by them. Children are consulted only on minor details, such as teaching aids and devices. Rarely do they participate in making major decisions from the first grade through the graduate school.

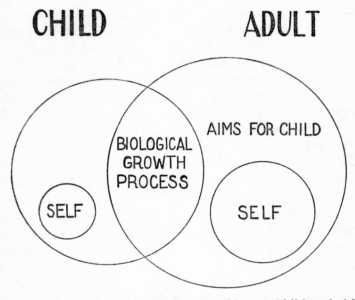

Chart V. Psychological Field Relationships of Child and Adult

2. Children work blindly toward adult aims, values, and standards since these seldom fall within their psychological fields. The outside authority who controls the curriculum sets the aims, goals, and values within his experience to meet his needs. Since his experiences and needs are broader and deeper than those of less mature children or college

students, his aims are usually outside their experience. Chart V shows these field relationships.

The overlapping area in the two fields shown in the chart is the process of growth which the adult does not accept. He grooves the child toward his aims or goals, which are outside the child's field. Since a child cannot long operate blindly toward the goals of another, he pursues his own purposes related to his own needs, while to the observer he appears to be facing the subject-teaching situations. And since his purposes rarely coincide with the aims of the teacher, he learns through his needs and purposes while the teacher teaches by his aims. Thus good human relations and desirable learning are lost to each.

3. In the teaching curriculum adults expect children to reach fixed ends, usually identified by correct answers. From the child in beginning reading who tells what the book says up to the senior in college who takes a teachers' examination, the emphasis is on fixed ends or "truth." Variations from this pattern are mere diversions, for they provide no credit toward high school graduation or a college degree. This tends to develop an individual who believes there is a correct answer to every life problem, and always searches for a superior authority to give it to him. He may attach himself permanently to an individual or cultural institution which gives him every answer without his having to search for or think about it.

4. Adults expect children to take fragments of the experiences of others and fit them together into a unified experience of their own, a process which is psychologically impossible. Fragments of secondhand experiences are never united into wholes any more than fragments of apples can be put together to form a whole apple. The parts that give quality to an apple or to an experience are differentiated, not summated. In a curriculum composed of fragments taught under authoritarian pressures, the child has to find other experiences

outside the school through which to build more or less unaided the internal unity so necessary for his normal development.

In one school system I found a boy who was a good illustration of these difficulties. On entering high school he specifically stated that after graduation he would enter his father's
wholesale grocery business. Nevertheless his counselor gave
him the college preparatory curriculum. After the first
examination of his second year he asked his geometry teacher
the simple, reasonable question, "What good will this
geometry do me in my father's wholesale grocery business?"
He was trying to clarify his own purpose within his own
needs while learning the fragments of experiences of others
presented by the teacher. Not recognizing this situation, the
teacher gave the boy the usual arguments for the value of
mathematics in improving thinking which should be an asset
in the grocery business. The boy showed his evaluation by
his behavior, for his work decreased, his attitude changed,
and his grades dropped. In March the teacher pointed him
out to me as a lazy, troublesome boy who would fail the
subject. By examining his school records, talking with him,
chatting with his other teachers, interviewing his parents,
visiting the wholesale grocery, I concluded that an alert,
intelligent boy was trying to mature himself by a normal
process in an unsympathetic, restrictive school which was
the chief cause of his difficulties. The school officials would
neither admit responsibility nor change the existing conditions. Fortunately, when I helped him come to a realistic
explanation of the situation, the boy so raised his grades for
the remaining period as to obtain the required average to
pass the subject. Thus does a bright boy with a clear need
and purpose become a troublemaker in the teaching curriculum.

The learning curriculum operates on a different set of
principles.

1. The experience is cooperatively controlled by those in the learning group. The direction, materials, organization, learning aids, standards of evaluation, criteria for success are all selected and managed by consensus within the group.

2. Members of the group work openly, consistently, and deliberately on their own needs, purposes, judgments. There is no blind action, for both the group and the individuals move directly toward the attainment of their own purposes within their experiences.

3. Everyone works toward the most intelligent decisions or the most deliberative action of which he is capable in a cooperative environment. Functional knowledge related to the action is present. Increased accuracy in differentiated parts is promoted. The fluid end as a direction in process is accepted.

4. The wholeness of the experience sets the need for differentiating the parts. Integrating wholeness is the primary purpose which controls the movement of the total experience from the very beginning. Parts are always refined in relation to such wholeness. Thus there are no stray fragments of experiences of others which cannot be used.

These differences can be summarized in a simple column comparison.

Teaching Curriculum	*Learning Curriculum*
1. Adult control and management.	1. Cooperative group control and management.
2. Children work blindly against adult goals.	2. Children work openly and intelligently to achieve their own purposes.
3. End of teaching is correct answers.	3. End of learning is intelligent social action.
4. Children are taught fragments of experiences of others, to be assembled later in some unified organization.	4. Children refine parts of their own experience within integrative wholeness.

The evidence shows two further items of importance. First, improvements in the teaching curriculum come through incorporating in it, to the extent possible, the basic ideas of the learning curriculum. Second, pupils badly adjusted in the former are placed in the latter to heal their personality disorders. Since the learning curriculum is the therapy for the teaching curriculum, it should be accepted for its preventive and positive achievements.

WHAT ARE SOME OF THE AGREEMENTS?

There is common ground between the two positions since they are differentiated from an original common whole. But the common ground is no longer significant educationally; it does not define either the theory or the practice. It is like the outward show of handshaking and good fellowship of the old grads at a college reunion. The next day they go about their life activities, forgetting both the principles and the practices of their common pronouncements. Educators assert common ground but follow widely divergent theories and practices.

The essential aspects of the common ground assented to in theory but widely interpreted in practice are:

1. Each position accepts experience as the basis for education, for it is the only thing that anyone can study or learn anywhere, at any time, in any culture. But no one person knows all past or present experiences of peoples, neither does he know what experiences he will face in the future. Yet everyone must draw upon the past and present to develop intelligent foresight for the future. Who shall select from past experience and how shall such foresight in present experience be developed? Here great differences in the interpretation and use of experience begin.

2. Each group recognizes the fact that children are necessary for a school. Without them there would be no educational institutions. Each group is genuinely concerned about

children and the educational opportunity offered them. But here this common ground stops. The authoritarian group studies the capacities, individual differences, achievement of children in order to fit them into the common mold of prescribed subject matter. The cooperative group studies these same variations in order to help children release and develop their potentialities for creative action.

✓ 3. Both groups admit that the child must be reared in the surrounding culture. But they differ markedly as to what shall be his relationship to adults who control his environment. Here the distinction between authoritarian and cooperative relations is vital.

4. The two groups agree that the final test of education is in the behavior of children and adults and both assert that they want better or more mature behavior. Here this common ground ceases. They do not agree as to the meaning of the evidence for or the educational program necessary to achieve such maturity. The accompanying flow chart, Chart VI, of the way each group educates children will sharpen this difference.

The problem raised on this flow chart is whether *Line 1* or *Line 2* offers a child a better opportunity to become a mature adult. Some evidence may be appropriate. First, the control of the curriculum has been on Line 1 for at least two thousand years. Some authorities say it extends back in the culture to the dawn of civilization prior to the establishment of formal schools. Second, in spite of the many isolated attempts to improve Line 1 during these years, the curriculum still operates on Line 1. Third, the inadequacy of the schools in teaching pupils how to mature effectively their general and specific behaviors is a charge against the teaching curriculum on Line 1. It is not against the learning curriculum on Line 2 since that curriculum is not as yet in general practice. Fourth, the ineffectiveness of the curriculum on Line 1 in educating children and adults to meet intelligently

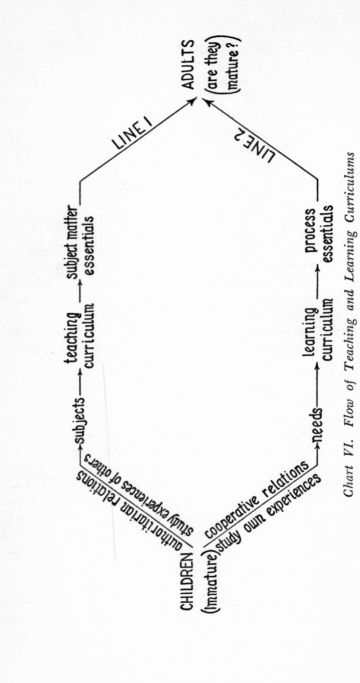

Chart VI. Flow of Teaching and Learning Curriculums

their needs in modern living has been shown repeatedly by various studies over the past century. Fifth, the possibly greater value of the learning curriculum on Line 2 can be supported theoretically through recent research in many fields which were not in existence when Line 1 was established. Sixth, the limited evidence available from practice on Line 2 supports the theoretical possibilities. Theoretically the time is ripe for rapid and universal change from the teaching to the learning curriculum. The implementation is difficult owing to further differences between the authoritarian and cooperative groups.

5. Both groups agree that one test of maturing behavior is that a child utilizes his past learnings to improve his future learnings. Here the agreement ceases. The authoritarians interpret this to mean that the child should use past subject matter to learn more subject matter, such as arithmetic to succeed in algebra, reading to learn geography and history, the expanded three R's to succeed in high school, high school subjects to succeed in college. The prerequisite or admission requirement system is based on this premise. The cooperative group agrees that a child utilizes past learnings to improve future behavior, for it is axiomatic that every individual picks up something from past experience to carry on in present and future action. But what does he select to carry on? The cooperative group believes this now is and should be the process of growth or learning which he uses to meet his needs. Specific subject learnings are important and have meaning only as they are converted through this process. Again the authoritarians test maturing behavior through book learning or academic knowledge taught in school. The cooperative group tests maturing behavior through the tendencies to action of the child in unforeseen life experiences inside and outside school. The school is a center for improving living instead of teaching fragments of experiences of others.

6. Both groups agree that on their tests of maturing behavior the results of the teaching curriculum are unsatisfactory. The majority of children in a good traditional school never learn enough subject matter to be able to use it to improve the quality of subsequent learning in that or any other subject. Every year parents, teachers, and administrators document this endlessly from their own experiences. College professors constantly refer to the increasing number of students with inadequate preparation to learn their subject as they, the professors, want to teach it. A reasonable estimate is that 75 to 85 per cent do not and 15 to 25 per cent do learn enough to be successful on higher levels. So both groups want a greater carry-over from past to present and future learning.

Furthermore, the use of what is taught in school in outside life experiences is on an equally low level. The reasons are that (a) little subject matter taught in an authoritarian school is at that time usable in outside life, (b) the child does not learn enough of it to apply, (c) the child does not see where or how to apply even the small amount he has learned, and (d) the child acts on a different kind of learning from that taught him in school.

What are the remedies for this situation? The authoritarian group wants to intensify or subtly refine the authority by increasing requirements, prescriptions, drills, examinations, prerequisites. The cooperative group wants to abandon the external subject approach and work with children on their needs, feelings, values, which are the dynamics of their behavior. The matter could be settled amicably if both groups would accept the biological process of learning and the dynamics of behavior, and devise a program best suited to mature people within them. But those who want power or now have power through a teaching curriculum rarely agree to such a proposal. They fear the results of reasonable inquiry. Hence the schools continue on Line 1.

HOW DID THE DIFFERENT CONCEPTS OF CURRICULUM ARISE?

Many students ask where these two different curriculums originated, why schools continue to operate on Line 1 in spite of the evidence against it, what is valuable enough in the teaching curriculum to keep and incorporate into Line 2, what attempts have been made to change from the teaching to the learning curriculum, whether these attempts have succeeded or failed, and other questions too numerous to mention. I shall summarize the background which students need in order to clarify their emerging meanings.

The three distinct approaches to the curriculum are the authoritarian, the revolt or child-centered, and the need-experience process. The first began at Alexandria in Egypt in the third and fourth centuries B.C., where a school was formed to teach the wisdom found in the books of the great Greek writers. This school was taken to Rome to teach the Romans the philosophy of the Greeks. The early Christian church employed it to maintain unimpaired its authoritarian doctrines. It was used to teach the revived classics during the Revival of Learning. The authoritarian-class school was brought to America by the early settlers and established to teach the content of the books written and approved by the authorities. At the time of American Independence, Thomas Jefferson raised grave doubts as to whether such an authoritarian-class school could ever educate the common man in the intelligent action necessary to maintain and enrich democracy. But nothing was done to change it.

A new version, which some writers have called a more scientific method in the authoritarian approach, came when Herbert Spencer in 1859 published his famous article on education entitled "What Knowledge Is of Most Worth?" He said the purpose of education was to prepare an individual for complete living as an adult. To discover what knowledge was of most worth one should analyze all aspects of complete living, thereby locating what knowledge should be taught children to prepare them for such later life. Spencer divided complete living into (1) maintaining self-preservation of life and limb, (2) acquiring the means of living, or work, (3) rearing and disciplining offspring, or family life, (4) carrying on proper social relations, or social-civic responsibilities, and (5) gratifying leisure tastes and feelings by appropriate activities. Implementing his analysis of complete living for the schools Spencer said the best knowledge was in the sciences of life—biology, physics, chemistry, mathematics,—and the sciences of society—history, sociology, and psychology. The classics, then the center of the school curriculum, were of little use to an individual in complete living.

While Spencer placed more emphasis upon newer subjects or life sciences, it was his method which lived after him. By 1900, under the name of job analysis, it was used in scientific management in industry and in education through vocational agriculture. Alexander Inglis accepted it as his technique in formulating the Cardinal Objectives of Education (1918) except that he selected seven aspects of adult living to Spencer's five. Bobbitt in 1918–20, following the same approach, classified the major fields of human action into ten groups which are a more detailed breakdown of the Spencer and Inglis lists. Charters employed this technique in organizing the curriculum at Stephens College, Columbia, Mo., in 1923–26, and also with Waples in the Teacher Education Study in 1928. Herbert Bruner used it to locate the modern problems for his modern problems approach of 1925–30. Paul Hanna applied it in setting up the scope and sequence for the Virginia Curriculum of 1931.

Job analysis is today used by all persons who approach the curriculum through the demands of adults, whether their results be called the Cardinal Objectives of Education, Persistent Problems of Living, the Core Curriculum, or General Education. It is the favored method of those who believe that

people improve their behavior by synthesizing isolated fragments of the experience of others.

Early in my educational career, I was fortunate enough to
have experience in using the job analysis technique in vocational agriculture. Later I made time and motion studies for
four different manufacturing organizations. In the early
twenties I applied this approach to curriculum by analyzing
activities of adults, elementary children, and high school
pupils. By 1925 I concluded that this technique could be used
satisfactorily only when (1) there were fixed and unchanging
products, (2) these products were made out of fixed and
unchanging parts, (3) the operator placed these parts together
in the correct order to achieve the predetermined product
with as few operations and motions as possible and with a
very high percentage of perfect finished products. The operator had no voice in determining the structure and value of
the product nor the relationship of the parts to produce it.
He was consulted on layout of parts for ease of handling, the
assembling motions, and the rhythm of work and rest. All
decisions for improvement of production were considered
with workers on an individual basis. The results of the recent
"alone and together" experiments were not available. The
effects of cooperative group purposes on output and morale
were just beginning to be studied both in industry and in
education. The many experiments in cooperative curriculum
planning among teachers in the period from 1920 to 1930
were the educational aspect of this group effort.

From the available evidence I conclude that job analysis
cannot be effectively used in education for the following
reasons. (1) The teacher and pupils are not working toward
ends fixed in advance or unchanging educational products.
They are moving in variable directions which are a function
of their needs in their life situations within their psychological
fields. They have in common a tendency toward the most
intelligent or deliberative action possible within their available experience. (2) These variable directions toward variable

ends must be achieved by an appropriate process in which both the developing meanings and value judgments of the children and the emerging professional insight of the teacher can be used and improved. (3) The pupils and teacher play an important part in determining the value of the everyday product of their efforts, which is their behavior. They should be its chief evaluators if they are to continue to move toward maturity. (4) Locating areas of group disturbance, finding individual needs and purposes, and using the need-experience process are vital to the improvement of learning for pupils and teachers. (5) Analyses of adult roles or pupil activities always assume existing conditions. There is no guarantee that the behavior analyzed was or is valuable. There is no real evidence to show that the designated parts produced the behavior, as there is in industry where the fitted parts compose the product. Furthermore, there is no reasonable expectation that in his adulthood a child will face the same or even similar situations for which he was early taught the parts. Finally, studies in the transfer of parts learned in one situation to another situation show little spread into the new situation even by pupils who had high scores in the original academic learning. The probability of future use by pupils of the tangled fragments of adult experiences is too low to give serious consideration to this method of curriculum building. (6) Behavior of an individual is a function of his need and the process by which he satisfies it within his field. The job analysis technique wherever used—in industry or in education —does not locate and develop these vital need centers.

Adults should study carefully their own behavior and that of others who have preceded them in the culture. But they should not reorganize results of their adult inquiries into subjects to be taught to pupils in isolation from the need processes of these students. Pupils should have the same opportunity to study their needs as did Herbert Spencer or any other person who makes analyses of adult life.

Those who believe in authoritarian human relations have

streamlined the original job analysis technique into two aspects of scientific subject matter. One is improved analyses of the cultural heritage better to select the subject matter to be taught. The other is studies of the results of teaching through the performance of pupils on objective tests. These show where to locate materials for the best pupil reaction or how to pace it with the developing experience of the learners. These refined procedures have brought two desirable results. Adults are clarifying their meanings of the past and are now taking a more realistic view of the learning results from their subject teaching. Both of these mean re-evaluation and rearrangements of materials to reduce frustration of pupils who are too immature to find need-value in what they are taught. But the educational outlook remains the same, for these changes are only a slightly more human way of administering the old authoritarian demands. They can never satisfy the emerging needs of the pupils born with a tendency towards cooperative interaction. All such attempts to analyze adult life or the culture or the needs of society to determine what should be taught to children in home or school have resulted only in perpetuating traditional controls which are the chief cause of the present ineffective educational results.

The revolt from this authoritarian adult approach was begun by Rousseau (1712–78) and followed by Pestalozzi (1764–1827). Rousseau expounded the "natural law" and asserted that a child could not grow "naturally" when he was forever surrounded by restrictions to make him a miniature adult. Pestalozzi carried Rousseau's ideas into the school by emphasizing the child and his behavior although he did not resist authoritarian adult demands to any great extent. In America this revolt was fostered in the pragmatic philosophy of Charles Peirce (1870–1908), and William James (1842–1910), and in the instrumentalism of John Dewey (1859–1952). Many private and public schools were organized or modified on this basis.

By 1918 this revolt became the Progressive Education

Association, which advocated an educational bill of rights consisting of freedom for teacher and pupils against external controls, child initiative and activity instead of the usual teacher dominance, real firsthand active experience rather than secondhand experience from books, child interest as the basis for the educational program, learning based upon creative self-expression, and the development of wholesome personalities as the direction and end in view of the educational program. They changed the center of education from learning subject matter for complete living as an adult to the development of wholesome personalities of children as evidenced by their behavior on an immaturity–maturity scale. But the members of the P.E.A. used too much energy in revolting against the authoritarian controls and too little in studying how to implement their bill of rights into better educational opportunities for children.

History shows that every revolt usually runs a short course unless it can evolve into something more positive in purpose and action. By 1930 the negative energy was spent and the P.E.A. was given advice on the adoption of a more positive direction by many persons in various cultural fields. Some advocated a return to the analyses of Spencer, but on a more scientific and critical basis. They wanted to reappraise the American cultural tradition to locate more dynamic and less sterile knowledge to teach pupils who, as adults, could redirect or reconstruct the social order. To them, Spencer's method was sound but his analyses were poor. Either he did not select dynamic learnings or they were not taught in a dynamic way.

Another group advised the P.E.A. to emphasize the process of learning as the determining factor in personality development. About this time (October, 1930) the P.E.A. organized its Commission on the Relation of School and College, which developed what is known as the Eight-Year Study. Two years later the issue of direction became prominent in the deliberations of the Commission. The adherents of the Spencer viewpoint won, and a Directing Committee to support it was formed. In the end comparative studies showed that schools which emphasized the process of learning gave pupils the best preparation for college, whereas schools that held closest to the old subject matter gave pupils the poorest preparation for college. So the P.E.A. broke into two groups, one moving into cultural analyses on an international scale and the other studying the process of learning best suited to maturing personalities. It is safe to conclude that the revolt of a half century ago is spent and there are now two positive approaches to the curriculum. One is authoritarian subject-teaching method and the other is cooperative need-experience process.

While the events just described were taking place other groups were affecting the curriculum. Those moving consistently toward the need process were mental hygienists, Association for Childhood Education International, psychiatrists, sociologists, cultural anthropologists, social workers, psychotherapists, and field theory psychologists. Those promoting the authoritarian adult approach were subject matter specialists through their subject associations; educators and psychologists interested in the scientific movement in education; special groups developing educational tests, measurements, and research; and all educators at all levels who through their respective institutions or professional organizations accept the cultural control of education. And this means a large proportion of all educators with their numerous educational groups. While there are overlapping opinions of members of any group, since persons in conservative organizations may become liberal and some in liberal groups may become conservative, this evaluation of the general direction of their movement for many years is reasonable. Educational organizations generally take the conservative cultural position, while those working more closely with the behavior of people tend to place more stress on the process.

This brief summary of the historical background of the two approaches to the curriculum helps students rearrange their own past experiences to focus them more sharply on current problems and issues. Persons using the adult analysis approach are satisfying their needs on Line 2 (see Chart VI, p. 98). If they stopped at this point there would be no Line 1. But they have a compulsive drive to make pupils study the results of their Line 2 analyses, which constitute the Line 1 curriculum. Again persons who conceive new and dynamic analyses of the culture contribute to the Line 2 curriculum, for they enrich the environment from which a student can select better materials for his own creative assimilation. Unfortunately they destroy their contribution by their methods of teaching. Furthermore, the tighter adults organize their need materials for the Line 1 subjects, the more difficult it is for pupils to break the scope and sequence to find the few aspects which they can use for their need-satisfaction. The organization is like the shell on a walnut. The harder the shell the greater the difficulty in extracting the meat.

Finally, any person really attempting to improve living, from Socrates to John Dewey, always works on Line 2, through his needs. But he gives other people freedom to assimilate the results of his need-efforts on Line 2 by the same process through which he created them. If the early Alexandrians had been intelligent enough to select for their school the process used by Socrates with laymen in the market places or that used by Plato and Aristotle in satisfying their needs, anyone can speculate upon what might have happened. Yet we must now try to build a better future upon their decision at that time.

WHO SHOULD MAKE THE CURRICULUM?

The most important curriculum question is: Who should make the curriculum, with the corollaries of when, where, how, and under what conditions? This question has many parts. Who is making the curriculum now? Should these persons continue to make it? If so, how can they improve it? If not, how can other groups make a better curriculum?

From the authoritarian point of view the curriculum is now being made or designed by adults. Such designing has three phases: (1) Making a careful analysis of important aspects of living to find the major demands upon an individual in each of the roles he must play in adult life. Such analysis is continued to the point where the knowledge, skill, habit, or attitude necessary for success in these adult roles is clearly defined. (2) Organizing the results of such an analysis into an over-all plan for the curriculum. Plans now in use go by such names as "subjects," "broad fields," "core," "modern problems," "functions of social living," "persistent problems of living," and "general education." (3) Furnishing such over-all plan with suggested materials for implementing it to the teacher to prevent conscious or inadvertent omission of any significant phases of modern adult living.

There are a number of important phases in applying this authoritarian approach to curriculum making in a school system. (1) A general over-all or master plan for the school system as a whole is set up to define the basic areas and to insure a well-balanced, consistent program to meet all the predicated needs of pupils. Originally such a plan was drawn up by a few subject specialists, by supervisors, principals, and other members of a central office staff, by a few experts in planning procedures or by a combination of these groups. Now the favored method is to have the plan made by a committee or committees of teachers and other educators selected from the school system as a whole. (2) Each school staff develops its over-all program within the framework of the general plan furnished by the central office. (3) Each individual teacher within a school implements the particular program agreed upon for that school. (4) Each teacher plans with her children on-the-spot teaching activities related to the material to be taught within the over-all program. (5) Final evaluation of the results of such teaching through the learned behavior of pupils is made by the external adults responsible for formulating the original general plan.

There are two broad aspects of such planning. One is planning in advance or planning for the children prior to working with them in the various classes. The other is planning on the spot or in the teaching situations with the children, but within the limits of the prescribed framework. In each of these two aspects the teachers are rapidly assuming major responsibility and becoming the dominant influence. Parents, supervisors, experts, and others help them formulate the over-all plan. Children are represented to the extent that their elders are conscious of their needs and are willing to take them into account. This is a meager representation indeed. Most children have little opportunity to express their needs in authoritarian schools and most teachers have not yet learned how to read behavior so as to infer the need within the self of the behaver. The teacher usually plans some broad areas of social living to satisfy his needs and hopes that his greater wisdom will be beneficial to the child.

In their on-the-spot planning together, teacher and pupils keep within the framework of the broad areas of the over-all plan in order to maintain in their program the continuity, scope, and balance which adults expect. Broad areas of adult social living are outside the psychological field of children but within that of the teacher. There is ample evidence that needs of children do not fall within these adult categories, that their disturbances cut across all aspects of their living within their fields, and that when they are free to plan, they develop their own needs without regard for the paper programs of adults. They cannot be allowed such freedom, as it upsets the balance of the over-all plan.

Authoritarian educators hold that the curriculum is made primarily by teachers with the help of parents, supervisors,

administrators, experts, and children. They believe this is
and should be so, for teachers are best equipped of all adult
groups to assume this responsibility. There are three major
differences between this point of view and that of one hundred
years ago. First, the authoritarian control is now with the
teacher in a school, which locates it closer to the children.
Second, the subject matter is now selected and organized to
produce scope, sequence, and balance around modern adult
problems rather than specialized subject knowledge. Third,
teachers now utilize more of the experiences of children in
teaching the new subject matter. But the job analysis
technique and the authoritarian control are still present,
although they operate more subtly. The present theory and
practice are only a refinement of the approach of Spencer and
Bobbitt. They do not represent a new point of view, neither
do they produce a basic change in the educational program
for children or college students.

   As they see it, these adults are making the curriculum for
children. According to their own evidence, however, the
learning results are unsatisfactory. From the behaver's point
of view each pupil is making the curriculum through his
self-selections from the available materials in his environment.
According to his admissions, which are his behaviors, the
results are equally unsatisfactory. If the child is a self interacting with his environment, this modern version of the
traditional approach merely reorganizes the environment
from the more isolated subjects to some more inclusive
arrangement of the problems of adult social living. It gives
little help to the pupil in improving his perceptions of himself
or in understanding his biological growth process. Thus children and college students go on searching for themselves in an
environment organized to teach them the general and specific
knowledges they should have as adults.

   Who should make the curriculum? Children or pupils or
college students or behavers should make it. They have made

it in the past and will continue to make it in the future. How can adults work with them so that behavers can make a better curriculum? This question is simple to answer but difficult to achieve in practice. One suggestion will be given here since it will be discussed throughout the book. Preplanning or planning in advance and planning on the spot or planning in process go on in every life activity. The learnings which constitute the individual's self are his preplanning for every experience and his tendency to action is his on-the-spot or process direction. And so it is with teachers and pupils. But the teacher must change the nature of his preplanning in order to work cooperatively with pupils in process planning. He must study his adult need-experience process so as to feel, conceptualize, accept, and use it in improving himself. His self-security must emerge from fixed ends to an ongoing process. He must recognize results in his own improved behaviors before he is adequately prepared for on-the-spot planning with children. Traditionally the quality of the pre-planning is the quality of the subject matter selected to meet adult needs. In the cooperative approach the quality of the preplanning is the quality of the person who works with the pupils. Herein lies a fundamental difference, for a disintegrating person can teach subjects, as every reader of these words knows. But only a teacher who is moving toward higher operational unity on a maturity scale can help children or college students find and improve themselves through their own need-experiences.

A BACKWARD AND FORWARD LOOK

Parents and students raise one question about the foregoing material. "Is this progressive education? If it is, I certainly cannot accept it or I would not be allowed to use it in my school." After finding from them the great mental and educational hazards associated with the respectable word "progressive," I summarize.

1. Every individual is progressive. He must be to remain alive, for all life is organized energy that is constantly changing its internal structure and modifying its surrounding environment. Each organism moves resourcefully in the direction of its own life-fulfillment. All energy released in this purposive manner results in change called progress or progressive action. The amoeba which grows to the size where it divides and becomes two is progressive. The child who grows from birth to adolescence is progressive. The adult who detects even the slightest modification of his behavior over a designated period of time is progressive. If all life is progressive and every individual is progressive, why should people be so concerned over this word? The answer lies in the nature of the direction and the speed of movement. People disagree over whose direction shall prevail and how many generations shall be consumed on the road.

2. I have discussed three different meanings of progressive. Educators who refine the teaching curriculum call themselves progressive. Those who introduced the monitorial system, changed the rural school into a graded school, grouped pupils according to ability, promoted objective tests for measuring the results of teaching, devised remedial programs for every subject, and standardized administrative devices for giving and recording credits were the great progressives of their times even though they tightened authoritarian controls over pupils. But those educators who revolted against authoritarian direction also called themselves progressive. They advocated the elective system in colleges; tried to abolish the arraying of pupils through marks, grades, and promotions; rebelled against adult domination of children either in school or in the home; worked to reduce academic subject requirements in the preparation of teachers; and took many other measures to undermine the old educational structure. Many of them were denounced as progressive by those who were refining authoritarian controls. Parents and educators who

believe in the need-experience approach to life and the school curriculum are also called progressive. They move to eliminate the dichotomy between growing and learning which exists in traditional education. Thus it is difficult to know which concept of progress is held by a person who supports or denounces progressive education.

3. Time is also an important factor to be considered. Traditional progressives think of change as slow or gradual, composed of many small increments over many generations. They dislike the speed of the revolters who would abolish certain practices immediately or the insistence of the process advocates that the change from Line 1 to Line 2 should be completed within the educational lifetime of a child, or about twelve years. They are concerned over the radical nature of such progressive proposals, for they cut too deeply into or destroy the roots of their traditional program. These time and depth factors produce adjectives of conservative and reactionary, or progressive and radical to designate positions on a scale of educational change. While biological sciences support both gradual and abrupt change, the evolutionary record shows that organisms able to make a quick radical adaptation to a changing environment tend to survive while the slower gradualists perish. Educators should ponder this fact while they make present decisions in shaping the future of the schools.

Students are disturbed by the method of polarization which I use, have used in preceding chapters, and will continue to follow in this book. It confuses temporarily those who have been taught that there is a correct and an incorrect answer to every life problem. An older person tells a younger one the correct answer and thus keeps him away from error. Rarely do they see their past either-or's as a low autonomic form of polarization designed to promote their arrested development, especially in what they call moral behavior.

Furthermore, they generally believe that in situations where a correct answer is difficult to find, differences should be compromised by taking a middle-of-the-road position.

Polarization occurs whenever an individual recognizes in his psychological field a new center competing with his established figure–ground relationship. He examines both the old and the competing poles until he differentiates, refines, and reorganizes his experience around an emergent figure heretofore non-existent. He does not view one pole as right and the other wrong, nor does he take a position between the two on the original level of differentiation, for neither action raises the quality of his experience. He creates the new figure around which he reorganizes his field. Outside persons can help him locate his poles and examine the differences, and teach him a process for their conversion into new qualitative experience. He makes the thoughtful judgments which his traditional right-wrong education does not foster. Thus students are not so concerned with the poles as they are with what the polarized method of examining life and education does to them or makes them do to themselves. Polarization of experience is one aspect of normal interaction. It is both a preface to and a reality in the rise and identification of need. Without it life would be complacent unto death, for it would cease to exist. The real issue is not the existence of polarization but the way to deal with the need which accompanies it. In the next chapter I shall discuss need as the dynamic in all behavior, both personal and professional.

Chapter V

WHAT IS NEED-EXPERIENCE PROCESS?

Every organism is a system in which each part is so related to every other part by cooperative interaction that it tends to maintain throughout its growth a delicately balanced state of form and function, striving always to restore itself if altered in any way by internal or external conditions. Growth is not a random process. It is a steady, purposeful march toward organized unity expressed as a unique, integrated, maturing self. Human life is a complex and open system which is extraordinary flexible, sensitive to external conditions, and capable of converting environmental disorder into organic order through the self as the operating center. A basic condition for growth toward a maturing self is that each individual must work on his own needs. He must locate, understand, conceptualize, and direct his energy intelligently, for the origin and control of his behavior lie within him even though they are affected by external conditions.

Every school of psychology has a term to define this inner urge for growth. In people it is called wish, want, need, purpose, goal, interest, or desire, depending upon the point of view of the individual. While these words have different meanings, all are used to indicate internal beginnings of the

116

process through which each person develops in structure and behavior into an integrated self. In this book, I shall use the term *need* to indicate this internal energy. Since it cannot be studied by itself apart from its external movements, I shall in this chapter explain more fully its meaning as an aspect of the need-experience process.

WHAT IS A NEED?

A need is a state of disturbed equilibrium which the individual himself feels so keenly that he must do something about it in order to restore his balance. This definition can be broken down into a number of aspects, which are indicated below.

1. Any particular state of disturbed equilibrium exists only in one individual. Every other person has his imbalances, but no two states are alike since no two people are the same. Every person can feel *his* need even though he cannot consciously describe or focus it. Outside persons should help him locate, define, and raise it to the level of conscious action.

2. Needs represent different degrees of disturbance to the individual. Some with little depth can be satisfied promptly and are called transitory or superficial needs. Others which cut so deeply into the self that they require time for study are called permanent, abiding or genuine needs. The school should help pupils locate and study consciously their genuine needs so that the energy can be directed toward self-improvement. They are necessary for qualitative learning and should be the basis of the school program.

3. The individual must do something about the need in order to restore his balance, for he cannot develop satisfactorily in imbalance with his environment. He can be in disequilibrium for relatively short periods of time only. His developmental rhythm is from equilibrium, to disequilibrium, to equilibrium, and so on throughout life, but the direction is constantly and purposefully toward the higher

levels of action, which I earlier described as maturing behavior.

4. Learning occurs in the need process by which the individual moves from disturbance to equilibrium, from the disorganized situation to the organized whole. The quality of the process determines the quality of the learning. A high quality of learning does not generally result from an inferior process, neither does inferior behavior generally accompany a high quality process. Educators can help learners raise their level of maturity by showing them how to improve their process of need-satisfaction.

5. Only people have needs. They are characteristics of living organisms that develop a conscious self and have the inherited ability to learn how to act on thinking. While lower organisms have no such needs, they do have disturbances which are similar to them. They have protoplasmic irritants, chemical imbalances, enzymatic rhythms, and fluctuations of hormonic levels. Such imbalances are close to the bottom of the upset scale, whereas conscious needs are near the top. Some persons use a different term, such as "drive" to indicate tissue imbalances and reserve need for higher self-disturbances. Whatever the term employed all people have needs regardless of where they were born, the color of their skins, the culture in which they were reared.

Societies, institutions, or cultures do not have needs. Society is the term used for a group of people working together to satisfy their needs. Institutions are set up by people to act for and with them in achieving such satisfactions. Culture is a record of everything acquired by man through his groups and institutions. The needs are in the people, not the society, institutions, or culture. The needs of society usually mean those of a few people who control the group. When a superintendent of schools says that our community demands a certain type of education, he refers to the need-satisfaction of a small, articulate, powerful group. When educators and others speak of using cultural needs as the basis for an educational program, they are executing the demands of a few people to have certain aspects of the culture taught to children to satisfy their own needs. But the definition of need is everywhere the same. It is a disturbance which some individual is attempting to resolve in order to restore his balance.

6. Many persons assume that their needs are the needs of others. They project their disturbances upon others and imply or openly assert that outside persons have the same upset, when in reality they are totally unaware of its nature, for it is quite foreign to their psychological fields. Such a projected need is to the other person a predicated or imputed need. Parents impute their needs to their children and demand that they satisfy these nonexistent disturbances. Adults impute to children needs for learning the three R's or other designated subject matter when children have no real needs for which such knowledge is a need-satisfaction. In home, school, industry, religious groups, community organizations adults impute their needs to children, or persons in higher authority predicate theirs to persons in lesser positions.

A child has little opportunity alone or with others to locate, define, focus, and study his own needs intelligently. In his early years he is psychologically pushed around while trying unsuccessfully to learn the need-satisfactions of others. Herein lies a potent factor in the development of immature behavior.

WHEN DOES A NEED ARISE?

1. A need occurs when the self lacks the behaviors to deal adequately with new and novel conditions arising in its psychological field. A need never occurs when past learnings have sufficient quality to control or contain the field, since experience flows smoothly or adequately. Need is a stimulus for new experience, but it is not the new experience. It is the energy ready and poised to become a new experience, con-

tinuing until the need-tension abates. So need is both the beginning of and the sustained energy for the better experience necessary to self-enhancement. It will continue in this direction even though thwarted at every turn by external conditions. Thus need is a lack of and a self-demand for more adequate experience.

2. Need is the phenomenal self undergoing a reorganization. Every situation that occurs in the flow of experience affects the self. But temporary imbalances do not produce the deep upset which marks the beginning of new experiences which will re-integrate the self-structure. If every situation had so profound an effect, the self would lack consistency and there would be no dependable tendency to action discernible in its behaviors. Temporary, momentary, superficial disturbances emanating from the protective sheath should not be mistaken for real needs which are the deeper imbalances of the inner self.

While a need is deep enough to result in reorganization of the self, it should not be a threat to the self. Whether it is or becomes one depends on many factors, such as (a) the individual's existing maturity or the way he perceives himself when he feels a deep imbalance, (b) his tendency to action accepted in the past which he will use in the present upset, (c) the strength of the external forces in his environment or the demands made upon him by others as he sees them. If he believes others are exacting and unreasonable, expecting him to act on imputed needs and denying him the normal growth process, they become a threat to him. Threat occurs when the imbalance is so overpowering that the self tightens defenses for protection instead of relaxing them to increase differentiation in the perceptual field. A need deep enough to cause reconstruction of the self, must arise in a phenomenal field free from threat and full of sympathetic guidance in the growth process which produces the higher quality of experience. Threat is not the need; it is the behaver's perception of field conditions when the need appears. Every psychotherapist knows that a client must remove threats if he is to achieve a normal reconstruction of the self.

3. Need arises only in relation to aspects of the psychological field to which the self is sensitive. Usually these sensitive areas have been differentiated as conscious meanings which in the past have brought need-satisfaction. These past meanings are the individual's selectors that determine those aspects of the current field to which he is sensitive and from which arises the imbalance for an improved present experience. When one person responds to another he is actually responding to his own response, which is his meaning of the behavior of the other. So he is responding to the meaning he has of himself. Meaning has three aspects: It is selective. It is a plan for action. It is a prediction of a result of action in a given situation. The relationship may be expressed as follows: Need→present meanings→action→inadequate satisfaction, results in→new need→new experience→better meanings→ better action→adequate need-satisfaction.

Meaning is not a mysterious something which inheres in objects, for no object has meaning independent of the behaver. To the observer meaning is the action directed toward or the overt behavior related to the object or event by the individual. To the behaver meaning is his selective internal energy-conversion of the object or event which becomes his observed behavior toward it. Thus the crucial aspect in building qualitative experience lies in improving the internal energy-conversion of the object-meaning stimulus which is the old and inadequate behavior. By acting on past meanings the individual discovers the lack of quality in his behaviors, which gives him a need. To obtain need-satisfaction he must have better meanings. Therefore he contrives new and unforeseen relationships between his environment and himself. By creative insight he evolves and differentiates the energy directions, heretofore unknown to his psychological field, which resolve adequately the need-tension. Meanings are the

selectors of as well as the actions in experience old and new.
Aspects of situations to which an individual makes no response
do not exist. In satisfying his needs he should extend his
sensitivity to new aspects of experience so as to increase the
range and accuracy of his meanings through normal creative
differentiation.

4. Need usually arises as an imbalance in the figure, or
highly differentiated aspects of the field, although it may arise
from the ground, or the relatively vague, fuzzy, and indefinite
aspects. In either case the onset is felt as a gross total disturbance of the self. Whether an imbalance emanates from the
figure or from the ground makes a difference to the meanings
the individual will project into it, and the way he will direct
his actions to resolve it or the source affects the quality of the
need-experience process.

The normal assumption is that all aspects of the field including the inner can be remade through conscious differentiation. This, however, is not the case. Some ground behaviors
are only partially accepted by the self. Originally, they were
autonomic responses to predicated needs or outside pressures
of adults. They may now be keenly felt as gross total imbalances which the individual cannot raise to the level of
deliberative action. He therefore secures the services of a
psychotherapist or a psychiatrist to help him release more of
the ground so that he can differentiate it into figure. Through
such release he can use a greater area of his field in developing
the sharper and clearer meanings necessary to more adequate
behavior. Thus existing ground material may become the raw
material for the enriched new experience.

5. The needs of an individual arise out of the realities of
his phenomenal field as he experiences them. His unified field
is his one and only, positive and actual, authentic and certain
reality. His needs are always real to him, even though they are
not so recognized or appear as distortions to an outside observer. He cannot change his reality into that of another, for

his reality is his self. Thus the observer from his field may reject the behavior of another as unwarranted by the conditions as he sees them. But to the behaver it fits perfectly into the emerging patterns of reality in his field. The observer does not realize that the perception of outside objects and conditions is reality to the behaver, for no external object has reality in its own right. Its meaning or value to him in satisfying his needs is its reality. The teacher of a first grade surrounds the child with many beautiful books, yet he does not read. The teacher may feel that such behavior is unwarranted. But the child's perception of the books is his reality, even though it differs from that of the teacher. To him books are still in his ground and he must differentiate them into figure before he will be able to read. Thus meaning which governs behavior is the reality which changes with changing differentiations in the field.

Students raise many questions relative to the meaning of need. Do all needs result in the reorganization of self? Are there needs which do not originate with or involve the self? When a person says he needs a better job or a new automobile is that a need? I reply to such questions by emphasizing two points.

First, they should distinguish between a need and the action to satisfy it. To help them see this difference I ask them to select a need and study it by the need-experience process. Each person passes in an outline under three headings: This is my need. This is why I select it. This is how I propose to study it. Experienced readers carefully examine each outline, writing their comments and suggestions for the student to consider as he wishes. I make a group analysis of the papers and report the findings to the class as further evidence which each can take into account as he desires. The chief characteristic of such outlines is that students express need as a direction of action against the environment. They propose to resolve their disturbance by changing external conditions, when they are unaware of the nature of their internal tensions which brought on the drive or of the process by which they determined the direction of action. I suggest that each search himself to find the focus of his disturbance, for his direction of action or quality of behavior is only as sound as his conceptual insight into what upsets him.

Second, all imbalances or needs involve the self, the resolution of needs always modifies the self; but there is wide difference among individuals in both direction and degree of such modification. When need-tension is satisfactorily relieved by rearranging old meanings or tendencies to action, modification of the self is slight in the direction of preserving or refining its old organization. I refer to such tensions as *problems,* to distinguish them from needs. I call the method that is used "problem-solving" to show low self-reorganization, even though there may be much rearrangement of the external environment. The parent tries to change the behavior of his problem child, the teacher has problem children in reading, university officials have problem students who accept outside pay for winning or losing basketball games, the high school teacher finds a problem in teaching his subject to pupils who cannot read the books, the superintendent faces a problem of obtaining adequate housing for children, and so on.

Most people correctly designate their disturbances as problems since they have no intention of seriously modifying themselves. They always try to readjust the other person, as parents do their children and as professors do the students making unsatisfactory responses to their teaching. A need can be resolved adequately only when there is a profound change in the organization of the self. Each individual begins life with many needs and few problems but gradually changes the ratio to few needs and many problems. His continued growth toward self-enhancement lies in how well he manages the few needs rather than in how well he solves the many problems.

The concept of need can now be more sharply focused. Shall children work blindly on the needs of adults or shall they work openly consciously on their own? The teaching curriculum is organized around the needs of adults not the needs of children. This is acceptable to authoritarians, who hold that children are too immature to know their needs so adults must tell them what to do. The learning curriculum is organized cooperatively by children and teachers around the needs of children.

What difference does it make? I frequently illustrate it in a college class by stating that I am disturbed over the lack of ventilation in the room and asking someone on the back row and not so disturbed to adjust the windows. He raises them at the bottom or lowers them from the top or both and then looks at me to see if the result is satisfactory. If I nod my head he sits down. If I shake my head he tries again. If I again shake my head, he makes further adjustments and will continue until I register approval or until he catches the meaning of the performance. Since he has no internal need for directing his action, he cannot gauge the adjustment to his need. Since he does not know my need, he can relate the window openings to it only as I indicate to him my evaluation of his actions. He derives a need to satisfy me so that my pressure on him will be removed. Thus he achieves need-satisfaction, but not my need-satisfaction. He learns his own need behavior, not the relationship of his behavior to my need. Such behaviors learned under external pressure have low quality since the student does not discover, expand, develop, enrich his ability to study his own real needs. The control is external by me through my demands, but internal by him since he learns his own need responses. My external demand should be that he select a genuine need of his own and learn how to study it by his biological growth process with such help as I am able to give him.

It makes a big difference whether a school is organized

around the needs of teachers or those of children. Adults can, if they wish, work cooperatively with children on their needs, but children cannot, even if they wish, work cooperatively with adults on their needs. Since need begins and sustains action, the depth of need-tension determines the amount of energy released. The understanding the individual has of himself determines the level at which such energy will function. If the schools expect children to release much energy operating at high levels, they must be organized around the needs of the learners.

WHAT IS A NEED-EXPERIENCE PROCESS?

Students have difficulty in clarifying their meaning of "process" since they believe improvement in life and learning is associated with rearranging increasing number of external objects and events in their environment. It takes much time and self-searching to view life and learning as creative, interactive movements of a living organism to select external objects to convert into organic energy necessary for its own growth. Students are more familiar with the word "method," which means a systematic, uniform, orderly way of teaching children bodies of knowledge which adults want them to learn. It is a neat, tidy, regular progression from a known (to them, unknown to the child) beginning to their preconceived fixed goal. Usually students use the word "procedures" to mean a series of logical steps in a fixed line of action along a narrow pathway where vision is cloudy and limited. They use the word "technique" to mean a sequence of movements in refining behaviors in order to attain dexterity, expertness, skill in some nonhuman aspect of the outer world of objective knowledge, craftsmanship, or business productivity. All these words describe ways of grooving the experiences of children into an organization of the external environment set by adults, which is the educational approach of the teaching curriculum.

In the broadest sense, process is a shorthand word to include all movements of an individual from the onset of need to the release of tension, whether the direction be toward the disintegration or the enhancement of the self. A desirable process is a way of using need energy to achieve a higher quality of experience than that which constituted the need and a higher integration of the self than that which precipitated the original disturbance. This qualitative need process is described by such words as exploration, search, inquiry, appraisal, deliberative action. The need is the beginning; deliberative action is the flexible direction; and the process is the total way of moving from the initial need to the concluding action. The end in view is not a set of facts or a body of knowledge, neither is it a skill or a correct answer. It is the best working judgment or the most critically appraised action of which the individual is capable at that moment. Process is not a teaching method, neither is it a fixed procedure or a set of rules to be followed. It is a creative study of the need situation within which the thoughtful direction evolves. The individual does not disregard previous experience. He uses all pertinent past experience and all appropriate new experience in achieving his deliberative action by learning how to appraise the old and how to select the new. Process, then, is a functional reorganization of past and present experience in a new need situation in the direction of self-enhancement.

The need process is a continuous flow of interrelated dynamic situations. Three aspects of this movement are selected here for differentiation and clarification: (1) finding a need worth working on, (2) determining the direction in which the need-experience shall be developed, (3) managing a series of situations or activities so as to achieve the new quality of the emerging experience. These three aspects of the process are as vital to need-fulfillment of the child with his limited experience as they are to the adult with his broader experience. They may be studied from three points of view: (1) the behaver in the moving process trying to resolve his need satisfactorily, (2) the outside observer with a different need and not actively engaged in the process, (3) the professional educator or adult within the experience trying to help children understand and use their need process more effectively. The first two points of view are found everywhere; the third operates only when older persons teach younger people how to manage their lives, as in school or home. These three basic aspects of the need process will be discussed from behaver and observer viewpoints, with special reference to the actions of the professional educator.

HOW ARE NEEDS LOCATED?

Each individual must locate his most important needs, for he has neither time nor energy to study effectively all his disturbances. He makes choices or selects upsets to which to give attention and thought; without such continuous evaluation of disturbances his life would be disorganized, uncertain, and essentially hopeless. From experience in working with professional and nonprofessional groups, I conclude that adults fall into three broad categories in selecting the needs on which they work.

1. Members of the first group assert they have no needs, and they are honest in this belief. Many students tell me this when I ask them to select a need through which to learn the need-experience process. Such people have many common characteristics. They move in a relatively fixed environment in which the existing self operates satisfactorily. They find nothing in the environment which contradicts the self or causes suspicions of inadequacy of self. They live by unquestioned acceptance of values introjected in their early years by parents and others who demanded fixed behaviors for all life activities. They find few occasions to differentiate new figure–ground relationships in their psychological fields.

Their tendency to preserve intact the existing self is so great, and their inadequacy in dealing with upsets is so profound, that they limit their activities to a circumscribed environment where upsets rarely occur.

These persons follow the middle of the social or educational road, seldom being for or against anything. They make every effort to ally themselves with persons in power, doing exactly what their superiors demand. Such people have arrested their development at the point where perpetual complacency overcame them. They consider themselves fortunate in keeping their internal and external environment narrow enough to avoid conflicts. When uncertainty does arise they withdraw from it by narrowing the area of adaptation or finding someone in authority to give them the exact answer. They are energy systems with the two usual dynamics of intaking, assimilating, integrating and outgoing or outmoving in relation to fellow men. But they have so reduced range and movement that changes in behavior cannot be observed from the outside for they are almost nonexistent to them.

2. The second group—the majority of people—select what they call needs by the sore-spot method, simply picking the sorest spots of the moment. These occur where there is the greatest external pressure, more specifically where people are most articulate or where existing conditions are likely to get out of control. Such people invariably work on external symptoms, applying salves to allay surface irritation while ignoring the internal conditions which caused the outbreak. They never really grow up, for they have little time to locate and work on their real needs and they have no process for working on them effectively even if time were available. They take pride in becoming trouble-shooters or experience-smoothers, applying the traditional snake oil remedy to all personal or educational problems.

3. A minority group plans life activities around genuine

needs and finds time to deal with them on a realistic, de-liberative level. They purposely move in a fluid environment where the self finds new conditions contradicting past be-haviors, thus polarizing experience and making reorganiza-tion necessary. They oppose and reject introjected standards by bringing all behavior under conceptual examination. They accept and live hopefully with change, trusting their ability in individual and group thinking to guide them to higher levels of self-organization. Although this third group is the most constructive of the three, many individuals who compose it lack real understanding of the need-experience process so necessary to generate the improved meanings neces-sary for their continued growth.

While adults in all three groups may to themselves as be-havers have an entirely satisfactory life, outside observers may draw from their actions quite different conclusions. Yet the actions of the behaver are and will continue to be motivated by his beliefs rather than the evaluations of the observer. Outside persons must find ways to stimulate those with no needs, help the sore-spot applicators dig for under-lying conditions, and guide the searching expansionists into sounder process directions.

To improve the quality of his behavior every individual must learn how to distinguish between needs and problems or how to search for and select needs which have possibilities of developing into higher quality experiences. An outside observer may help him in three ways which are used by parents with their children, by teachers with pupils, by psy-chotherapists with clients. The first is to observe his behavior, the second is to ask him to write answers to questions that reveal his likes and dislikes, and the third is to talk with him directly about what he thinks his needs are. The first is the only reliable method with young children, who are un-able to give a reasonable statement of their internal disturb-ances. The second and third are widely used with adolescents and adults. All three should be used by the observer wherever possible. Anyone who lives intimately with children—parents, teachers, social workers—should be able to read behavior better than he reads books. Present behavior of a growing child is more important in determining what he will become than is the verbal learning which he is taught from books.

A real need always undergirds behavior, as all behavior is an attempt to satisfy need. Rarely is there a direct relation between need and behavior; the latter may be released by a circuitous route to confuse the observer and protect the real self. To obtain an accurate inference of need, behavior must be observed under conditions in which the behaver shows a high degree of correspondence between his internal disturbance and his overt actions. While such conditions rarely exist in either the home or the school, they are indicated here as a convenient check list.

1. The child must be free to explore widely the environment within his range of experience. He must have opportunity to make many new, varied, wholesome, interesting contacts. Outside persons must encourage and support his natural curiosity or outgoingness, for by direct sensory experience he takes in the impressions which are converted into meanings which constitute his growing self. A highly controlled environment prevents the child from indicating his real disturbances through his behavior.

2. In the rich environment described above the child must be allowed (a) to select the objects or activities which engage his attention, as they are his directions of action to satisfy need; (b) to express freely in many media the feelings which result from his perceptions in his expanding psychological field. These freedoms are best carried on in groups in order to give each child an opportunity to show what are his developing patterns of human relations. The age-range in such groups should be as wide as individual personalities can encompass, in order to show the observer how young children

adapt to older ones and how well the older include the younger in activities of common interest.

3. The cooperative process of planning together should be used to show we-ness or groupness or outgoingness of a child toward other people. He can reveal the number of children with whom he finds common areas of need or common purposes within activities, and thus indicate the logic or maturing organization of his experience. These cooperative activities also provide opportunity for releasing and guiding many blocked tensions before they become troublesome tendencies to action.

4. The environment must be permissive in order that adults may find out what each child is self-selecting from his experiences. Means of determining this with a very young child are the questions he asks, the informal conversations he has with others, the toys, games, or stones he cherishes, the stories he enjoys, the life situations he dramatizes, as well as his facial expression and body movements as he finger paints or squeezes clay, his smiles of satisfaction as he reads. All of these and many other behaviors indicate his selections and their conversion to the satisfaction of his needs.

5. The adult should help the child check his purposes and value judgments by every free and friendly means at their disposal. Usually this is not difficult in a permissive, cooperative environment rich in activities appropriate to the child's age and maturity.

The two most widely advocated methods of discovering needs through what the behaver writes are free and controlled association tests. The former was orginated by Frances Galton (1822–1900), perfected by Sigmund Freud (1865–1939), and used extensively in psychoanalysis with soldiers in World War I. It is still common in all modern forms of nondirective therapy. The adult usually asks the child a number of questions which focus attention on his environment or himself: (1) What do you like best in or out of school? (2) What would you like to do in or out of school that you cannot now do? (3) What do you like about yourself? (4) What do you dislike about yourself? To these may be added other questions such as: (1) What is the most interesting thing you have done at school this year? (2) What is one of the places you would especially like to go to in your town or city? (3) What was one of the happiest days in your life? All questions are phrased in relation to age and experience of children and only a few are used at any one time. Usually they are paired so that information given on one can be checked against that of another.

The controlled association test elicits very specific responses in limited aspects of experience designated by the author through the content and form of his questions. The child is not free to select and present his experience as he feels it, but must select and organize it within the framework of the directed inquiry. Standardized achievement or objective homemade tests are the most common forms for such controlled responses. Their value rests on whether they promote conditions which cause the child to release himself or whether they introduce factors which cause him to protect himself. On this there is much difference of opinion among educators and laymen.

The third way of discovering needs, as noted earlier, is to ask pupils what their needs are, either in small discussion groups or through individual conferences. While there are arguments for and against each, the group method is most satisfactory for secondary school pupils. The adult group leader should be expert in discussion techniques and should be someone in whom the pupils have confidence—usually not an official of the school. A few staff members in some schools may have developed such a high quality of human relations that pupils will give them reliable information about their needs in any group discussion. They are, however, the exception rather than the rule. When high schools are managed cooperatively this condition changes, since pupils are revealing and meeting their needs continuously through their educational program. The adult leader uses an interview technique designed to release experiences until real selves are uncovered. While he varies the approach and tailors the discussion to the particular group, he is always rewarded by the pupils' keen insight in locating their needs and in evaluating the opportunities offered by the school for their satisfaction.

A few general conclusions are drawn from studies of the needs of children made during the past thirty years. (1) The school seems to be a dead institution. The interest of children in what goes on there is highest in the first grade and decreases each year to the lowest point in the twelfth grade. The percentage of children liking school in the first year becomes the percentage disliking it in the twelfth year. (2) Each year children have more and deeper needs which the school does little or nothing to help them meet. They try to solve them as best they can without the benefit of advice from the school personnel. (3) The pressures of the school tend to groove all children into conforming behaviors. The atmosphere is unfavorable to creative interests and expression. (4) The children have many fears toward requirements, adults, other children, and their own ability or worth. They feel that the school neither cares about giving them nor is willing to give them the encouragement and strength to deal with such fears successfully. (5) There is little relationship between life in and out of the school. Children make little use of what they are taught in school to improve their outside experiences. They think of the school as composed of many routine and uninteresting chores that have to be done for various reasons. (6) There is little understanding by educators of the anxiety which the school fosters in pupils from elementary through graduate school. The demands are artificial, the failures are contrived, the competition is unhealthy, the depreciation of learners is based upon false life evaluation, the rewards for success are social group status and consciousness at the price of regressive retreats into the past or intellectual discussions of the present. (7) Children have ample real needs upon which to develop a full program of education from the first grade through the colleges. But these needs cannot be used by adults to prepare in advance a graded subject curriculum for teachers to teach. Rather they can be used by teachers and pupils cooperatively to develop a learning curriculum when and if external adult controls are relaxed.

The studies from which the above observations are drawn were all made in authoritarian schools. Their lack of realism in dealing with the genuine life activities of children is profound. In such schools children cannot bring their needs to the attention of the controlling adults or obtain reasonable consideration of them when shown by word or deed. Yet the genuine needs of children are the basic power which impels them to improve their experiences and to raise the level of their behavior. To thwart them or to overlay them with inferior needs derived from adult pressures is to lower the very quality of learning which the school is organized to promote. The evidence is overwhelming that children will satisfy their genuine needs in some way regardless of what the school offers them. Educators should use every possible means to develop school programs openly and fearlessly upon the deep and abiding needs of children in order to help them feel, use, and accept the cooperative process of deliberative action. The school can then help everyone progressively achieve the new integration and better operational unity which is his biological and cultural birthright.

WHAT IS THE DIRECTION OF THE NEED PROCESS?

Every behaver of any age in his own moving need process has the one direction of preserving and enhancing his real self. He wants to discover and release his potentialities and develop them into his real self, not his protective self nor his idealized image of himself. The real self is the deep source of his life, of his active forces, of his creative insights, and of his unique individuality. Within it are the springs of his emerging meanings, the integrative organization of his dynamic learnings, the operating center for his incoming and outgoing energies. He can develop these potentialities into his unique self only in an external atmosphere of warmth, of good will, of healthy friction with others who give him an inner security and freedom to release his own real feelings and thoughts. He must live in an environment in which he can be truthful to himself, he can be active and productive, he can work with others in a cooperative spirit of mutuality, he can select and assume responsibility for his behaviors.

It is a sad commentary not only on our schools but on all our cultural institutions that these favorable conditions rarely exist. Hence the individual meets his needs under thwarting conditions that cause him to develop a protective self. The energy that could and should be released toward self-realization is either blocked or dissipated in building up an idealized image of what the self could have become were it allowed to develop. The struggle of the organism to build an integrated self, the resiliency of its recovery after severe onslaughts by external field conditions, the dogged determination with which it moves toward the completion of its potential capacity, is one of the profound creative phenomena of all times. And the professional service of the educator is to facilitate such becoming.

To achieve continuous movement toward self-enhancement the process in every need experience must involve the most deliberative, thoughtful, social, human behavior of which the individual is capable within the given conditions. Such deliberative action must be learned. No child is born with it but each inherits a capacity to learn it. While it takes time to develop such learning, each child has an automatic nervous system to maintain physiological life activities until his cerebrospinal system matures enough for him to deal with life problems on a conscious level. His early autonomic actions are sometimes called *impulsive,* whereas his later behaviors are called *deliberative.* In growing up a child shifts his operating center from the autonomic system and impulsive action to the cerebrospinal system and deliberative action. In either case the whole organism operates in each act, but different

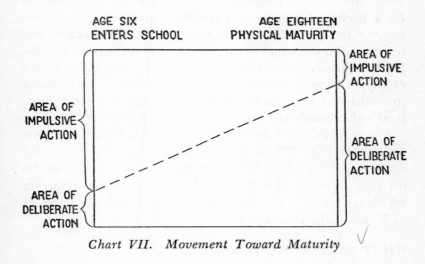

Chart VII.   Movement Toward Maturity

organs function to a different degree with a different emphasis and in a different figure–ground relationship.

A flow chart (Chart VII) shows the relation between impulsive and deliberative action at various ages. Most actions of a six-year-old are impulsive, but some are truly deliberative. The exact relationship between the two is not important, for it varies widely among children. But the direction of action should never be in doubt. Each succeeding year a child should be more deliberative in more experiences. By the time he reaches physical or legal maturity he should be capable of continuing to move toward ever more deliberative behavior. To help him educators must re-evaluate every school experience by its contribution to such deliberative process and to such self-realization.

No experience is neutral. Either it moves the individual toward maturity or it pushes him back toward immaturity. The addition facts in the second grade, the European back-grounds of American history in the sixth, the geometry in the tenth, the English literature in the twelfth, the requirements for a Bachelor's degree or a certificate to teach must be ex-amined from a different reference point. Fortunately one instance of a devastating experience will not wreck the bio-logical tendency toward maturity. But the prolonged pressure of a few experiences toward immaturity without opportunity to counteract them is the stuff out of which mama's boys, papa's girls, teachers' pets, or neurotic personalities are made.

Maturing does not mean that all behavior at all times must be deliberative. There are occasions in specific situations when impulsive action may be a mature response or may be the best way to deal with conditions. It is not a specific act which counts, it is the tendency to action which a series of such specific behaviors implies.

WHAT IS NEED-FULLFILLMENT?

The rhythm of life is a continuous flow of energy which is outgoing, intaking, converting, selecting, incorporating, dif-ferentiating—all words to describe the constant change within the organism as it interacts with its environment. The energy moves in waves whose width, height, and depth vary with internal and external conditions. They change as do the waves of the sea, sometimes barely discernible, at others in a deep swell, and in severe storms reaching great heights. The calm after a storm is similar to the recovery after a need. In one the tension is reduced to relative evenness of wave motion, while in the other there is reasonable quiet and complacency within the organism. And neither the sea nor the individual is the same after the storm or need as it was before. The great difference in their calmness is that the sea energy is spent aimlessly and the life energy is directed purposefully toward its own fulfillment.

Recovery from or fulfillment of a need creates changes in the psychological field which constitute a new integration and a better operational unity of the self. The conditions which brought on the original need can never be restored, so the individual can never go back to his equilibrium prior to the upset. He can only go forward to a modified organization of the self. Regression, which is described as a backward movement, and disintegration, which is a breakdown in self-unity, are both forward movements, but in an undesirable direction. They do not fulfill the life purpose of self-enhancement. No person can regress to or disintegrate into any earlier behavior, since all conditions including himself are different from what they were previously. Thus he never gets back into equilibrium; he always goes forward into it. The tension is reduced, the rhythm of life is quieter, the self is relatively undisturbed, but it is not the self it was before the upset. So recovery is the new equilibrium of a dynamic, confident self more adequate to deal with the new needs which are certain to arise.

Students are frequently disturbed over the meanings of terms such as recovery, satisfaction, and fulfillment. They think of recovery as improvement after an injury or operation or disease. To them it means getting back health and strength or re-establishing conditions which existed prior to the occurrence, a return to the original state. This can never exist after a physical injury, an emotional outburst, an intellectual effort, or any self-disturbance. The individual may walk after a fracture or think after a concussion or breathe after a lung resection, but he is not his prior physical or mental self. To think of the concept of recovery as a new equilibrium based on an emerging perception of self and

environment requires time to be acceptable, but its acceptance is essential if recovery is to be an element in behavior conversion.

Satisfaction implies that conditions in the phenomenal
field have changed and that the upset has more or less dis-
appeared. The individual feels happy, comfortable, elated,
but this may not mean a higher operating level that comes
only through deliberative action. A child has satisfaction in
his temper tantrum, an adult feels joyful over his neurotic
persecution of others, the authoritarian parent glories in his
power to manage members of the family, the teacher takes
pride in maintaining standards by eliminating students.
These are need-satisfactions but not need-fulfillment, since
they are neither in the direction nor on the level of self-
enhancement. They do not release potential capacity or fulfill life purposes. Fulfillment means that an individual is so
resolving his need as to give reasonable assurance of his
higher integration. To obtain need-fulfillment he must have
satisfaction in the process by which it is accomplished. This
is difficult to explain to persons reared to believe that satisfaction or fulfillment resides in specific parts or fixed-end results
of an experience.

On page 141 is a flow chart (Chart VIII) showing the development of a need through deliberative action and need-
fulfillment into a mature self and through impulsive action
and need-satisfaction to an immature self. While this is never
an either/or relationship, the chart defines movement and
sharpens the difference between two major directions of
growth and behavior. The deliberative process generally leads
to need-fulfillment, the impulsive process tends to result in
temporary satisfaction but lower integration and poorer
operational unity.

Sometimes students confuse frustration with need, yet the
two have quite different meanings. Frustration refers to in-
surmountable barriers in life situations which cause the in-

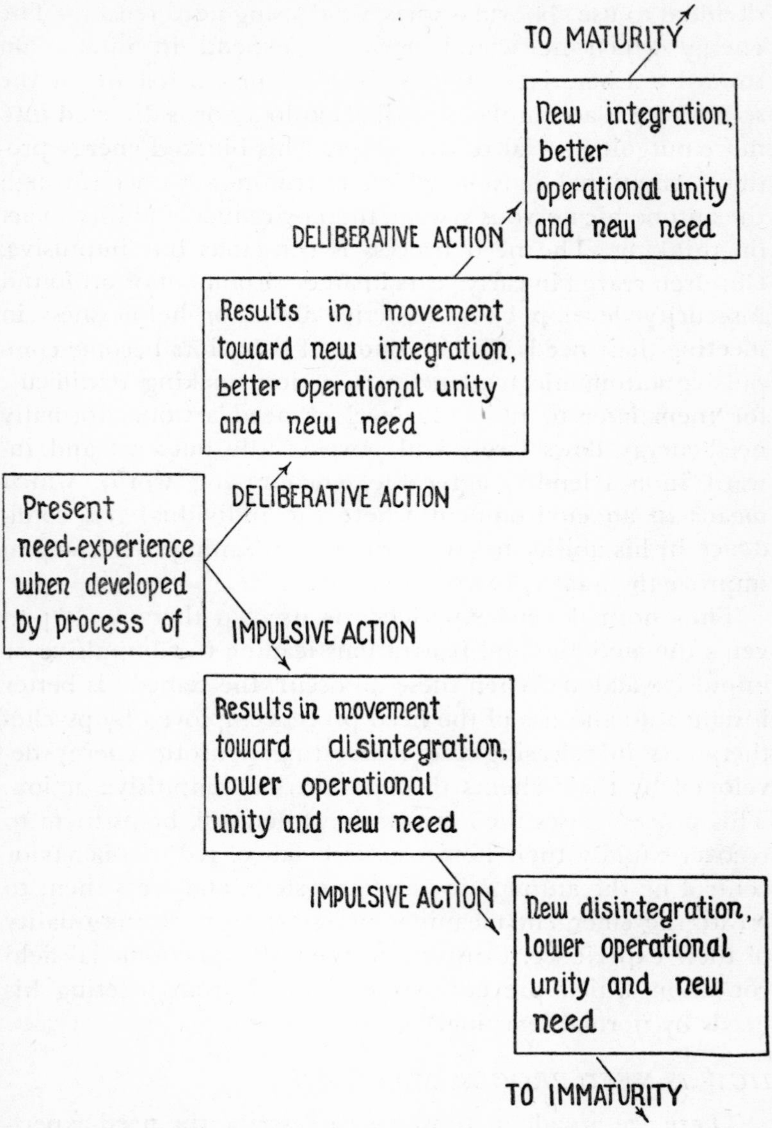

TO MATURITY

New integration, better operational unity and new need

DELIBERATIVE ACTION

Results in movement toward new integration, better operational unity and new need

DELIBERATIVE ACTION

Present need-experience when developed by process of

IMPULSIVE ACTION

Results in movement toward disintegration, lower operational unity and new need

IMPULSIVE ACTION

New disintegration, lower operational unity and new need

TO IMMATURITY

Chart VIII.   Direction in Need Process

dividual to use abnormal ways of releasing need tension. The energy which he would normally expend in interaction toward deliberative action is blocked or turned in on the self, where it accumulates until it explodes or is directed into more outgoing social relationships. This blocked energy produces emotional tension which is readiness to act through the autonomic nervous system, thereby reducing ability to act on thinking. The need process is conscious but impulsive. Children reared in early years in an environment of profound insecurity develop basic anxieties about or helplessness in meeting their needs. Their abnormal behaviors become compulsive autonomic tendencies to action, making it difficult for them later to raise the level of need action. Normally need-energy flows freely and purposefully outward and inward in a friendly, agreeable, encouraging world, which means in an environment where the individual has confidence in his ability to create the new meanings necessary to improve the quality of his experience.

Thus normal need-experience is its own therapy. It prevents the anxieties and frustrations leading to compulsive or impulsive action. When these do occur, the remedy is better insight into and use of the need process employed by psychotherapists in releasing and redirecting neurotic energy developed by their clients through years of impulsive action. This process raises their frustration tolerance, helps them to recover rapidly their homeostatic balance, reduces behavior control by the autonomic nervous system, and frees them to create the emergent meanings necessary to raise the quality of their experience. Frustration, then, is a phenomenal field condition which prevents an individual from meeting his needs by normal learning.

HOW IS NEED PROCESS MANAGED?

There are no adequate words to describe the need-experience process, since it is a holistic, biospheric phenomenon and most available terms explain development and learning as linear rather than circular responses. New terms such as autonomy, which means interest centered in the self, and homonomy, which is interest centered in others, do not describe the holistic, circular interaction. Furthermore, there are no adequate terms to explain deliberative action as direction in need-experience. The need is the beginning, the need-fulfillment is the variable recovery, and the deliberative quality of the series of moving situations is the promise of the fulfillment. Since I am unable to catch this movement as an observer and frequently lose sight of it as a behaver, I shall follow the usual procedure of locating and describing fixed spots on the biosphere. They do not occur in the neat order presented here, inasmuch as they operate continuously and simultaneously.

1. The need, lack, upset, or imbalance must be explored, since the area and depth of the psychological field involved in the disturbance must be determined. The purpose of this exploration is to locate the controlling figure–ground relationship so as to bring into focus and differentiate the marginal experiences, find the real center of the need, and select the inadequate meanings to be improved. The quality of such exploration is important to the final quality of the total experience.

2. The individual must search for appropriate new experience to leaven his psychological field. Regardless of how well old experience which constituted the need is explored, past experience is never adequate for resolving the need on the fulfillment level. New experience does not mean more of the same kind as that which the individual has already built into behavior, but a different kind. New experience tends (a) to extend the range of the psychological field, (b) to polarize it through neglected or heretofore unconsidered evidence, (c) to increase sensitivity toward other persons, especially those with different experiential backgrounds, (d) to furnish the basic leaven from which new meanings may

emerge. This search for new experience goes on simultaneously with exploration of the origin of the need.

3. The individual must make process decisions in order to
direct his efforts and study their relationship to the experience as a whole. Process decisions occur wherever there is a
choice of action, conduct, or behavior either by an individual
or by a group. These judgments and choices should not be
made for the individual by outside persons, thus robbing him
of the opportunity to discover and release his creative and
integrative insight, which is the stuff from which new meanings arise. Releasing these constructive and integrative forces
in his expanding and enriching field matures the individual
more rapidly than does the slower and more discouraging
method of trying to control his development from without.

Making process decisions has a number of aspects. These
are: (a) Working with others so as to make judgments by
consensus. Voting may indicate that no real reason exists for
a decision since the basic need or issues are not clear. Further
study will bring a clarified need and consensus, thus eliminating the divisive effect that voting has on group unity.
(b) Changing direction by new decisions wherever there is
evidence through action that old decisions are no longer adequate. Thus decisions become both the direction of and the
basis for revision of action. (c) Understanding and accepting
the sound mental hygiene that decisions are purposeful directions for action made upon the best accounting of all
available evidence at the moment of judgment. When subsequent experience shows that such decisions are no longer
useful or have little future promise, they are changed without regret, fear, or other emotional upset. (d) Continuous
appraisal of all decisions and actions prior to the moment
when the next decision is to be made. This keeps fluid the
figure–ground relationship within the moving field and thus
gives opportunity to differentiate aspects heretofore unclari-
fied. The greater the pertinent area considered in the new

judgment, the greater the possibility for meaningful reorganization of the field.

4. Each individual must have free opportunity to self-select from the moving experience those learnings which in his judgment best satisfy his need. He should be helped to make his selections as conscious, deliberate, and realistic as possible by clarifying his reasons for such choices and by anticipating their effect upon himself and others. Pupils should not be expected to select the same learnings from a common need-experience, for each has a different field structure. Parents, teachers, and adult leaders should help each person make the best choices within his field but should not compare or evaluate him against others singly or in groups in order to praise or belittle his honest judgment.

5. The individual group studies experience in retrospect to locate, define, and evaluate the process in order to use it better in subsequent need-experiences. While such evaluation should always be relative to the experiences of children, it should be as broad in scope and deep in meaning as the group can accept. Since the quality of need-fulfillment is a function of the quality of the process, and since the process is the stable yet modifiable continuity from one experience to another, a conscious evaluation of a process is the best single learning which any individual can acquire from past experience. Teacher, parent, or leader must recognize that need process is a circular learning experience not the linear teaching of traditional education. There are no predetermined fixed ends to which the behaviors of all persons must conform.

A sharper distinction can now be drawn between the teaching and learning curriculums. The teaching curriculum is composed of a series of fixed fragments of experiences of others forced into the psychological field of the child through straight-line teaching, with external demands and rewards for accepting them without change. The learning curriculum is composed of a series of need-experiences selected and developed by children through a circular learning process toward need-fulfillment, with the guidance of mature adults, expert in helping them to understand, accept, and use such process. The results of two thousand years of recorded history seem to be sufficient evidence for thinking people to decide which is preferable as a system of education in our democratic society.

A BACKWARD AND FORWARD LOOK

Two points here stressed are always discussed at length by students. The first is that all behavior is an attempt to satisfy a need. Many educators and laymen believe that behavior is caused directly by some external force. They have difficulty in seeing it as the efforts of an individual to resolve his need tension. The many routes taken by people to externalize their need energy is also an absorbing mystery to those taught to believe that behavior is a simple, direct reaction response to an outside stimulus. As soon as they accept this new relationship between need and action, many persons begin to see learners, including themselves in their college classes, in a different light and with a clearer meaning of the learning–behaving process.

The second point is usually raised as a question, "Does every individual *know* he is moving in the direction of enhancing himself?" Students have two major reasons for asking this question, each of which they support by observations of the behavior of others, especially of children. Some believe that behavior is purposeless. They reject the conscious, purposeful, creative character of life managed by the individual in interaction with his environment. Others accept purpose in learning but assert that it is not always in the direction of self-enhancement. Each group cites many illustrations of observed behavior which in their judgment deny both purpose and self-enhancement. The difficulty is with the reference point.

Behavior to the behaver is always purposeful, is always directed toward enhancing himself, and is always the best behavior toward that end that he can release under the existing field conditions. No children and few adults are able to discuss directly the concept of self-realization as direction of behavior, even though all know the meaning of it autonomically. They talk about how they feel; how others treat them; how well they achieve their purposes or goals in immediate experiences; how, when, and why they create new objects or meanings; what attitudes and values they accept from past experience. These are criteria by which they test the effects of their behavior on themselves, keeping what is good and rejecting what is hurtful. A person never does anything which he believes autonomically or conceptually will depress him as a person, as this is contrary to his life-fulfillment. But to an observer his behavior may be leading toward self-deterioration since it will eventually isolate him from people or shield him from normal interaction with the outside world or turn his energy into himself to become an egocentric personality. So the behaver and observer from different reference points give entirely different meanings to the action.

Students always ask a series of related questions on the material of this chapter. "Does the teacher create the need for the pupil?" "Does the teacher create need in the pupil for the subject matter which he will teach?" Underlying all of them are assumptions such as these: (1) The teacher gives the pupil the need which he wants him to have when he wants him to have it. (2) The teacher directs the need energy toward learning the subject matter which he will teach anyhow, even though the pupil sees no value in it. (3) The subject matter will be accepted by the pupil as necessary to need-fulfillment. (4) The subject matter is the beginning, the direction, and the end of action.

There are six different assumptions underlying this chapter:
(1) The need of the pupil grows out of his interaction with
his environment, which includes his teacher. But he finds it;
the teacher does not select and give it to him. (2) The pupil
directs his need energy toward the most reasonable action
of which he is capable with or without the help of the teacher.
(3) The subject matter which the teacher has to teach has
little or no direct value to the pupil in satisfying his need,
since adults never selected and organized it for such purpose.
(4) The pupil creates his own need matter within the experience out of what he takes in from the surrounding environment. (5) The teacher helps the pupil locate his need and
assists him in resolving it so as to increase his power in mutual,
reasonable, thoughtful action. The external culture selected
and converted into need energy varies, but the process continues from need to need or experience to experience. (6) The
need is the beginning, need matter is the converted energy,
ever more qualitative experience is the direction, and self-
enhancement is the end of action.

These differences are neither easy to see nor easy to accept
by persons with years of education or experience in subject
thinking. In the next chapter I discuss further the process by
which a need is developed into a qualitative experience.

Chapter VI

HOW IS NEED-EXPERIENCE DEVELOPED?

Need is a disturbance of the self or the operating center of the individual that arises out of his interaction with his environment. Without selfhood or self-awareness there is no disturbance which constitutes need, even though there are in lower forms of life and in man in earlier stages of development protoplasmic irritants which keep the life process operating. Since the self is the conscious life or the entire organism in purposeful action, the individual feels his need all over. It begins as a gross total uneasiness, gradually becoming consciously and conceptually focused until he locates its scope and depth. With young children or immature adults, need remains too long as a gross total disturbance since they never locate definitely the nature of their uneasiness. Others pinpoint the upset so rapidly that its more general origin is overlooked. In either case the behavior lacks some aspects of the process necessary for developing the higher quality of experience for which the individual is searching. Others must help him better to locate his need and differentiate more direct, realistic, and meaningful behaviors.

While each individual feels his need all over, his total self never interacts with other total selves in his psychological field. Never is all of his experience involved in the total experience of others. Rather, selected parts of it are polarized toward selected parts of the experience of others. When this moving interaction becomes sufficiently prolonged either in scope or in depth to challenge existing behaviors which constitute the organized self, an area of need appears. This is not given to any individual by someone else. Each discovers his area of conflict which he must resolve, but what produces need in one person may cause no self-disturbance in another in the same situation. A teacher may be distressed over the lack of interest of pupils in his subject. A parent may be upset over the unwillingness of his child to follow proffered advice. Life is full of illustrations of the fact that interaction produces need in one or more persons but not in others since they find nothing to challenge the existing organization of the self.

Since need arises out of interaction among people, one of the first steps in the process of resolving it is to explore all of the existing field conditions of the total group. Deliberative action cannot be reached by studying only the polarized area. It must be seen in its differentiated relationship to the larger group experience. And the quality of the action necessary to resolve it rests with the people who produced it. They must direct their future activities so as to increase the sensitiveness of every person to himself and to others, especially to those behaviors which cause the conflict. A person can be defined operationally only as a tendency to action in situations under existing phenomenal field conditions. Since each self lives in a psychological field of other selves, each exists in some form in every other self. Thus each individual is a tendency to interaction in a dynamic series of life experiences. Since need arises out of social interaction and must be resolved in social interaction, the need-experience process of need-fulfillment is sometimes called *the social process* or *the group process*.

ARE THERE GROUP NEEDS?

Students agree that people live in groups and that teachers have many pupils, but they differ sharply on whether there are group needs. Some accept individual needs but reject group needs, while others object that this is impossible, for each teacher would then have to work with each child on his individual need apart from every other child. Some believe there are group needs in addition to individual needs and that the teacher works with these common group needs. Others immediately point out that group needs do not and cannot exist since a group is only the quality of interaction among individuals. When this is high "groupness" appears, when it is low "groupness" is absent. All agree to the social origin of need and most believe that it must be resolved by a social group process. Few, however, can locate what a teacher works with or teaches under the need concept. Students see clearly what to do when teaching subjects, but in the need-experience process everything seems vague and indefinite, even intangible.

✓Group needs do not exist. A group is qualitative interaction among individuals and a quality has no felt disturbances. These are in the individuals who operate so as to produce the quality, better to resolve their respective tensions. Individuals do have common areas of disturbance out of which individual needs arise. These larger upsetting areas appear because of similarities in many life factors, such as process of development, rate of growth, attitudes and beliefs of parents and teachers, physical environmental conditions, and the mores of the surrounding group life. Movements of children to grow into adequate selves under such similar conditions cause many common areas of disturbance to appear. Since the particular series of events which precipitates them in one person is not the same for others, parents and teachers may uncritically conclude that children have separate needs when in reality their actions represent only individual impingements within a common area of disturbance. The teacher or parent helps members of the group search for the common area underlying their specific actions to produce the quality called groupness which aids each to fulfill better his own specific need.

One spring in City A, near the source of a river, a serious typhoid epidemic broke out, affecting many people. Within a few days children in the fifth grade of City B, located downstream, came to school with many and varied questions about this epidemic which had hit friends living in City A. Will the children in our city get typhoid? Where does it come from? Is it in the water we drink from the river? Does City A dump its waste (sewage) into the river for us to drink? What do we do with our waste? Do we put it in the river for other people below to drink? Should we boil our water? Can we get typhoid by living with people who have it? And so on to over a hundred different questions within a week. While the external expression of the upset was personal to many children because of family situations, the teacher sensed a common area which she could help them study so as to understand and use better the process of deliberative action. For four months they worked together on the area approximately one-half of each day. On various occasions the children gave names to the experience. Once the center was germs, later it was water, but near the end they agreed to call it "The Life History of Sewage," which they understood well enough to explain to other children in the school, their parents, and interested citizens. They concluded that their effective water purification system would prevent a typhoid epidemic in their city. They decided they treated the people better in the cities below than City A treated them, since they had a modern sewage disposal plant while City A turned its raw sewage into the river to pollute the water for others. By working together as a group on the common area of disturbance each was able to resolve his particular need better than if he had worked alone on his upset.

HOW IS A COMMON AREA OF DISTURBANCE LOCATED?

Since life is a continuing series of imbalances and recoveries, every individual must carefully select the needs and every group must locate the areas of disturbance on which to work toward deliberative action. A few well-selected needs or common areas of disturbance thoughtfully studied will do more to enhance the self than many needs or areas examined with lesser understanding. Some areas have only minor importance in the larger life perspective; others eliminate themselves through new figure–ground relationships around deeper upsets; a few persist in spite of all ordinary readjustments of the field. The teacher helps children locate these deep persistent disturbing areas by sifting, evaluating, and selecting those vital to their educative experience. He encourages children to express freely in many media their specific directions of action, which are the evidence he must examine in order to determine whether a common need area exists. Such an area has three characteristics. (1) It represents a penetrating upset for all members of the group. (2) Since the teacher is most concerned that children learn group dynamics, study of the area will extend over a considerable period of time. (3) It is broad enough for the teacher to help children manage the experience by the need-experience process to reach need-fulfillment.

The teacher releases the existing environment to allow common areas of disturbance to emerge more fully. He does that by (1) exploring with children many and varied new first-hand experiences, (2) encouraging freedom of expression in many media, (3) extending and enriching the cooperative process of living together, (4) helping individuals to improve

the quality of their selective judgments and values by stim-
ulating their original creative insight. He carries on these
activities wherever possible in or outside school until children
begin to contribute freely, openly, and directly of themselves.
Such opportunities are always available if the teacher is sensitive to them.

The program of living has at least three different levels of
exploration of need or points of emphasis going on simultaneously. (1) On the first level the teacher is exploring, enriching, studying the many daily upsets which children release in
a cooperative environment to see whether they represent real
needs and possible common areas. (2) On the second level the
teacher works more extensively with the children on a few
needs selected from the many proposed, to locate a common
group area which they can develop into a qualitative experience. (3) On the third level the teacher studies with the children over a large but variable portion of each day some need
area already reached by consensus through the two preceding
levels. Thus a large part of the life of children in school falls
into three large variable areas, the most important of which
for qualitative learning is the third. A few of these experiences throughout a year will lift markedly the quality of living. The same relationship is equally basic in the home or in
an educational program for high school or college students.

Some differences among problems, needs, and areas of need
can now be better differentiated. A *problem* is a disturbance
in the environment in which the self is only superficially involved. There is a mild irritation in the outer protective
sheath which never reaches the real center or self-concept.
It can be resolved by rearranging present external conditions
along with only slight modifications of the outer shell of the
self but with no direct effect upon the inner self or self-
concept, the source of consistent tendencies to action. A *need*
is a disturbance of the real self which can be resolved satisfac-

torily only when the self-concept is reorganized on higher operating levels and the surrounding psychological field is creatively remade.

A problem is a superficial disturbance, whereas a need is a deep-seated upset of the inner self. Two or more people interacting in the same environment may locate a disturbance which is a problem to one and a need to another. A college professor has a problem when students do not learn his subject matter, whereas his students have a real need to resolve their basic insecurity developed under such conditions. A teacher may refer to a problem child, whereas the child is trying to solve unaided some profound inner disturbance. Educators generally speak of mathematics, history, or reading problems, as their solution does little to raise the operating level of the self. Many persons who are afraid to face themselves become expert in solving problems to divert attention from their own inner insecurity. Since a problem is only a slight disturbance of the outer shell of the self, its solution is a nondeliberative or inadequate direction of action. While all behavior is an attempt to satisfy need, problem-solving does not stem from a real need, hence the behavior is superficial and ineffective. This is why the teacher must explore the area surrounding the overt behavior to see whether a real need or a superficial upset lies back of it. When the behavior of children, college students, or adults stems from real needs common areas of disturbance are generally found.

Two frequently used approaches to locate a common area of disturbance for group action can now be distinguished. One is to make an inventory of problems suggested by individual members of the group, determine their order and importance, and study them seriatim as a committee of the whole or form subgroups for each, both of which are directions of action apart from a clear understanding of the underlying need. This approach is generally inadequate since individuals suggest as problems the sore spots on the top of their minds or those which they think the leader or professor would like to list. Once they are proposed for study, it is difficult to push behind them to locate the more fundamental disturbances. Many teachers use this approach because they believe they should not act to assist the free release of problems by students. The result of their abdication is a low quality of experience for everyone.

A more fruitful approach is for the teacher or leader to suggest at the outset something which will cause members to focus, release, and reorganize past experience. When I meet adult groups for the first time I ask volunteers to describe briefly the most interesting experience they have ever had. After a number of these, I ask for their most uninteresting experience. I then suggest that we analyze these experiences to find similarities and differences, together with the underlying reasons. Common areas of disturbance invariably emerge along with a feeling of mutuality or we-ness which raises the level of interaction above the individual problem response. I merely apply in a group situation a basic principle of individual counseling: whatever a client creatively releases with the sympathetic aid of the counselor comes closer to his real self than anything he will release unaided. The group then studies the common area by the need-experience process, which clears their original problems on a higher need level.

The chief issue between the two approaches is whether a more qualitative experience results from studying directly a series of superficial problems or whether it comes from locating and examining the common underlying need area out of which they emerged. In the former, individual problems are studied directly but can be satisfactorily resolved only for a relatively short time, to reoccur later in similar form. In the latter, the problem is resolved indirectly by a group process in a cooperative field which releases ability to deal more adequately with subsequent upsets. When a need process is used in a common area, the surface problems will either disappear entirely or be incorporated into those needs, emerging closer to the real self. The more the real self is revealed to the real self for what it is, the higher is the possible level of action.

Neither college professors nor elementary school teachers will have problem pupils in their classes if they locate common areas of need and study them intelligently or take better into account all of the field factors, including themselves, in their dynamic relationship. A third-grade boy had so much difficulty in one school that his teacher called him a moron. Later he transferred to another school where the new teacher was very sympathetic, beginning immediately to help him build up his faith in himself. One day in an interchange of confidences the boy said to her, "What is a moron?" The teacher replied, "A moron is a person who does not understand people very well." The boy thought a moment and said, "I guess the last teacher I had was a moron. She did not understand me very well." The boy and his former teacher had a common area of disturbance, but since they never found it they could not study it intelligently.

If a teacher prefers the problem-inventory approach, he should not discuss, array, or organize the proposed problems. He should use them as an entrance into the deeper sources of experience by questions such as these: What are the common antecedents to these problems? or, What do they have in common? Later when a common area begins to emerge, he should ask, what is the relation of this common background to these problems? or, What bearing do these antecedents have on the interpretation of these problems? Finally he comes to the real question, How can we study the common area so as to effect a solution of the problems? In this way the earlier problems to be solved by a change in the environment will generally become needs or opportunities to change the self. Chart IX shows this relationship.

HOW SHALL THE COMMON AREA OF DISTURBANCE BE STUDIED?

While need begins as a gross total disturbance, most people usually can define its general limits within the self and the environment or can locate roughly the area of impingement. They tend to resolve it by direct action, modifying external conditions to remove the specific sore spot without examining

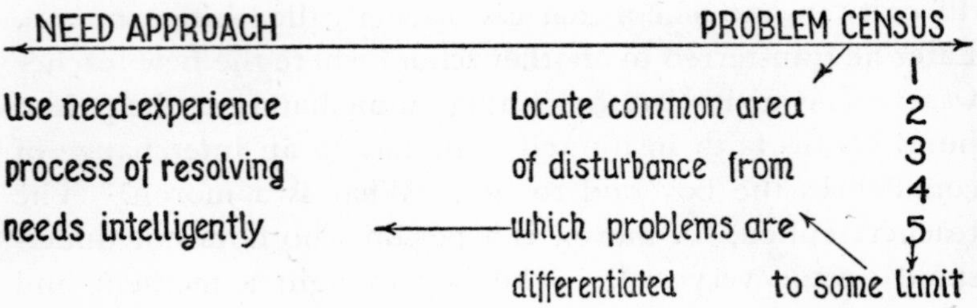

NEED APPROACH	PROBLEM CENSUS
Use need-experience	Locate common area
process of resolving	of disturbance from
needs intelligently	←——which problems are
	differentiated to some limit

1
2
3
4
5

Chart IX. *Need Approach to Group Problems*

the area of disturbance to find the conditions which caused it. They eliminate the surface symptoms rather than the underlying causes. By locating the need in the external environment, they use a problem-solving technique to resolve it. Rarely do they study themselves as a factor in it. They make a few minor external readjustments and continue throughout life as the old selves, accumulating deeper uncertainties and anxieties.

A variety of these uncritical approaches can be identified. They are: (1) the frontal mass attack of trying to break down the barrier by imposing force; (2) the pot-shot technique of chipping away at the difficulty from any or all points where a foothold can be gained; (3) the weak-spot technique or searching for a soft spot and trying to bore a hole through it; (4) the round-house technique of moving around it without meeting the problem realistically; (5) the escape technique of setting up and solving a similar problem in the world of phantasy, where conditions can be changed at will and success is always achieved. No one of these shows promise of resulting in a direction of action which enhances the self, for too many of the important factors in the field are inadequately considered.

The first step toward deliberative action is to explore the common group area of disturbance to find (1) the conditions which caused it to appear, and (2) other factors in the field which must be better taken into account. Since need arises when one self is polarized toward selected aspects of other selves, the common conditions which compete with or thwart so many selves simultaneously must be located and studied in order to modify their direction in future action. To continue them would only mean rearranging the prejudices of the people concerned with little reconstruction of any self on higher levels. I call these polarized factors the *A factors*, or antecedent conditions. Since every need occurs in a field organized around the self as figure, one antecedent condition is usually the over-dominance of the figure to the neglect of the ground. To study the need adequately, the ground, or what I call the *B factors*, must be identified and clarified, thereby changing the structure of the field so that *A factors* have a different meaning to the self. Out of this clearer perception of both figure and ground factors new relationships, which I call *C factors*, emerge. These are new meanings heretofore nonexistent in the field, but now created by members of the group through release of more of their total experience.

The possibilities for enhancing the self lie in the C factors, which are created through better perception of the field dynamics. Thus the basic reasons for locating and studying the A and B factors is to insure higher quality in the C factors. While all three of these sets of factors were potentially present in the original need field, the A factors so dominated it that the others were recognized but given relatively little importance, were consciously overlooked, or were subconsciously rejected. Also in the field is a teacher or leader who has a wider experience than other group members. With their consent he introduces new and heretofore inoperative *D factors*, after the other three have been examined or during the study of the others so long as the group creatively accepts them. As soon as C meanings emerge, each individual will be more

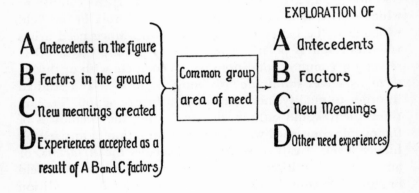

EXPLORATION OF

A antecedents in the figure
B factors in the ground
C new meanings created
D experiences accepted as a result of A B and C factors

Common group area of need

A antecedents
B factors
C new meanings
D other need experiences

————→toward deliberative action————→to self-enhancement

Chart X.   Exploration of Area of Need

receptive to new experience than when the field was dominated by the A factors which constituted the need.

Life always moves forward, never backward. Observers may conclude from his behavior that an individual is going backward but he believes he is going forward. So forward may be backward and backward may be forward, depending upon who makes the observations. Exploring the area of need is always forward, even though group members locate the conditions which produced it. This exploratory relationship is shown in Chart X.

The purposes of the exploration as the teacher or leader sees it are (1) to discover the limits of the upset, (2) to locate the center of the area of disturbance, (3) to help each individual clarify his specific impingement within the area, (4) to aid each individual to conceptualize and differentiate a larger area of his experience by changing his figure–ground relationships, (5) to encourage the emergence of new meanings, (6) to locate trial directions of action, (7) to find areas where new enriching experience is desirable, (8) to aid each person in obtaining a better understanding of others through their mutual cooperative social interaction, (9) to help each individual recognize the level of his logic of experience and see how it is affected by the group process.

I was asked by the educational staff—administrators, supervisors, and teachers—of a school system to help them modernize their school curriculum from the first through the twelfth grade. From a preliminary discussion of the problem as they saw it and from an examination of personnel records, I drew the following conclusions. (1) The school system was of the traditional academic type. (2) The professional staff had a subject matter background and experience since departmental teaching existed beyond the second grade. (3) There were no innovating experiences that challenged the subject outlook. All experimentation was within the academic framework. (4) Teachers were concerned over (a) the failure of so many children to learn the required subject matter and (b) the increasing number of problem children. (5) Administrators were alarmed over the growing public feeling that the schools were not teaching the three R's effectively and the increasing demand that something be done about it. (6) The attitude of the staff and the public toward a thorough study of the situation was favorable.

From these conditions I inferred the existence of a genuine common area of disturbance deep and broad enough for me to help everyone resolve it by the group process of deliberative action. I knew that my success as a leader rested on how well they understood this process and how effectively they could carry it on after my services were terminated. Their desire to modernize the school curriculum was the medium necessary for such learning. While we were getting acquainted, I tested the thinking of these educators by asking, "What do you believe is the direction in which we should move to improve the curriculum? Will this direction satisfy you, the parents, and the public?" There was consensus that the solution of the problem lay in bringing up to date the courses of study which had not been revised for fifteen years.

This was the answer I expected, as it fitted perfectly the A factors in the preparation and experience of staff members and in their existing educational practices. They expected me to help them develop these new courses of study. Yet as their leader I knew that the upset was too deep to be removed by new materials. (1) Their direction stemmed from the A factors which caused the need to appear. (2) There were many B factors which had been overlooked. (3) Creative C factors had not and could not emerge under the existing dominance of the A conditions. (4) The perspective of the staff should be widened with new and different types of experiences, introduced so as to increase a favorable attitude and high interest in finding a solution. (5) The center of the area of need was not the one proposed but had to be discovered. (6) Time necessary for a better exploration of the field had to be found, even though the group was set to rush into a rewrite job. (7) This exploration must take place within the dynamics of behavior of staff members so as to add to their favorable attitudes.

The behavior of an individual anywhere at any time either in or out of professional education operates around the following dynamics: (1) the affection, belongingness, wantedness which he felt in the early years of his life, together with the feeling of status which he has in the present, (2) his educational preparation for his position, (3) the nature of his professional experience, (4) the quality of his professional acceptance and status past and present, (5) the values which form the innermost core of himself, or his self-concept, which operates in the existing need and which he wants to preserve and perpetuate, (6) the structure of the surrounding environment in which he works, (7) his physical or energy capacity and the level of his safety margin, (8) his over-all personality integration, (9) his immediate and specific personality relationship to the need to be studied. An individual behaves in any given situation through a dynamic organization of selected meanings derived from these sources.

I could judge some of these dynamic factors from available personal data but I desired more live evidence from free and open interaction with staff members in small and large groups. From such discussions I drew these conclusions: (1) The controlling and nonmodifiable value for the moment was that the schools should preserve and perpetuate the three-R-knowledge purpose of education. (2) A few persons had real doubt as to the value of present methods of teaching these three R's. (3) There were some whose personalities and meanings were fluid enough to undertake innovating experience. (4) Many persons had such highly established and rigid personalities that, at the moment, they lacked both the desire and the ability to contribute toward an intelligent resolution of the problem. As their leader, I accepted their basic viewpoint of value and direction. I assured them of my own belief that the three-R-knowledge purpose of education in the country as a whole was inadequately achieved by pupils. I asked how we could best study their results in their local situation.

Agreement was soon reached on the following points: (1) Study available information on the achievement of pupils in the three R's or skills-knowledge purpose. Standardized achievement tests had been given for many years. The high school staff had just completed an occupational survey of their graduates over a ten-year period. (2) Study available sources of information inside and outside the school on how to improve methods of teaching and how to raise the quality of learning. (3) Promote innovating experience within the system to discover new ways of teaching the required skills and knowledges. To me these proposals were inadequate since all were within the A factors. They were a re-examination from a slightly different reference point of the conditions which had previously been explored.

Every school has pupils who are usually the B factor in educational situations. I introduced questions opening the area of what pupils felt and thought about the three R's as currently taught and how such feelings affected their achievement. Individual teachers volunteered evidence obtained from their discussions with problem children, special-class pupils, and parents. The group decided to organize three committees to assume responsibility for each of three lines of activity. Committee No. 1 studied existing data on achievement and also new evidence from pupils. They made case histories of problem children to find out why they became unadjusted. They located the needs of pupils by various methods. They obtained interest ratings by pupils of required subjects as they were now taught. The committee reported that for the first time it saw achievement from the point of view of children or learners as well as teachers and that the two points of view were far apart. By their various studies they brought into figure and clarified the behaviors of the learners which were originally in the ground. These new meanings conflicted with their old subject values, thus polarizing their field. They faced the dilemma of leaving the two points of view opposed to each other or of further clarifying each and thus reorganizing their whole psychological field including themselves. Eventually they followed the latter course but in varying degrees.

Committee No. 2 studied the methods used by the best

teachers in the school system. Later they visited schools in many outside communities to observe their best teachers. Representatives from these outside schools met with the committee to clarify meanings of teaching and learning. At the same time members reviewed the literature on teaching and learning. They became much interested in child growth and development, in studies on self-selection by learners, in personalities and how they are developed, in cooperative or organic and authoritarian or aggregate groups both in theory and in action. The first break came when they saw how the structure of the environment affected the quality of the self-selected learnings of pupils. Since quality of environment is a function of the quality of interpersonal relations, they discussed outside demands and requirements upon them and their pupils with new meaning. Shortly they reported that in their judgment the point of view in teaching and learning the required skills and knowledges that was prevalent in the school system did not harmonize with the best available evidence on how children learn and that it should have major revisions. Finally, they concluded their difficulty lay in the fact that the teacher controlled what he taught, but the pupil controlled what he learned.

Committee No. 3 assumed responsibility for helping all interested teachers to set up innovating practices with their respective classes. Administrative approval for such action was both willingly and helpfully given. Innovations ranged from a nonreading curriculum in the first grade to the development of materials cooperatively with pupils to meet their needs in biology, social studies, and English in senior high school. Two teachers cooperated with four groups in a trade school better to relate academic work to pupil needs as they recognized them, much to the satisfaction of everyone. A parent-teacher group which volunteered to study some difficult behaviors of children and adolescents eventually emerged as a community group studying personality, especially the way in which it is developed and modified. Members of a senior class exploring the meaning and development of personality met with this adult group for interesting and valuable interchange of experience. This committee concluded that there were unlimited possibilities for innovating experiences in new areas which the staff should explore, since they had important implications for improving teaching and learning.

The exploration described above was carried on for two years. Near the close of the first year I again asked the staff what was the direction of intelligent action. Their original clear-cut decision to revise the old courses of study had now changed to uncertainty or no desire to rush into such action. Other alternatives were proposed but they were loose and vague. In the fall of the second year there was consensus that revising courses of study was not now so important as many other activities; it was no longer the center of the disturbing area. Many persons remarked on how naive the original conclusion now seemed, but it was the best judgment they could make at that time. By the close of the second year the new center and direction for the future was to encourage each teacher to carry on innovating experiences cooperatively with pupils, to give him help in going forward with such action, and to readjust administrative requirements in order to make this possible. And the courses of study still have their ancient imprint.

HOW IS THE CENTER OF THE DISTURBANCE LOCATED?

One purpose in exploring the disturbing area is to locate its center or what may eventually become the direction of deliberate action. The best available trial centers are frequently selected and explored until some are eliminated, others emerge, and a new direction is differentiated from the broadened perspective. Rarely can a group of adults locate immediately a center of disturbance, and such ability almost never appears with children.

In one school system I found many over-age adolescent boys and girls in grades three to six. To be promoted they had to learn the subject matter for the grade or remain in it for two years. They were retarded, uninterested in the "children's stuff" which they were taught, and literally bursting out of the desks designed for smaller children. These forlorn, unhappy, listless individuals, damaged by the authoritarian school, were brought together in a special class in a junior high school where they could have many social contacts with older children. An understanding, sympathetic teacher, free to innovate, decided to move away from their old hurts to activities based on their needs. His problem was to find them. In two months of quiet living together, including many group excursions to interesting places in the community, the teacher gained their confidence. After group discussions and individual conferences, at odd times during the day, on the street after school, they began slyly to tell him or to pass him notes stating their important problems which authoritarian controls had surrounded with emotional blocks.

When they felt free to discuss together some of these more personal matters, they agreed upon six important questions they would like to answer. How can we find out "what is going on inside of us?" "Why do other people think we are queer or why do they think there is something the matter with us or what is wrong with us that other people don't like us?" "Why do our parents think that we are no good, worthless, never going to amount to anything?" "How do you act with boys and girls when you are with them?" or "How do you act when you are with a particular boy friend or girl friend?" "Can we get a radio for our room so that we can listen to some programs we like?" "Can we go to more different kinds of places on our excursions than we have been going to?"

They agreed to explore three proposals: to get a radio and study radio programs, to take excursions to more different places of interest, and to find out what was going on inside of themselves. The final center became a streamlined version of all those originally suggested. It was to improve their relationships with people in school, at home, in social groups, on the job, as they would soon leave school to go to work. For three years they studied cooperatively this area of need, with remarkable results in maturity for everyone.

Sometimes adults believe they have found the center of their disturbing area when in reality they are offside, having inadequately explored the antecedent conditions. One summer I had in class the head of the English department in a large high school. After the opening session she came to my office to state that she had come to Teachers College at the expense of the board of education and that she was authorized by the English teachers to write a course of study in grammar for grades seven through twelve. She concluded, "The time is short. I want to begin work immediately. I understand you have many thousands of courses of study in your library. Will you please tell me where to locate those on grammar so that I can study them promptly." I, as her adviser, wanted to explore with her the area of need, to find why the English teachers decided that a course of study in grammar was the direction of intelligent action. Shortly she stated that the oral and written expression of pupils was very unsatisfactory in English and other classes.

Since this was probably the area of disturbance, I explored with her the evidence considered by the English teachers in making the judgment to write a course of study in grammar. The evidence was all of the A-factor or figure-type which constituted the need. No B or ground factors were studied, no new C factors had emerged, and no new D experiences were added. I suggested that our grammar courses of study were rarely used, they would always be available, and that she relax as six weeks was ample time for her to complete her assignment. Since she was mobilized for immediate action in her accepted direction, I had to inject some D factors. I asked if she would explore other ways of improving the quality of oral and written expression. She replied, "I will if you want me to do so." At the end of a week she was still exploring. Before the close of another week new meanings or C factors began to merge. She revealed them by statements beginning with "I now see," or "I wonder why we overlooked," and culminating in "I now feel very uncertain as to the value of grammar in improving the quality of oral and written expression for the pupils in our high school. There are so many other ways that seem more promising." At the end of six weeks she went home with much material on the more promising ways of meeting the group disturbance and with a carefully documented paper on why a more intensive study of grammar could not meet the needs of pupils or teachers. She freely admitted that her group was offside because of uncritically appraised English values and lack of knowledge of how to work intelligently with a need. So I helped her examine in retrospect the high points in the process which we had used and plan ways of introducing it to English teachers when she returned. She must have succeeded since she still has her position, the pupils have no course of study in grammar, and the teachers agree that the newer proposals bring satisfactory results.

HOW ARE THE NEW EXPERIENCES SELECTED?

When I ask students, "What are new experiences?" I find almost immediate consensus that they are excursions, trips, activities, projects, or going to new places and doing new things in direct first-hand relationship with the environment. Sometimes they suggest reading books in unexplored areas. Rarely do they refer to a more critical examination and appraisal or reconstruction of past experience. It takes time to see that lifting ground factors to figure factors where they can be better conceptualized and creating virgin meanings by such readjustment are new experiences. Yet the new meanings are as necessary for qualitative learning as are the new excursions, activities, projects from the outside. New experience refers to the internal reconstruction of previous learnings as well as exploring unknown areas in the environment. And the quality of the group will facilitate or retard the emergence of the new experiences.

There are many reasons why both internal and external aspects of new experiences are important in the need process.

1. Everyone has a basic biological drive for new experience in the cultural environment in which he lives. It is so necessary for maturing the self that the energy is always available unless blocked or misdirected by previous experiences. In this case the leader must help the group soothe these prior hurts so that normal energy may be re-established.

2. New experiences are the leaven to raise the level of old experience. Old meanings continuously wear out, but they cannot be thrown away as are old shoes. They are psychologically thrown away by reconversion into new meanings through better insight into their origin and use. When experience is stabilized by hurtful interaction, the creation of new meanings is limited, for new contacts with the surrounding culture are reduced. They are both the substance and the catalytic agent or psychological enzyme for remaking the old field—including the self—into a more dynamic new one.

3. New experience, both internal and external, is vital to the circular concept of learning. When it is reduced or denied, the energy movement is reversed because external forces tend to control the field. Behavior degenerates into producing responses acceptable to others. Learning becomes the straight-line relationship which is so effective in arresting maturity. New creative experience is constantly necessary to upbuild the self.

These new external experiences in the surrounding culture should be cooperatively selected by the need group through self-determined values, some of which are here suggested.

1. Wherever possible, they should be common total group experience. They are generally superior to subgroup or individual experiences in producing quality, since they offer a better basis for interaction. When the experience is confined to a few or to one person only, the group is less able to clarify it or determine its value in developing the need.

2. The new experiences should be firsthand rather than secondhand. Reading about something is less valuable than actual firsthand contact with the people, materials, processes which were the data used by the author. The meanings created in a firsthand experience by an observer or a participator may be quite different from those accepted and published in a book. The closer one is to reality the better is his basis for creating and clarifying his meanings. This does not rule out secondhand experience, but only indicates its relative value.

3. The outside experience should be within the common area of disturbance and should extend it as far as possible without disorganizing the group. New experience accepted into the field under high need has a better chance of survival or has a greater ground value in subsequent experience than new experience forced into it under low need. When need can no longer encompass it, new experience should cease regardless of how valuable it may be to the teacher or leader.

4. New outside experiences should evolve from studying that A and B and C factors already in the field. The basic potential for learning should be released, expanded, and guided. The rush for new outside experience prior to the interactive examination of conditions already present is frequently a neurotic compulsion to action without prior thought of possible consequences. Since some new outside experiences will be added, they should be selected and used by the total group as effectively as possible. Making these necessary judgments is a vital part of the cooperative management of the experience.

WHY ARE PROCESS DECISIONS MADE?

Every individual or group must make process decisions to determine the direction in which an experience will move. Every decision is a guide to action whether it be impulsively or thoughtfully made, the difference being in quality only. Refusing to make judgments or letting things alone to see what will happen or running away from a situation which cannot be faced are all process decisions. As soon as a child is able to distinguish between himself and others, parents should encourage and guide him in making such judgments by taking ever more factors into account, by better anticipating the effects of his decisions, and by increasing his willingness to accept the results of his actions. The school should help him improve this ability.

Individuals and groups always make decisions in the light of their own meaning of conditions in their psychological fields. They never make them on the interpretation of their field held by an observer, even when he uses external compulsion through rewards for accepting his judgment. A person may be within the group physically, yet be an observer of its actions. He does not have to be actually apart from it to have the relation of an observer to it. The parent in any authoritarian home is an observer of the behavior of his children. The teacher in any authoritarian school is a paid observer of the actions of children. Neither the parent nor the teacher is really in the group, in the sense that he works cooperatively and interactively with the younger members. Under such conditions the observer tries to maneuver the younger persons into accepting his decisions. He rewards the child for denying him his right to develop his own judgments. Such a procedure damages both behaver and observer, for when the behaver becomes dependent, constantly relying upon the observer for decisions, the observer no longer respects him. The original need-satisfaction of the observer in promoting dependence change to need-dissatisfaction when he eventually sees the results of his efforts. Both persons make process decisions from different points of view within the common field and both are losers, whether in home or in school.

Process decisions made by individuals or groups within their own fields may not be acceptable to outside observers. As I write these words I make choices or value judgments or decisions. I include some ideas, many I reject. The quantity of material eliminated seems enormous in view of the time necessary to collect, sift, and interpret it. I made the best possible decisions during the first draft. I try to make better decisions in this final revision because of new meanings evolving from previous efforts. These selections are within my field in relation to my need as guided by my purposes. An observer, in this case a reader, may agree or disagree with them, but he is not examining my meanings in my psychological field. He is evaluating his meanings in his field through the medium of these printed words. Whether he accepts or rejects depends upon what they make him do to himself, which will be affected by (1) the extent to which I agree with or challenge his basic meanings and (2) the extent to which he can use a deliberative process to resolve any impending threat to his self. The judgments made by a child or a college student in an experience, or the meanings created by a reader of this book, are neither right nor wrong for the observer or the behaver. They are only his best judgments which each must accept, explain, defend, or modify when necessary.

Even though a common area of disturbance exists, the judgments of behavers as to desirable action may vary as much as those between behavers and observers. That is why the Justices of the Supreme Court of the United States study the same briefs on both sides of the same case, listen to the same arguments in Court, read the same underlying law, clarify their meanings by group discussions, yet arrived at five-to-four decisions. The meanings which organize their psychological fields are dissimilar, even under the best common group experiences. There is even greater variation among the judgments of children. Observers must pay more attention to the adequacy of the process used by anyone in making his decision, rather than to their agreement or disagreement with his overt actions.

All process decisions are tested by the quality of the action which they produce. This includes changes in the individual, in the external environment, in the process of interaction. All behavior is due to choices made in the ongoing activity, regardless of how they were made. And all present decisions affect subsequent behavior both internal and external. Neither behaver nor observer should ruthlessly rip overt action from the moving experience to judge it by external standards. They should judge it by the process which takes into account both covert and overt responses in normal field associations. External standards minimize, eliminate, or reverse such normal relationships. In life, decision and action cannot be separated and cannot be abstracted dynamically from the process by which they arose. Every individual should see and accept their emergence in his experience.

Process decisions are not clearly understood until examined in retrospect. Each time an important choice has to be made all earlier related decisions should be examined. But such continuous evaluation is not enough. Near the end, the entire experience should be reinterpreted by the changed selves approaching need-fulfillment. Group evaluation of the total process from the origin of the disturbing area to the final self-selections refocuses the various aspects so that each individual has an opportunity to clarify his own meanings of the dynamics involved. This is the final critical judgment of the experience by those actively engaged in it.

HOW ARE INDIVIDUAL LEARNINGS SELF-SELECTED?

Each individual takes something from every experience, or traces of every experience exist somewhere in him. These he self-selects, accepts, incorporates into himself to become new meanings, new organization of his field, new overt behaviors. What he selects and accepts he really learns. Since the self-selection cannot be denied by outside pressures, since it operates constantly throughout life, and since the selections are so important to the growth of the self, parents and educators should help each child improve the quality of his selections through every appropriate means to the end that they may contribute more fully to his self-maturity. The need-experience process is their ally.

There are a few points about self-selection which apply in all group situations whether the members be adults, children, or both.

1. Self-selection is expected and accepted by everyone as a normal aspect of learning. It takes place in an open, direct, aboveboard manner, without external attempts to restrict the process or control the results. All human and nonhuman factors facilitate self-selection; field conditions promote rather than hinder it.

2. Individuals in a group are not expected to self-select the same learnings from a common experience. Facts, meanings, skills vary with individual needs. To require everyone to learn the same knowledges and skills does not prevent each from self-selecting what he accepts to meet his need. It merely drives his self-selecting underground and thus prevents the teacher from helping him to improve its quality.

3. The teacher should not pass qualitative judgment upon or show external approval of selections, as this encourages some persons to believe that theirs are better than those of others. Such is not the case. Quality is the relationship of selections to need-fulfillment, which cannot be externally equated with that of others. Such external judgments cause pupils to doubt their ability to self-select, to accept uncritically the judgment of the teacher, or to ignore advice and take what they want. Thus a learning opportunity is lost.

4. The teacher or leader relies upon the group to help each member improve the quality of his selections. Group inter-

action on his proposed selections is more valuable in improving their quality than are the judgments of the teacher.

5. Everyone should self-select the process which is the common yet variable learning by which he fulfills his need. This operates to restrict self-selection only when the process itself is denied.

A crucial opportunity for emphasis in improving self-selection occurs when the need-experience is drawing to a close. The leader helps everyone become more conscious of what, why, how he selects the learnings which are valuable enough to accept. For many years I have been trying to discover better ways of helping learners of all ages do this under the life conditions which they face in homes and schools. I have experimented with and rejected many different approaches, but will describe the best available one at the moment in the opinion of college students.

I work with a group of full-time students studying the broad area of how to improve the educational program with children in the eight-year elementary school. The members generally come from all over the United States and a dozen or more foreign countries. At the opening period we begin to develop unity and after a few meetings we are able to operate on a high level of group interaction. While studying direction in the educational programs offered children through such questions as these—Where is the present direction? Where did it originate? Is there a better direction? How do we know it is better?—a student suggested that present direction inadequately considered the emotions of children. After some exploration, students decided to study emotions as a committee of the whole since no person knew much about their origin and development or how they affected the behavior of children. Since emotions represented a new area or a new center in an old area of disturbance, I suggested, during the exploration, that at the close we study the learnings selected by individuals better to help each improve their quality.

There was no external pressure for credits or grades to groove such selection. Earlier we had discussed some characteristics of group process including self-selection, so each student knew he was entirely free to choose whatever he felt best satisfied his needs.

The study continued for one three-hour period a week during eight weeks, or approximately twenty-four hours for the group as a whole, not including individual and subgroup activities carried on outside. At the beginning of the sixth week, in planning how to help each other improve his self-selections the group agreed that the problem had at least four aspects. The *first* was to obtain a statement from each person of the learnings which he selected. He should write briefly his selections under these headings: (1) These are the learnings which I select. (2) These are the reasons I select them. (3) This is how I am now using them or this is how I hope to use them in the future. The purpose of these three rubrics was to aid each student to make more deliberative choices and to facilitate tabulation of the results.

The *second* part was to analyze the learnings for group trends. I agree to do this and to present the results for further examination. The *third* was to study the selections of individuals in the group as a whole from three points of view: What is the relation of the selection to his need? How does his selection compare with those of highest frequency in the group as a whole? How can we help him improve his meaning of his need and his learnings selected to satisfy it? The *fourth* part was to examine our process of selecting and evaluating to see how teachers could use it to aid children in improving the quality of their self-selected learnings from their experiences. Since many students were parents, applications to rearing children in the home were also considered.

I tabulated the selections that were actually expressed, eliminating those included by implication only. The 115 papers ranged from 1 to 21 selections, with a median of 4 and an aggregate of 601. Omitting the statement that the emotions can be educated, on which everyone agreed, the five highest selections were: (1) A curriculum based upon the needs of children offers them the best opportunity for desirable emotional growth. (2) The basic needs of children for affection, security, belongingness, self-acceptance must be met in the educative process, whatever curriculum is used. (3) Teachers should be more emotionally stable themselves in order to help children develop emotional stability. (4) The emotional drives should be guided or directed by thinking appropriate to the experience of the children. (5) Emotional stability is an important factor in improving the quality of learning of children. Under the third aspect of the problem, on use of the selected learnings, 40 per cent said they were using them now to increase their own emotional stability, and illustrated their procedure and results. The other 60 per cent discussed how they proposed to use their selected learnings when they returned to their various educational posts. All students agreed that the changes in them through the self-selective process were an important preparation for their professional jobs.

After this group summary, students examined their papers to see their relation to the five learnings of highest frequency. They agreed immediately that no paper had all five, four, or three of the highest. Soon 15 persons decided they had two of the five, and 80 persons knew they had one of the five. Later 35 persons believed they had none of the five.

We discussed the reasons for this variability within a common experience. Then they asked me how many of their first five I would select and I answered, "One." "Why is this?" many asked immediately. I replied, "I approach the area with my need and experience, therefore my relative value of learnings differs from yours." There were wide differences in the selections of teachers with much or little experience, between majors in psychology and nonmajors, between teachers in this country and those of other countries, between those who were using their learnings now and those who planned to use them in the future, and many others. Promptly many questions arose, as the class log indicates: "Would children have similar variability of selections from an experience if they were free to select? If you gave us an examination based upon your selection of learnings for your need would that be fair to us based upon our need? If we selected our top five learnings for an examination, wouldn't it be unfair to most of us? How can you educate children in common learnings if there is such variability of self-selection? How can children grow up to be stable without common learnings? Does this mean that how you learn is more important than what you learn, or how do the two go together? How can we help a child select better learnings when he does not know what his needs are and most of the time we do not know what they are either? Why weren't we shown something like this in our undergraduate teachers colleges? How can you teach a subject and allow a child to self-select? How can you teach us this subject and allow each of us to select what he wants to take out of it? Is there no common subject matter that everyone must learn?" These and many other questions were discussed to the satisfaction of the group.

I then suggested that we ask individuals to allow the group to consider their selections in relation to their needs. This was unanimously accepted and there were immediate volunteers. I wrote on the blackboard the needs and selections of each student until ten had reported. I then recorded the selections of ten others which were different from those already given. The group studied each case to help the person better understand his need so as to improve his selections.

As moderator, I refocused the discussion whenever it wandered afar. I kept the emphasis upon understanding the need and the choices rather than upon approving and disapproving either or both. At times this was difficult because of the tendency of educators to give a right or wrong judgment upon the work of others. Soon one volunteer said, "If

I had seen my need before I wrote that paper as I see it now I would have made different selections." Others agreed with him. Now members began to analyze their papers freely before the group, showing how they could clarify their need and improve the quality of their selections. Many such analyses included very personal needs which had heretofore been kept within the self. The group quality passed from understanding into empathy as each merged in the developmental process of others and through insight recreated his own meanings into a better self. At the close of the last period such changes were well expressed by one member who said, "I never knew before that I could be so interested in what other people said when I knew what they were saying was wrong. Now I am not sure that they are wrong. It sure gives you a funny feeling inside." And thus was each free to select from the discussion what he wished and to use it in his own way.

Near the close of the semester the process of the course was identified and critically appraised. There was general agreement but not consensus that it should be used with pupils. All were keenly aware of the difficulties in schools adhering to subject curriculums, where ends and means are fixed for pupils and where their needs, self-selections, and normal process of growth are relatively insignificant. After returning to her position for a year, one teacher said, "In the past I have treated children in school as a captive audience. Now I see them as partners in the cooperative management of our own living together. And what a difference it makes to everyone!"

A BACKWARD AND FORWARD LOOK

While discussing how to develop a need, students release many creative meanings. (1) "I see now that the process begins with the origin of the need in the individual and continues until the need tension subsides." (2) "When you work with groups the process begins with the exploration to locate a group area of disturbance and continues until each individual has need-fulfillment." (3) "The group process must have all of the characteristics of the biological growth process to lead toward deliberative action." (4) "In applying the need-experience process, the leader or teacher always explores back of or on the antecedents of the observed behavior. He works on the observed behavior only when it may destroy the life of the behaver or someone else such as a child walking across a busy street against the lights in rapidly moving traffic." Another student replies, "Yes, but he must do this by the need process, which stumps me. I use the good old authoritarian method." (5) "The real learning takes place in the individual through the meanings which he creates. I never knew before that each individual creates his own quality in his own experiences." "Yes," says another, "but he will create his meanings which become himself in any environment." "True, but to achieve his highest quality he must not only have an environment that respects his right to do so but also aids him in doing it." (6) "Self-selection is the most difficult part of this process for me. I do not see how you can get a child or a high school student to select the specific behaviors you want him to and know he must have. How do you know [he says to me] that each of us will self-select out of this experience the things that you think are important and that all of us should know?"

And so the discussion moves from theory into practice, involving not only subjects in schools and colleges but many aspects of home and family life. Some questions open deep areas of need which can be treated adequately only after careful investigation of a particular home. "How can you use this process in a school or a college when you have something exact to teach, as spelling words or calculus?" "How can I teach a child skill in performance at the piano when he can only obtain it by practice?" "How can I teach my child food habits or how to care for his toys or any other specific behavior so necessary for him to grow up with others in a home?" "How can I apply this process to mechanical drawing?" "What about nursing skills?" "Could you teach a doctor or a dentist this way?" And then come the most devastating questions of all. "I am a parent with two young children. Both my husband and I work. How can *I* find the time to teach them this way? There is barely enough when I use authoritarian methods."

After the deluge subsides, I point out that every child *really* learns what he knows by the growth or need-experience process regardless of the way in which he is taught. He accepts into himself to use creatively only those learnings which he has creatively assimilated. A child who really learns to spell words taught directly, finds by himself how to assimilate them through his need-experiences. To assert that a professional pianist learned to perform through practice is to admit inadequate observation of or lack of understanding of the total process of which practice is only one aspect.

A nurse treats the whole patient regardless of his particular disturbance or her specific directions for relieving it. Her knowledge of the growth process is vital to such service, for she must have creatively assimilated her skills to use them effectively in helping a whole person regain his health. No patient would knowingly consult a diagnostician, surgeon, or dentist who had mechanically learned his professional skills. He seeks the analysis, judgment, and action suited to his particular self which only creative learning can produce.

Since most children are unable to reconvert reverse authoritarian teaching into a normal growth process, they have an acute and profound problem of improving the quality of their learning. Time is not important since the cumulative effect of a creative process offsets the slow and ineffective results obtained by direct teaching of specific behaviors. Other factors prevent its use. Many adults believe that a child should not or cannot learn a cooperative need process because they do not understand it or know how to use it themselves.

Especially are they unwilling to accept the deliberative action which emerges with it.

In the next chapter I examine in more detail the nature of groups and how they affect the development of individuals, since every person is born into and lives with groups in some form throughout his earthly years.

Chapter VII

HOW DOES A GROUP AFFECT GROWTH?

Children are born among people. They grow up, work, play, worship, or live and die among people organized loosely or formally into groups, such as the home, school, club, sorority, fraternity, church. Sometimes the word class is used to designate such organizations. Sociologists refer to classes in a culture as upper, middle, and lower, with various divisions in each. Schools generally designate as classes the many different arrangements of pupils for instructional purposes from kindergarten through university. Sometimes another word such as gang is used to apply to certain types of organizations, especially among youth and young adults. These three words have degrees of social approval and acceptance. Group is favorably considered; class may or may not be, depending on how it is applied; gang generally connotes an organization of people subversive or detrimental to or in rebellion against the accepted social practices. But whether the organization be formal or informal, whether the purposes be socially accepted or rejected, each individual grows up with people united in some way to carry on their life activities. And each group, in some tangible, observable, or noticeable degree, influences or conditions the behavior of its members.

184

Thus the group or class or gang continuously affects the growth or learning of people.

Each child grows up in and each adult belongs to a number of different kinds of groups. For purposes of clarification, I shall call them primary and secondary groups. The former are small, informal, and intimate. Interaction among members is open and meaningful; functional unity is high; mutuality, security, compatibility are the operating climate, and continuity is usually extensive. Secondary groups have a larger membership, interaction is through subgroups rather than direct, meaningful functional unity is less tangible and more difficult to maintain, mutuality is limited, security comes through some surrogate, and continuity is high. All of these characteristics are due to effective organization rather than to psychological unity from common needs and purposes of its members. Most individuals belong to relatively few primary groups, but hold membership in a larger number of secondary groups. This larger number may vary from the few of some people to the large number of the joiners, who release energy accumulated through compulsive striving for affection, by becoming members of any organization in which they think they are really wanted. Over a period of years each individual finds his group quotient. He locates the intimate groups and the size, range, complexity of the secondary groups, which gives him a feeling of belongingness and self-enhancement. Unless he finds some powerful disturbance through interaction, he will probably operate within the limits set by such groups for the remainder of his life. Thus the kinds of groups in which a child is reared to physiological maturity help him become the self that he is and, by the process of his membership, affect his continuing social relationships throughout life.

In this chapter I shall examine in some detail the inter-personal relations of children with their peers and adults, to shed some light on the age-old problem of how membership in groups affects their growth, especially their development into normal, continuously maturing people.

WHAT IS A GROUP PROCESS?

The term "process" has been used in various contexts in previous chapters. Here I shall explain further its meaning to distinguish some behaviors of people which are usually associated with the word group. A process is described by such words as movement, change, action, development, behavior, depending upon the point of view of the individual. It is continuous, dynamic, directional. It begins at conception and lasts until death. It is so completely coexistent with life that when process ceases life also ceases. These descriptive terms may be brought together into one sentence: *A process is a continuous, dynamic, directional life movement of an individual within his phenomenal field.* This movement includes everything that takes place inside the individual, as well as all his relationships with his external environment. It is what he thinks and the unconscious data that he registers in his viscera. It is what outsiders hear him saying or observe him doing, together with all that they construe within such action. It has both covert and overt implications. It is everything that he does, feels, or thinks. It is everything that others see him do, believe he feels, or infer he thinks.

This continuous life process is called experience, which is defined as the continuous interaction of an individual with his environment. Experience or life moves through a series of disturbances called situations, which are not of equal duration, depth, or value. While they are all upsets in the individual, some are problems which can be adjusted by using old behavior patterns with relatively minor modifications; others cut so deeply into his previously constituted self as to be called needs. The latter are of longer duration, greater area and depth, and call for major reorganization of the self by the growth-learning process in order to promote self-enhancement. The series of situations arising out of and integrated through the need-action process is sometimes called *having an experience* instead of just experience, since it has a unit quality which gives it a name or at least a definite and distinctive recognition. Regardless of how the individual or others may view his life, whether he accepts it or regrets it, whether others approve or disapprove it, a process of some type is ever present. So the growing child in his environment and the adults in theirs should have the same common area of need. They should all work together to develop such high quality in the process of living, growing, learning that each self may continue its upward movement in the never-ending quest for self-enhancement.

When I explain to students that all life is process, someone immediately asks, "What is group process?" Whenever two or more people work together on anything for any purpose, by any method of study, inquiry, or human relations, the process used is group process since two or more interacting individuals constitute a group. Reversing this statement, group process means that two or more people are working together on some need or problem toward some recognized end, by some form of interpersonal relations, with some covert or overt effect on each. A few students immediately point out that this definition of group process is too general. Any form of human relations can qualify under it, even the most arbitrary and ruthless persecution of a weak person by a more powerful individual. Of course this is true. Other students reply that every act of any individual is modified by others and in turn affects others, hence life process is really group process. This is true also.

But a distinction must be made between the social behavior of an individual and the behavior of social group. The former refers to the actions of a single person in relation to other people, individually or collectively, within his own phenomenal field. The latter has to do with what constitutes a group, how it operates to develop and maintain its groupness, and what effects it has upon the individuals who compose it. In either case, the same number of people may be involved, but there is a different relationship among them. In social behavior the movement is largely from individual to individual, whereas in group behavior there is a tangible qualitative interdependence of each upon others which operates three ways: individual to individual, individual to whole, and whole to individual. When this three-dimensional relationship breaks, the group ceases to exist. Everyone knows that some associations with people are unsatisfactory since they tend to depress the self, while others are desirable since they tend to elevate the self. There is a quality in human relations which can be distinguished and explained intellectually, even though the more subtle emotional effects are difficult to symbolize.

This quality in the relationship of individuals is the group and the way they work together to produce it is the process. It is not the social behavior of individuals, it is not any old way by which people work together, it is not any effect which one person may have on someone else. Group process is the way people work together to release an emergent quality, called psychological climate, group morale, esprit de corps, or cooperative unity, through which each discovers and develops his inner capacities, realizes better the nature of his self, releases more of his past experience, and learns how to create this emergent quality in all life situations. This does not affirm a group mind existing apart from the individuals who compose it. Neither does it mean that individuals in a group generate a common mind superior to that of any member. For there is no common mind or superior group mind which imposes actions on anyone. By the need-experience process, individuals release into the environment potential creative ability heretofore unknown to them or to others. A higher level of thinking emerges than was possessed by any individual prior to the qualitative interaction. Thus interacting individuals furnish the environment in which to bring forward their creative meanings, thereby giving each the opportunity to become a better self. It is the need-experience process previously discussed which produces the quality called the group. And only as individuals conceptualize it while they use it, can the group continue to function on a high level.

WHAT IS AN AGGREGATE GROUP?

The word group should be applied to people only when they develop the high quality of internal relationship which results from resolving their disturbances through cooperative interaction. Yet it is frequently used to describe interpersonal relations that are on a very low operating level. An adjective must be inserted before "group" to let the listener or reader know its position on a qualitative scale. The term "aggregate" is most frequently used to specify that the group is merely the mathematical sum of its parts—of the individuals who compose it. The word "authoritarian" indicates the dominant internal structure which causes the operating quality to be low. Some writers use the term "categorical" to describe this group. It means that the organization and probable action can be defined and classified in advance of the actual operation of the members. Others have given it the pathological name "heterogenous," meaning that its source of origin lies outside the organism. In sociocultural concepts this group originates from or is formed by some outside person to meet his needs and purposes and is structured by him to that end. Technically, it is not a group, for a group is based upon we-ness or unity or morale, characteristics which such an aggregate does not possess. It is described in practice as a class or an aggregate although the term group is most frequently used. The aggregate group is the psychological field supporting all forms of authoritarian human relations in all life activities in all cultures throughout the world.

The aggregate group has many functional characteristics, a few of which will be stated.

1. The source or origin lies outside the group.

2. The group has a status person designated by the outside source of origin to control it from within. The position is relatively permanent. The particular individual occupies it so long as he has the confidence of his superior, which means so long as he manages the behavior of the group in the direction of and acceptable to his outside authority. Some writers refer to this individual as a status leader to distinguish him from a real leader who has a relationship of mutual interdependence with all members. Yet any individual with internal status from an outside source of authority has the difficult, if not impossible, task of becoming an emergent leader of the group. His best hope lies in becoming as benevolent in his internal relations as his outside authority will permit.

3. The group is managed around, through, or by the person who is the status leader. What he wants or demands is the focal operating center.

4. The group is organized to a greater or less degree, depending upon the ability and the purpose of the status control. Regardless of the degree or quality from his point of view, the group never has unity, for unity can never be put into a group from the outside. It is *found* by individuals from within. Many people mistake for unity the rigid organization, the good discipline, the regimentation, of an aggregate under external authority. Any interested person can disprove this belief by examining critically how a modern paternalistic family operates or by studying the rise and fall of authoritarian cultures. Learning how to exist in an aggregate organization does not prepare an individual to live in a unified group.

5. The intelligence of the aggregate is the intelligence of the status control. The authorities assume that he knows, and that the members are inadequate in knowledge and in the means of acquiring it. This is why he has to manage them. Yet

his control limits their possibilities of ever developing their potential capacity, for their thinking must always be below his and in the direction which he determines.

6. The communication within the group is direct from the status control to each member. Each person reacts to the control but does not interact with it or with others in the group. The communication among the various members has such a low human quality that it can hardly be described as interaction.

7. Preplanning and developmental planning are all managed by external individuals operating through the status control. All major decisions are made for the members. They are allowed to use their judgment only in situations of relatively minor importance.

8. The membership-character of each individual is determined by how well he meets the externally designated or structured ends. This decision is made by the status control. He arrays them in mathematical sequence from highest to lowest, an arrangement in which no individual ever has real security and belongingness with the status control or with his fellows. Members develop various adaptive mechanisms through which one becomes a star while another is called an isolate.

9. The responsibility for the success of the enterprise to which the group is committed rests with the status control. He is held accountable by the external authority which sets the group in motion. He must manipulate it to do what his superiors want. A few failures cost him his position.

10. The internal evaluation of the success of each member is always made by the status control in terms of the qualitative demands placed upon him by the outside authorities for their purposes. The status leader himself is rated by his superiors on their judgment of the success of his group by their standards. Thus he is not psychologically free to develop and use his intelligence, a field condition which he willingly

accepts and transmits to the members of his group. Each member finds the kinds and degrees of followership which he and the leader can tolerate so that neither will be removed from the group by the superior powers.

The psychological structure of an aggregate group under its authoritarian leadership takes many forms, two of the most common being the chain and level relationships to the status leader. When the number is small, everyone faces him separately, as in family life where the father is the authority. When the number is large, small subgroups form within the whole group in relation to the leader. They do not follow patterns of social classes brought into the aggregate from the environment. They represent the psychological effect of the leader on their need-satisfactions. Where the psychological effect is similar or where the attraction is mutual, the individuals get together. They form various sociometric patterns to compete more favorably for the psychological favors of the authoritarian leader than can an individual alone. Since the interpersonal relations of an aggregate group are competitive, and since the leader can make or break the individual—and frequently does, unintentionally or deliberately —each person strives for the most favored status possible.

The chain and level organizations of aggregate groups are shown in Chart XI. In the chain type, a small number with mutual psychological effects unite under a spokesman better to promote their influence on the leader. They do not represent a resistance to the leader organization, but rather a persuasion of the leader unit. They wish to reduce or change the direction of or transfer to some other "chain gang" the psychological pressure which they feel is hurtful to them. They use all the techniques of influence at their command. The level organization operates differently. Level 1 represents the inner circle, the *avant-garde* or leader's pets, all working individually in relation to him but all feeling a mutual psychological security. Level 2 is a chain organization of resistance to the leader due to many factors, one of which is the inner circle. Such resistance may be quiet and subversive, or it may flare into open revolt against him and his inner circle. Level 3 consists of individual isolates competing with each other for the attention of the leader and other members of the group. They are only present in the group physically, for

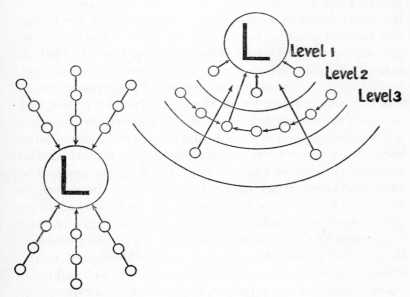

Chart XI. Chain and Level Organizations of Aggregate-Authoritarian Group

psychologically they are thrown out by factors which they cannot control.

The aggregate-authoritarian group is the form of organization of most institutions in all cultures of the world today. It is basic in homes, schools, and churches, which have priority in the education of children and youth. In the United States the class is the teaching and administrative unit from the first grade through the university. While any reasonable person will admit different degrees of control within these aggregates in various schools or individual classes, he cannot deny that aggregate characteristics are operating. Internal variability is due to the amount of humaneness of a particular teacher. Every child finds wide differences in the benevolence of his teachers, a college student feels marked variation in the human insight of his professors, everyone in the home responds to the changing kindliness of the father. But the real problem is how this aggregate group affects the growth, learning, maturity of its members. Here the outlook is not promising even under the most benevolent conditions.

The aggregate group operates on linear concepts of growth and learning. It never was in the beginning, is not now, and probably never shall be concerned about growth as a creative, self-selective process moving in the direction of self-enhancement. For such concepts are anathema to the authorities who organize the groups and use them for their purposes. The aggregate group is set up to develop specific behaviors, to select and elevate those who can qualify in them, and to reject, discard, or eliminate those with no such capacity. The narrowness of the scope and direction releases and develops the capacity of no one, not even those who succeed to the satisfaction of the status control. The aggregate is based upon authoritarian human relations. Every member is exposed to, reared in, and expected to exemplify them in his behavior. The low interpersonal morale tends to incite conflict within the individual or toward his fellow men.

Experimental studies of aggregates support the mental, emotional, and physical hazards in such structures. No form of group organization can eliminate all such risks for everyone at all times. The high incidence of self-threat, within adequate methods of dealing with it, causes the mental hygiene difficulties of aggregates to be abnormally high, even among those who appear to be meeting the desired external requirements. Since the aggregate is organized to promote linear concepts of learning according to the demands of those in authority, it has all the unhealthy concomitant outcomes of such a psychological field. In homes and schools the drive for specific behaviors disparages selves and individual experiences, limiting the development of all.

The greatest weakness of the aggregate group is that the child is not taught and does not learn a process of deliberative action in all life activities for his continued growth after formal education ceases. He may grow up chronologically within aggregates, he may learn the specific behaviors which give him status, but will never rise to great height on a maturity scale unless he has opportunities for richer, fuller, more creative experiences outside such groups. When home, school, and church are organized as aggregates, many children have only slight possibility of finding outside experiences where the normal growth process can function. Adults commit the educational paradox of asserting that they wish their children to grow up to live by general behaviors associated with mature selves, while they organize their major institutions through aggregate groups in which the development of such maturity is effectively restricted.

WHAT IS AN ORGANIC GROUP?

An organic group is the name applied to a number of individuals working together by a process of meaningful interaction which releases in them a latent emergent quality of wholeness previously unknown to any individual. It is found exclusively among human beings, since they alone are capable of developing the thinking necessary to achieve such quality. Some persons use the word "superorganic" to describe this phenomenon, since it clearly transcends mere organic structure or sensory experience. All of them recognize that this quality emerges when interaction is such as to release the potential capacities of people. Since this emergent quality is the growth process which every organism is born with and uses to keep itself intact, I shall use the term "organic group" to apply to people working under such conditions.

The concept of the organic group is of relatively recent origin. It was unknown to peoples in ancient times, when they used the aggregate as the pattern of organization of their various social institutions. It is a product of the growing researches in the life sciences, ranging from basic biology to the more recent studies in group dynamics. It is called organic since individual members function in a similar dynamic relation to each other and to the whole as do the various organs of the body to each other and to the whole. It is called cooperative and interactive since cooperative interaction is the basic process by which the body maintains its unitary wholeness under the various conditions of its environment, internal and external. Granted that there are meanings, values, norms which hold people together and which are above and beyond any wisdom of the body. Yet the operating self, which is the person, is a unity of organic wisdom with superorganic meanings derived through thoughtful criticism and enrichment of sensory experience. The normal way to develop a meaningful self is to extend upward into the psychological area the basic process of learning already established by inheritance in the organic area. In this dynamic interaction within an organism there are some very clear operating principles which offer a clue to cooperative relations within and among groups.

1. The organism as a whole determines the quantity, quality, and direction of its energy output. The quantity is associated with the strength of the need or the depth to which the upset affects the already constituted self. The quality is in the process of meeting the need or the way in which need-fulfillment is obtained. The direction is toward need behaviors which maintain, preserve, and improve the operating wholeness. The direction is paramount since operating wholeness is the very essence of life itself. And it is remarkable how the organism struggles to maintain such wholeness under the most devastating environmental conditions.

2. The organism as a whole regulates the energy output or work of the various parts or organs. All energy is expended through the various parts and all bodily functions are carried on by them. The whole stimulates or retards such action. It concentrates forces at a given point, as in the case of the white corpuscles going into action against a localized infection. It fights against all conditions within or without that tend to destroy its unity. But the organism as a whole is not something added to the parts to give them unity. It is not the sum of its parts plus this regulating entity. The organism as a whole is the cooperative interaction among the various parts whereby each participates in every directional judgment and action. When one part tries to dominate another the process is disoperative and a divided self or a disorganization of inward coherence results. The behavior associated with a disoperative process is described by the observer as neurotic or psychotic. Thus the integrating whole is the normal process of interaction among the various parts, each working in relation to their shared directional decisions.

3. Each organ of the body has a specialized function to perform for the good of the whole. This gives it a permanent but variable membership-character in promoting the organic quality and a continuous status with the whole and the parts. This specialized ability is recognized and respected by all organs. No one tries to usurp the function of any other. And the organism as a whole recognizes that it cannot maintain itself without the specialized services of the parts. It does not place one function on a higher level than another or favor one organ over another. When some part is temporarily unable to perform its services, thereby threatening the integrity of the whole, other organs either stimulate the sluggish one to a normal performance or devise means of taking care of its duties. Such wisdom of the body is now an accepted fact.

4. The unity and direction of the organism are maintained

by the highest form of the cooperative interactive process known to man. The sensitivity of each organ to the performance of all others is maintained at all times through main avenues of communication, which are the blood stream and the nervous system. Some organs have their own private messengers called hormones, which they secrete into the blood if danger is apparent and more energy is necessary. Leadership moves from one to another, depending upon where the need of the whole is centered at the moment. While every organism develops tendencies to action as a means of dealing with internal and external forces, these tendencies do not deny the principle of organic cooperation. At times they make cooperation difficult, as in the case of neurotic persons, but the cooperative process still works to overcome the denial conditions.

5. Each organ self-selects those elements which are best for it as an organ, as in foods to rebuild its tissues and maintain them in healthy working condition. The organism as a whole self-selects those learnings which in its judgment are best for its developing unity. Such selection takes place on the autonomic and conscious level.

6. There is continuous differentiation of new adjustments both in structure and in behavior, except when serious damage prevents such differentiation. The damaged heart develops new blood channels. When varicose veins are blocked, the leg increases the size of other veins to carry the blood supply. The healthy kidney expands to carry on the functions of the diseased one which was removed. The lungs develop seals to enclose and arrest the spread of tuberculosis germs which attempt to destroy them. In the same way individuals develop behaviors to compensate for difficulties of adjustment or select learnings which promote more mature relationships. Variation is in the degree to which they are capable of utilizing it. But these principles of self-selection and differentiation do not deny the process of cooperation. Neither do they reject

the regulation and direction of the organism by the whole. For the whole does not set itself up as a dominating entity, forcing the parts to live within its status demands. From the biological evidence available, cooperative action in organic groups is the normal basis of life, while cultural authoritarianism in aggregate groups is cancerous tissue arrested in embryonic differentiation.

The organic group has many functional characteristics. A few of the most important ones will be enumerated.

1. It is autogenous in origin, the members coming together to resolve common needs.

2. Leadership emerges from within and continues so long as it functions to achieve group purposes through cooperative action.

3. Unity and functional organization are developed internally around the group's own purposes in relation to its own need.

4. All of the planning and all of the major and minor decisions are made by the group itself.

5. Large directional policy decisions which regulate the work of individuals or subgroups are made by the group as a whole.

6. Decisions as to policy or action are made by consensus, not by majority rule. Consensus means that every member recognizes and assents to the mutual fitness of the judgment or action to achieve the purposes which are commonly accepted.

7. The work is carried on by individuals and small groups. The responsibility for such work is delegated by the group as a whole. It should be both genuine and challenging to everyone concerned. The whole group holds subgroups accountable for the adequate performance of their duties. Individual initiative and creativeness in carrying on such activities are encouraged at all times.

8. The group as a whole sets the esprit de corps or climate

of opinion or psychological atmosphere in which each individual or subgroup carries on its work. This is a creative emergent from the cooperative interaction among the members.

9. The group as a whole helps each individual member clarify his own concept of need, refine his own meanings, improve the logic of his own experience. It encourages his creative contributions, helps him to evaluate his own self-selections, shows him how to appraise his own value judgments.

10. Responsibility for the success of the total group enterprise is assumed by everyone, each contributing in his own best way through free and open interaction among members which is maintained at all times.

11. Cooperative and continuous evaluation by the group of its own decisions and actions is made in the light of the developing need-experience.

The psychological structure of an organic group under its perceived, achieved, and distributed leadership takes many forms, the most common of which is a network relationship in simple patterns in small groups and more complex patterns in larger groups. The sociometric picture tends to take one of the forms shown in Chart XII.

The nature of the organization depends upon many internal factors, the most important of which is the climate of opinion fostered by the initial leader. He knows the group process and how to help others use it to fulfill their needs. He keeps their energy process-centered rather than focused on the leader, a goal, or other individuals. This gives him greater security with them and they have greater mutuality with him than in any other form of working relationship. Empathy is high, for all sense that the process releases and develops them. As the leader highlights, and members accept, the process, the various sociometric patterns change. Merely establishing interaction among the members, or developing good rapport with the leader, or evolving a high general morale is not enough to constitute an organic group. These approaches are helpful and in a desirable direction, but they lack the quality which aids each individual in understanding how to release and use his own abilities intelligently in social situations. So the psychological structure varies and the patterns change, but in the direction of better utilization of the need-experience growth concept.

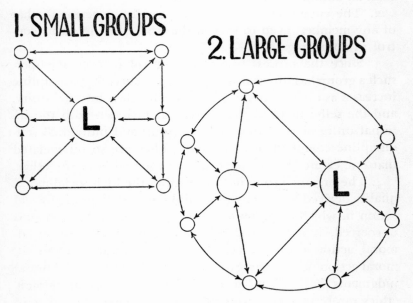

1. SMALL GROUPS

2. LARGE GROUPS

Chart XII. Organic Group Patterns

Organic or cooperative groups have intelligent unity and a serviceable organization. The unity comes through common directional purposes set up to achieve deliberative action within perceived needs. The organization is the systematic arrangement of the working parts by the group toward satisfying the desired purposes. It is a service to the unity and is continuously modified as new centers of unity develop. There is little possibility that it may perpetuate itself to become the status control of the authoritarian group. Participators learn to see and evaluate organization for what it really is—a means of satisfying their needs. The unity is intelligent, since it is based upon the best thinking that the group can generate within the favorable climate, using all available resources. The evidence shows these values.

1. A cooperative group releases more potential ability than an authoritarian group.

2. The emerging thinking has a quality superior to that of any member, even to that of the leader or the status control in an aggregate.

3. Since the process fosters self-control in each member, such a group has internal self-discipline. This group discipline increases as each individual improves his own internal unity, and the self-control of the individual increases with the internal unity of the group. Thus, group and individual self-discipline complement each other. They are so interrelated that one cannot be satisfactorily achieved without the other.

4. The organic group has in its unity the high social-moral quality derived from acting on thinking or deliberative social action in which common consent and acceptance, active and uncoerced, is the test of behavior. This intelligent social-moral action contrasts sharply with the autonomic social-moral action of the aggregate. In crises when new social-moral judgments have to be made, individuals with autonomic ethics rarely rise to the occasion. By studying the causes of delinquency in the United States or by examining the human relations of people under totalitarian rule, one finds ample evidence to support this statement. The low moral tone of the world today is a product of such autonomic teachings in authoritarian groups. To improve it children must be reared in institutions where they learn organic unity and action.

Throughout this book I stress the fact that the life in any organism begins with and continues through a process of cooperative interaction. Some form of communal or group life is universal for all animals, since it has a survival value, for both the individual and the species, which no one can achieve for himself alone. A sort of unconscious proto-cooperation or autonomic mutuality extends so far down among the simpler plants and animals as to lead some biologists to assert the actual inheritance of social behavior. Natural mutuality is one of the great principles of biology. The survival value in proto-cooperation is directly related to two important factors: (1) sufficient numbers to allow for maximum mutuality but not to decrease interaction by overcrowding, (2) many past mutated genes, perhaps millions of years old, which furnish the store of concealed potential variability, necessary for creative adaptation under changed environmental conditions in order that the species may survive.

When organisms come together they create something which helps them grow more rapidly and live longer. Goldfish in colloidal silver water will secrete a mutually protective substance which will extend the mean life of groups of ten in this poison approximately five times the length of the mean life of fish existing separately. Grouped *Daphnia* survive longer in an overalkaline solution than do isolated fleas because grouped animals give off more carbon dioxide, which neutralizes the alkali. Sea urchin eggs and larvae in groups secrete an extract that is growth-promoting. They also secrete an extract that is growth-inhibiting. When alone, more of the growth-inhibiting than growth-promoting extract is produced. Experiments with the protozoan *Oxytricha* show that each nucleus is provided with a growth-producing substance, much of which is lost in the surrounding media during cell division. There is a speeding up of growth and cell division when many cells are together, since each cell loses less of the growth-producing substance to the surrounding medium because of the presence of others. Certain fish

seem to secrete in the surrounding water a chemical substance which stimulates growth. The greater the number of
fish below the overcrowding stage the greater the quantity
of the secretion and the more rapid the growth.

Space will not permit illustrations throughout all of the
species where unconscious proto-cooperation exists. However, four basic principles seem to underlie all instances of
such mutuality. First, organisms in interaction tend to
produce something which no individual produces or perhaps
produces insufficiently by himself alone. Second, the substance produced while in groups affects both the rate of
growth and the over-all life span of each individual. Third,
this substance so changes the general external environment
as to induce individuals to release previously latent mutated
genes which cause a species to survive, if existing in sufficient numbers, under certain changes in the environment
over which the species has no control. Fourth, these group-
centered interactions of a more or less subsocial altruistic
nature lead primarily to the preservation of the group or
some members of it, frequently at the expense of or sacrifice
of many individuals.

The similarity of the relationship between the behaviors
of lower animals on the autonomic proto-cooperative levels
and man on the autonomic or conscious levels, when in some
form of groups, is remarkable. The evidence is that persons
working together in any form of human relations affect each
other in the following ways. First, each individual secretes
something into the surrounding environment which becomes
a climate of opinion, an esprit de corps, or group feeling or
attitude within which each individual lives. Second, this group
substance or hormone or whatever it may be called affects
the growth and development of every individual member in
every aspect of the self. Third, individuals are unable to
create the group climate of opinion or environmental hormone when they exist by themselves alone. Fourth, such

group substance has an immediate empathic effect upon each member, causing him to release to others potentialities heretofore unknown even to him. Fifth, the developing groupness becomes a survival value to other outside groups and even to the species, *Homo sapiens,* as a whole. Sixth, group-centered interactions on a conscious, mutual, deliberative level not only preserve the group as a unit, but increase the personal advancement and longevity of each member.

By releasing emergent intelligence the individual is not sacrificed to the group as in lower forms of life. The group is preserved through reconstruction on higher levels in direct proportion to the survival and enhancement values of individuals. Authoritarian culture groups anywhere in the world, promoting their survival through liquidation of members by any means, are denying the proto-cooperative or autonomic mutualism which will one day insure their downfall.

When aggregate and organic groups are examined in the light of the preceding concepts their similarities and differences become clearer. Each develops changes in the surrounding environment not produced by one person alone. These changes affect the immediate growth of each member, the life of the group, and the survival of the species. But the hormones, values, meanings, process of human relations, which each group generates, uses, and tends to perpetuate through the life history of its members, are not the same. The differences appear in the quality of the self as a tendency to action in the existing and subsequent situations. The evidence seems to indicate that the cooperative organic group is superior to the authoritarian aggregate in these results: (1) It operates on sounder biological principles. (2) It generates more of the growth hormone. (3) It releases more potential capacity. (4) It promotes greater enhancement of each individual. (5) It reconstructs itself on higher levels. The problem now becomes a very simple one to state but a very difficult one to resolve. It is how to change quickly and effectively our major social institutions—home, school, and church—from aggregate to organic groups.

HOW CAN A CLASS BECOME A GROUP?

To see better what changes are necessary for a class to become a group the chief differences between an aggregate and an organic group will be summarized under three main headings called the beginning, the end, and the means, as these cause greatest concern to parents and educators.

First, the organic group *begins* with a common area of need or common needs within a given area recognized by members as important for them to resolve, whereas the aggregate begins with knowledge which is selected by the external control to solve his needs and which he wishes the class to learn. Second, the *end in view* in the organic group is the most deliberative action possible on its own needs, whereas the end in the aggregate group is to learn the body of knowledge designated by the external control to his satisfaction. In the organic group each member openly, deliberately, and constructively self-selects from the experience those learnings which he believes are most valuable to him, whereas in the aggregate he has no such open opportunity either to self-select or to learn how to do it more constructively. Third, the *means* by which the organic group moves from the incipient need to the deliberative action is cooperative interaction, whereas the means by which the aggregate moves from the beginning of the experience to the fixed outcome is a series of conditioned responses to situations set by the internal status leader, who represents the external control.

The problem is how to change the beginning, the end, and the means which together become the process. This can be achieved only when there is some common need or environmental reason for doing so that is recognized both by the external control and by the members of the aggregate.

Changing from a class to a group seems difficult to parents and teachers, for they tend to overemphasize some restrictive condition which prevails in their particular case. And so we analyze together various types of restrictions and how to work within them, until they reach three conclusions: First, the difficulty lies in them as much as in the external conditions, for many of them admit that they would not be willing to change even if the external restrictions were removed. Second, those who really want to change are handicapped by lack of knowledge of the group process and feel insecure in attempting to use it. Third, if they believe in and use the group process, they will view external conditions differently and may not find them so restrictive as they appeared at the outset. I encourage them to study and understand better the outside demands by finding out who imposes them, for what purpose, with what expected results. Also I suggest that they try out the group process to develop security with it and to determine the extent to which it can be used under existing conditions. Their final conclusion is that there are always more opportunities than anyone ever employs, for promoting groupness in the home or for developing it with a class of pupils of any age. If a parent or teacher understands need process, he can begin immediately to move in the direction of achieving organic quality, even though maximum development may be far in the future. And every such step improves the atmosphere for learning for everyone.

To help parents and teachers understand better how to move continuously and effectively toward group quality, I discuss the means under a series of related aspects which operate simultaneously. (1) The external authority which makes the aggregate group must be released so that internal conditions may be changed. This release must be given for the length of time necessary for an organic group to emerge. The authority must trust the judgment of group members. He cannot reserve the right to step in at any time to alter conditions which do not suit him or to revoke the permission to make internal changes. (2) The class must be free to locate and develop common areas of need around which its group-ness emerges. It must study its own need-experiences rather than those of adults. (3) The fixed-in-advance end to be achieved under aggregate control must be so modified or released that the group can substitute its deliberative action to meet its own needs. By so doing, the group does not reject all fixed ends which outside adults desire. The group wants freedom to learn them not as aggregate ends, but as means of achieving its own deliberative action. (4) The group must be free to manage the developing experience cooperatively by making the major decisions which determine the direction of action and by setting the conditions for the most effective work of subgroups or individuals. (5) The group must keep open all channels of communication while helping each member to use them in focus with the need-experience. (6) The group must allow each member to self-select those learnings which he thinks are of greatest importance to him within the emotional tone and human quality developed by the whole. (7) The group must consciously appraise the cooperative process as a way of developing the experience to their need-satisfaction. (8) The group members must understand, feel, use, and build confidence in the cooperative process as the underlying sequence in all qualitative living.

To make the change from an aggregate class to an organic group in a school is not difficult because there are many conditions which facilitate such action. Some of these are:

1. Organic groups are the normal human association for both children and adults. Authoritarian aggregates are abnormal. Every teacher of children knows that as soon as he relaxes his control a class will break up into small organic groups based upon need or interest. Such groups vary in size, in persistence, and in effective working relations. Their organizing needs are usually quite unrelated to the educa-

tional purposes of the teacher. The sensitive teacher must decide whether to disregard them and promote the aggregate organization or whether to welcome and help these small need units expand in size and relationship to encompass the entire class, thus giving it organic unity.

2. Groups may be formed in school around the needs of pupils to replace the aggregate classes now in operation. To do this with young children is sometimes difficult, but the situation in high schools is very simple. No pupil should be allowed in any subject in a secondary school unless he can show that he has a need which that subject will help him satisfy. And when pupils enroll on this basis the subject matter will be changed to meet their needs. Thus all classes will become groups. Since extracurricular activities are usually need groups, the basic concept can easily be extended to include regular subjects.

The same method can be used in college classes. If a subject is so important that everyone must study it, such as anatomy in medical education, need should definitely be aroused through a series of exploratory experiences in clinics or similar situations where the student can see how the subject matter functions *before* he learns it. Such exploration and enrichment of need through functional experiences should continue throughout the subject. The informal discussion groups which spring up in many college classes are based upon need. Some professors encourage students to form them and help them to function effectively. Even in the most authoritarian cultures, individuals form organic groups. Some are in tune with existing policies and some are opposed to them. The more authoritarian the culture, the greater the struggle to form organic groups. In no small measure this accounts for our own Declaration of Independence.

3. The authoritarian control in our institutions is usually benevolent enough to allow some variation in ends and means. Usually there is greater flexibility in means than in

ends. The strategy is to find out just what ends the authority demands, in as specific a statement as possible. To say that he wants a child to learn the three R's or to take college preparatory courses in high school or to obtain a general education in college is not enough. These must be broken down into more specific subjects and parts of subjects. The next step is to show him how these ends can better be achieved by a new process which releases more organic quality. And this can be made clearer and more acceptable to lay citizens than to professional educators as the following illustrates.

A few years ago I addressed an open meeting of educators and laymen in a city where the public was advocating educational reform. The program began with a panel discussion by local citizens, from which I concluded their main criticism was that the three R's were ineffectively taught. I opened my remarks by agreeing with them on the importance of the three R's and the inadequacy of the teaching. I then explained that the results which all of us want can be achieved only as the classes become organic groups. During the question period which followed, all of the objections were raised by educators. The laymen asked for clarification of points with emphasis upon how such a change could be made. Finally the situation was summed up by a man who said, "I think I understand what you are saying. I am a dentist. I have practiced my profession for thirty years. I still put in inlays, fit bridges, extract teeth, and make partial or full dentures. But the equipment and the process are different now from what they were when I first began to practice. If I used the same tools and methods as thirty years ago I would not have a patient. All you are saying is that schools will continue to teach children the three R's along with some other things which are equally important. But to do this effectively you must change both the equipment and the process, which seems to me to be a reasonable conclusion. I not only think such a change is necessary, but I have confidence in the ability of educators to bring it about as successfully in education as I have tried to do it in my profession." This dentist really understood and his remarks had a profound effect in releasing top controls so that teachers who really wanted to could develop organic groups with their children.

4. Many teachers are willing to move from the old aggregate approach toward a better way of growing and learning through a higher quality group. There are many more such teachers in the average school system than appears reasonable to an administrator who is usually looking for the conformers. These liberals hold that aggregate groups cannot effectively discuss, develop, and utilize the experiences of members for the improvement of their own learning. This great loss in working capital keeps learning on the low level of conditioned responses. They say that attempts to improve the quality of teaching and learning by forming what are called ability groups within the aggregates or by differentiating the requirements for children with different potential capacities or by any other of the many mechanical arrangements now in use, do not improve results since the original aggregate base still prevails. They are not happy that they or the children expend so much energy toward such unrealistic purposes with such meager results. These innovating teachers are ready to make changes in the direction of better qualitative groups, even though they are unable to predict definitely what the real outcomes may be. They are willing to trust the cooperative intelligence of pupils and teachers as they plan together.

5. Teachers and pupils who work in organic groups recognize the better learning and living and spread it to other groups, if they really know the process by which they achieved the higher quality. Instances of this are numerous. Exceptions are few. A group of sixth-grade children in an elementary school using the process of deliberative action was promoted to a junior high school organized in classes. In November of that year I met a number of them at a party where they

immediately began to talk about school. The conversation was summarized by a girl who said, "We have a serious problem in junior high. The teachers know nothing about our way of doing things. We have to figure out some plan to show them the group process and how it works." And they did. At the end of their three years that junior high school was not the same institution it was when they entered.

During the discussion of how a class becomes a group, I usually help parents and teachers see that their difficulties are universal, for all of our basic social institutions are more or less benevolent aggregates. The restraining influences, internal and external, which they face are field conditions for every parent, manufacturer, labor leader, social worker, or college professor. I analyze for them in some detail how these field conditions operate in the many colleges and universities in which I have taught and what a professor can do to modify them. Thus they conclude that the opposition they meet in their particular situation is not greater or less than in any other, that they have no peculiar problem to solve, and that they have more opportunity to move in the direction of organic grouping than they realized. A parent said recently, "There is in me so much inhibition due to early home and educational experiences. As I straighten this out these external conditions are not so imposing as I thought they were. When you free yourself, you can do many things that heretofore seemed impossible." Thus each, in his own way, studies the early effect of aggregates upon his present behavior and moves to change field conditions so as to develop the organic groups necessary for the self-enhancement of everyone.

HOW DOES THE TEACHER HELP A CLASS BECOME A GROUP?

The quality of the organic group is in the operating wholeness. This is first sensed by the internal members or outside visitors as a feeling tone. The atmosphere appears different. The human relations seem more tolerant and considerate.

The sentiments of the members toward each other are freer and warmer. Each person feels at home, is relaxed and comfortable, and is inspired with purposeful vigor. There is no doubt about the wholeness. The empathic atmosphere is actually present and it is really different from that of an aggregate. But the group may be the former members of a class with a status teacher. How has the former teacher worked to bring about this change? What has each of the former individuals contributed toward this feeling tone? These are two questions universally asked by students. And here are some suggestions on what the teacher does to help create such groupness.

1. The teacher or status leader or the older more mature person sets the atmosphere within which members work and out of which a class emerges into a group. Evidence available from studies of group dynamics in all aspects of living where the process is analyzed, support this statement as one of the common outstanding conclusions. A half century ago one frequently heard and read the statement that the teacher made the school. This is clarified to mean that the status leader sets the climate of opinion of the class and that the learning of members is encompassed by or never transcends the atmosphere which he sets. Since all status organizations have a hierarchy of positions, each status member at his level sets the atmosphere for learning of all persons below him. The teacher sets it for his class within that set by the principal for the school, who in turn reflects the emotional tone of the superintendent of schools. The key to any improvement lies not only in the teacher but in the larger atmosphere determined for the system by those of superior rank. Since each individual, whatever his rank, tends toward interpersonal relations that give him need-fulfillment, the status leader must change himself as a person, must reorganize his self-structure, must find a new direction and a different process of self-enhancement.

The interpersonal behavior of each individual has a much

higher degree of correspondence with his need than does all of his intellectual theorizing. Some years ago I heard William Jennings Bryan lecture before the students and faculty of a large university on moral behavior. He pointed out dramatically the relation between professed belief and action by saying, "When an individual asserts that it is all right to steal, never argue with him, always search him." A status leader helps an aggregate become a group by setting the atmosphere in which cooperative interaction emerges, but only when he has action belief in such process. And the reorganization of himself must certainly accompany such action.

To change the atmosphere of an authoritarian competitive class into that of a cooperative interactive group, the status leader must release the miseducative tensions which classes tend to build in individuals. To do this effectively, he must understand a number of points about atmosphere.

First, the atmosphere is usually set by the leader at the very outset or during the initial stages of his relationship with members. And this crucial period is very short. For the members "size him up" or make a quick emotional guess as to the direction of his behavior toward them. Second, the most important factor in changing the initial atmosphere is to remove from members the threat which is always present in a situation with a status leader. While he may not remove the status given him by some outside power, he can reduce its psychological consequences. Both his verbal assurances and his interpersonal behaviors are necessary to bring this about. Third, an atmosphere once established tends to be more or less stable over a long period, perhaps even for the lifetime of the group. This is true whether it be competitive or cooperative, whether it restricts and exploits or whether it releases and develops individual capacity.

Fourth, the status leader must change the aggregate rules of the game into new principles of organic relationships and he must show members how to guide their emerging behavior by them. And he must work according to the new principles the moment he enters the group. By his actions he shows members that he believes in them, respects them as persons; he encourages them to express their sentiments or to share their experiences; he acknowledges individual beliefs and opinions while helping each to appraise them critically; he treats all fairly and helps everyone feel at home; he makes each member realize that he counts for something as a person or has worth to others, for without him the quality of the group would be lessened. Fifth, he shows by his behavior that everyone has security, belongingness, wantedness, status, as a basic field condition since he is both a creative individual and a member of the group. He never allows anyone to suggest by word or deed the old aggregate concept that the leader has and should use security or other interbehavioral qualities as rewards to those who do his bidding. Security and belongingness are the field conditions necessary for everyone to release creatively into the environment more and better directed past experience through more of his real self. In good group atmosphere each self is revealed; in good class atmosphere each self is heavily draped. The teacher more than any other person is responsible for initiating and continuing these self-releasing conditions.

But atmosphere is not enough. The leader shows others how to work together on their activities by the purposes which they select. He helps them understand and use the group process for satisfying their needs so that they feel better, think better, act better, until they are really more mature people. They accept him as a friend, expert in helping them resolve their needs by a superior process leading toward more reasonable action. He focuses his services *to* them and not *on* them. Each recognizes his dependence upon the other for his growth. The teacher takes into the classroom only his needs that are legitimate for the classroom. These are to help learners resolve their needs in an atmosphere and by a process which lead them continuously to higher levels of self-enhancement. While pupils recognize his professional needs, they contribute to his personal development in the same way that he contributes to theirs, thus accelerating and improving the learning of everyone. Atmosphere and process are so internally interrelated that one cannot exist without the other. Each learns the process in a cooperative atmosphere which releases the capacity necessary to make the process effective. The leader promotes each with such internal sincerity that his belief can be observed and accepted in external behavior by those with whom he works.

WHAT DOES EACH MEMBER CONTRIBUTE?

A class cannot be changed into a group solely by the action of the status leader, no matter how deep his interest, how high his ability, or how much he understands group process. The favorable atmosphere which he initiates will gradually vanish or revert to the competitive levels of a class unless members are willing and know how to contribute their part. For group quality emerges from the interactions of members and must be nurtured by everyone. So I shall enumerate some basic general points for members to consider.

1. Each member must recognize that group quality or atmosphere or feeling tone is made by people. It evolves through their behavioral interrelations as they try to resolve some common area of need which disturbs them.

2. Each individual must perceive himself and others as referents in the same need situation, to reach the psychological level at which a social group field may be formed. Each transcends his existing point of view by relating it to or modifying it by that of others. Such a phenomenon occurs only in the individual as a product of his released creative activity. It is not something superior to the interactive process injected by supernatural forces. It is an emergent meaning and empathy in a mutually shared field.

3. The key to an adequate resolution of a situation or need lies in the interactions of people, not in their reactions to external objects or things in their common environment. While the latter may sometimes appear to be important, the relation between a person and an external thing, a nonliving object, is never so crucial as the psychological interactions between person and person, for both are energy systems that perceive, feel, understand, and self-select their own direction of action. The qualitative atmosphere of a group is a product of the psychological interaction of person and person, both of whom are mutually modifiable.

4. Each individual must recognize that anyone who is unwilling to modify his prior perceptions through interaction, structures the field in a fixed direction which tends to prevent the emergence of groupness. Since he denies creative insight in himself, he is usually unwilling to admit or allow it in others.

5. Each individual must work to reduce in himself and others the threats arising from their earlier aggregate fields. Each will then be free to modify his perceptions of external nonhuman objects or things, thus giving them a more realistic value to the need situation. His dominance by fear, through interactive release, is modified to purposeful goals.

6. Each member must recognize that high feeling tone can be maintained only so long as there is sustained effort to manage adequately a common area of disturbance. Such working together may or may not mean that the group as a whole takes action to change external conditions. Frequently need is cleared on a higher level when the favorable climate helps each better conceptualize and differentiate himself. He then takes such overt action as he believes best within his clarified perception of his field. Thus there are action groups and discussion or clarification groups, each depending upon field atmosphere for the quality of consensus action or of individual behavior. Intimate social groups are usually not

action groups but opportunities for members to feel, release, and express tensions to psychologically kindred persons who help each other reactivate their purposeful energy. The results appear in improved actions of individuals in many and varied life activities.

7. Each individual recognizes that members with heterogeneous abilities and experiences can contribute more toward emergent group quality than the same number of individuals with relatively homogeneous backgrounds and experiences. Group phenomena are both the product of and the conditions for deliberative actions of individuals. The greater the spread of ability and experience within the common need area the greater the possibility for extending and clarifying perceptions and for remaking figure–ground relationships in individual fields. But each must be free to release his ideas, meanings, values to the group as he sees them for the interaction of others as they understand them.

To achieve this group relationship each member performs certain services or studies his behavior toward others or carries on in a direction within the moving molar experience which I shall describe here as a series of molecular observations.

1. Each member accepts a common area of disturbance on which to work even though his need which falls within it may not be his first choice or the one which is most pressing. He is willing to move along in the area in the direction formulated by the group. He allows his particular versions of the need or interpretation of the situation to become a part of the total experience, but not a dominating control. He is ready to learn that his self-discipline in the interest of the larger group quality brings greater benefit to everyone including himself.

2. He helps the group locate the center of disturbance within the area and clarifies his own individual need in relation thereto. He focuses the major difficulty and works on it until a new and better direction emerges. He holds himself to the points at issue. He does not wander afield to drag in

interesting but unrelated material that would detract from cogent thinking. He is constantly trying to refine his responsibility to the group as a whole, knowing that in the end this will give him the greatest outlet for his own creative energy.

3. He is always willing to revise his thinking in the light of the dynamics of the situation. He does not push toward a previously determined, fixed conclusion based upon limited perspective and evidence. He searches for that creative insight within the group, and that new experience from without, that merge into a new qualitative stream of endeavor flowing toward a sea of better individual satisfactions.

4. He encourages each member to express his own feeling tone, his deeper sentiments, his integrated learnings, which compose his real self. He accepts their sincerity even though he may not agree with them. He respects individual personality by giving each person confidence in himself. He encourages all to create new insights and helps to direct them constructively in the situation. He is sensitive to every opportunity for upbuilding each self into more mature action.

5. He keeps his eye constantly upon the moving situations that constitute the direction of need action. He tries to locate and examine all factors pertinent to each situation the better to deal with each succeeding one. Thus he reduces personality conflicts, releases tensions while in the making, and gives freedom to everyone for need-fulfillment.

6. He is alert to keep out all conditions operating against the high level of quality which he and the others are striving to reach. The greatest of these is fear. Individuals tend to fear people that they do not understand: people in authority who can control them, restrict their abilities, and debase their personalities; people with greater ability and more ideas than they; people with fewer ideas who achieve their ends by subversive means. They fear their own meanings will not be acceptable to the group, so they will not propose them. They look with suspicion on this creative group quality which is released by cooperative effort. They fear change of any sort,

creative or regimented, as a foreign instrument designed to circumscribe and frustrate them more than do their established ways of behaving. All of these fears are not in any one person, but all are usually present in any class. They are difficult dynamics to overcome in developing group quality. Only through patient constructive effort by each member with the sympathetic leadership of an older person can they be so reduced that energy is released constructively on higher levels.

The second greatest influence against group quality is that some members will strive for and the leader will allow them to become an inner elite subgroup quietly managing the larger membership toward their preconceived ends. No alert leader will ever allow himself to be maneuvered into this technique of aggregates, and every alert member will study the signs of its formation so as to expose it promptly. The private pipeline of a few to the leader is one of the surest ways of denying group quality.

Both the status teacher and the aggregate pupils or the authoritarian parent and the managed children learn these new vital group relationships while acting deliberatively on their needs. They are first experienced as a better feeling tone, a happier place to work, a greater personal belongingness and status. As the atmosphere of at-homeness increases, the group discusses the basic dynamics and how to apply them in varied life situations. Eventually all accept interaction as the conscious guide to quality of behavior brought by every person to all new experiences. Thus do individuals mature themselves as they move from aggregates to groups.

A BACKWARD AND FORWARD LOOK

As students discuss the material in this chapter certain conclusions and questions may arise. First, they see more clearly than ever before that children are born, reared, educated with people, organized formally or loosely into groups, transmitting to these groups a process of carrying on their life activities. This process is a powerful factor in determining what children are becoming as children and how they will view themselves as selves when they are adult. Each of the two sharply contrasted groups, the aggregate and the organic, has its own distinct process and its particular effects upon the growth of its members. Since the direction of all behavior is toward maturing the self, students analyze these two groups to see what and how they contribute to such enhancement. They decide that the emergent cooperative quality of the organic group has a sure footing in a long record of social and biological evidence. The aggregate has much historical and modern social support, though it lacks basic biological credentials. Finally, students realize that when external cultural demands conflict with a unitary biological process, each child tends to arrest his development at a low maturity level, either by rejecting or conforming to protect himself from the abnormal pressure.

A second conclusion is that each group has its distinct atmosphere, that some form of growth and learning will take place in either atmosphere, that the life problem is to select the one which tends to discover the greatest amount of capacity of each child and develop it to the highest quality. All children can learn some of the three R's in varied amounts in any type of group, since they were born with diverse abilities to learn. All children can learn the three R's better when differentiating the self to reach higher levels of integration. Thus the group which facilitates the growth of better selves simultaneously promotes functional learning of the three R's and improved general life behavior, for they are both aspects of continuous becoming.

The third conclusion is that the home has a far greater effect upon present and subsequent learning than has been formerly realized. The greatest contribution made by the home to the life of anyone is the process of teaching and learning which it uses, thereby advocates, and almost indelibly impresses upon the emerging selves of children. This disturbs some students greatly, for someone says, "But parents do not know this. They believe their greatest contribution to children is in food, shelter, clothing, affection, and the like." Then another says, "I am a parent and I have always tried to do the best I could for my two children. I never realized before that I was teaching them the process of learning which goes with an aggregate group, which I will admit our home is." And then a chorus of voices, "Why don't parents know this if the basic learning is so important? Why have they not been taught that in school?" And so questions are released for temporary consideration pending further discussion later when more evidence is available for their examination.

Students have one persistent group of questions which breaks out anew at this point. "If the home is aggregate, should the child be placed in an organic group in school?" "What will be the effect on the child?" "On the home?" "Has the school a right to support one point of view when the home supports another which is almost the opposite?" These reach deeply into philosophical as well as psychological premises. While students are debating them, I point out that much can be gained for the child, the parents, and the teacher if the school moves toward organic groups. The cooperative biological process does not hurt anyone, as does the cultural atmosphere of aggregates. By the pragmatic test of visceral well-being, if not by conceptual analysis, children and parents know that the organic group is better for them. Any school as a unit or any individual teacher in it that helps children understand and accept this evidence, even for one year, moves them rapidly upward on a maturity scale. Thus they are able to cope more adequately with or to experience fewer detrimental effects from the outside aggregates of life.

In the next chapter I shall discuss how the need-experience process is applied in school and home. Each example illustrates a moving process, not a fixed procedure which anyone can apply seriatim in resolving his own life experiences.

Chapter VIII

HOW IS NEED-EXPERIENCE
PROCESS APPLIED?

As soon as students obtain insight into the nature and meaning of the need-experience process, they raise questions about how to use it in their professional and nonprofessional activities. The majority are teachers who want to know how to apply it from kindergarten to graduate school. Some nurses relate it to bedside care, others to the teaching of nursing skills, a few to improving the program of nursing education now offered in hospitals or schools of nursing. Social workers are sensitive to its value for their various activities. Theological students, chaplains, religious leaders have long discussions on how it affects their area. College presidents, deans, professors consider how it will change existing administrative and academic organizations. Psychologists and guidance counselors study its relation to existing theories and practices. Psychotherapists and psychiatrists are aware of its importance in permissive individual or group therapy. Deans of medical and dental schools have employed it to improve teaching and learning in their various subjects.

Everyone is interested in finding out how to apply the process to home and family life or just to life in general. All the questions raised by parents and educators can be grouped

223

in a few large areas. These are: (1) How can the need-experience process be applied to school subjects? This ranks first in importance since most persons were educated in or are now teaching in schools with a subject curriculum on Line 1. (2) How can it be introduced in a school as a whole? This is the concern of many teachers but is more especially the focus of supervisors and administrators. (3) How can it be applied in the nonprofessional aspects of life? These range from how to rear children to how to get along better with aged parents, from how to use the process in teaching children religious concepts to how to apply it in improving morale in industry. Parents and students hold that since it really is the biological life process, it should be used in every life situation and not be confined to education in schools. (4) What should a person know or what should be his professional education or what is the best life preparation of a person who uses the process effectively with others? In this chapter I shall present illustrations in each of the first three areas.

HOW IS NEED-EXPERIENCE PROCESS APPLIED TO SUBJECTS?

To apply the need-experience process to any school subject in any school, public or private, elementary or graduate, the teacher or professor must always keep in the forefront of his consciousness a few simple meanings necessary for a class to emerge into a group which can use the need or group process.

1. The teacher must unfix or make variable the fixed knowledge ends which usually dominate subject teaching. Students understand this but many are unable to see how it can be done and still keep intact a subject.

2. The teacher must allow the pupils to manage the experience cooperatively. They must explore it to find the area of need, to locate the trial centers, to decide the direction and plan of work, to determine the values which they will put into it and take out of it, to agree upon what is deliberative action within the area under the need as they see it. The

teacher as a member of the group has the same rights and privileges as everyone else. He neither abdicates nor asserts himself, but makes the quality of his experience available to others through interaction.

3. The teacher must be willing to change the entire subject matter of the subject if necessary. Rarely is this necessary if the teacher has a broad meaning of subject matter. But he must be psychologically adjusted to such a possibility.

4. The teacher must concentrate upon the process of developing the area of need so that the pupils' decisions are their best at that time.

5. The teacher must allow each pupil freedom to evaluate and self-select those learnings which he believes are valuable enough to keep. He should help each make his best selections, but he should not control them, even though he may disagree with the choices.

6. The teacher must find the quality of his efforts reflected in the better need-fulfillment, the higher operational unity, the more adequate interpersonal behavior of each pupil. The subject which he teaches is valuable only as it contributes to such outcomes.

One summer I had in class a teacher of four sections of World History in a large high school where the subject was a graduation requirement. She was matriculated for a doctor's degree in History in another university and came to New York with a friend who was a student at Teachers College. At the end of the fifth week she decided to try this process with one section, if I would help her make preliminary plans and give her advice throughout the year. To unfix the ends, I suggested that on the opening day she ask the class to try an experiment. This year they could select their own world history. *Their* selections would be better for them than those made for them by someone else, and they could make the selections intelligently since no living person knows what world history is. The historian selects what he likes best, the textbook writer puts in the history book what meets his needs, they can put into their World History what meets their needs.

I told her that many pupils would disagree with such statements, so she should be prepared to support them. And the best way was by an experiment which I felt sure the class would enjoy. I asked her to collect for the class *one* copy of each available world, general, ancient, medieval, and modern history textbook so that each pupil would have a *different* one, and to obtain books on the history of art, music, science, mathematics, family life, economics, and the like. The experiment was for each pupil to analyze his textbook, listing the topics which the author included and the number of lines under each. Since some pupils challenged the opening statement, they agreed to conduct the experiment. They found wide variability not only in topics but in amount of space given to each. But something more important developed. Pupils said that authors frequently disagreed in their interpretation of common topics. So they again examined the books to locate points of disagreement. When the experiment was finished, pupils agreed that authors disagree and that they could write their own world history. The teacher told me at that time that the class had read more with deeper interest and better insight than her former classes at the end of the year.

The pupils now had a real area of need to study world history as they desired. In discussing how to explore this, one pupil argued for the chronological approach, another insisted on beginning with a present problem. A girl suggested that they begin in the middle and go both ways. When the teacher asked her why, she replied, "We can't agree on beginning with the past or present so I thought we could begin with a period which is very much like the one we are in now, called in my book the Renaissance and in some others the Period of Discovery."

They accepted her suggestion. As they discussed what they

wished to study about this period, they appeared at the outset to disagree widely. They listed such questions as how do people earn a living, what is their home and family life, why are there two social classes, what is the nature of their religion, art, music, what do they do for fun, and many others. As a group they were interested in all aspects of life of the people, yet each pupil preferred his question to the others. And the teacher had two uncertainties. One was that the class might organize into subgroups, each studying its own specific interests, and so preclude a broad view of the life of the people. The other was how to work with the group as a whole on some need of their selection better to show them the need process. Her first uncertainty was relatively unimportant as each proposed question was only an entrance into the life of the people as a whole. The solution to the second was to ask pupils to select one topic to study as a committee of the whole so that all could better learn the cooperative process. They readily agreed to do this, but to her consternation they chose the art of the Renaissance about which she knew little, since her major field for her advanced degree was the history of political institutions. The teacher was now really disturbed. She wrote me an air mail, special delivery letter, beginning, "You got me into this, now help me out of it." I suggested that she tell the pupils she knew little about art, but that all of them together could find and use the available sources. They went to the art museum, consulted with the art supervisor, held numerous conferences with a commercial artist who made his library available, and carried on other activities too numerous to mention. Shortly they discovered that art was so interrelated with other aspects of life, that to understand it, they must study all types of activities of the people. So they merged their work with subcommittees studying specific activities, until near the end everyone began to grasp the meaning of individual, group, and cultural interdependence.

Some time before completing this area, pupils began to discuss what they would do next. A lead was found in two conflicting statements about democracy. One book said it originated with the Greeks, whereas another held that it was developed by the middle class which arose during the Renaissance. They agreed to find out what the Greeks really contributed to democracy. They surveyed Greek history quickly, and then concentrated on the Age of Pericles, which was the high spot in Athenian democracy. They concluded that the Greeks stated the theory as government of the people in the interest of all the people, but that they practiced relatively little of it even in their finest hours. So they decided to follow the lead that present practice of democracy accompanied the rise of the middle class, but before doing this they agreed "to mop up the Romans."

They now asked the teacher to select the period in history from which they could learn most about democracy. She selected the French Revolution, with its approaches and consequences through the Napoleonic era. With this completed, they decided to study the Nations of the Modern World to find out to what extent they practiced what democracy meant to them. They took Great Britain, Russia, China before the Communists came into power, and Brazil. Near the close of the year the teacher asked them to make their own self-selection of learnings which they freely shared with others. They discovered: (1) There was great variability in their selections, even though there was a common direction of democracy. (2) Each person had good reason for what he selected. (3) Many selections were concerned with attitudes and feelings rather than facts.

The teacher led in highlighting the process, exploring with the pupils the reasons underlying her actions, and helping them to interpret in retrospect their own decisions. The pupils unanimously concluded that this was the best way of learning they had ever had. Together, pupils and teacher unfixed the ends, managed the experience cooperatively, changed the subject matter, conceptualized the process, evaluated their own self-selections, and found the enhancement of self toward which every subject should contribute. And each received credit in a World History course.

Some teachers and students are unable to see how a pupil learns the subject matter of a subject by such a process. Of course the subject matter of a subject does not exist any more than does the need matter of a common area of need. So I tell them this story. In a high school of a large city, I entered a class labeled Latin I on the office file card. Mussolini was then in power and I heard a most interesting discussion of some of his contributions to the life of the people of modern Italy. At the close of the period I said to the teacher, "Is this Latin I?" "Yes." "But it is so unlike the Latin which I once studied and taught." She smiled and told this story. "I teach only Latin I. Shortly after the beginning of the year, I found many pupils who were not interested in and were unable to learn conventional Latin. I had to make one of two choices. Either keep them in it and fail them at the end of the year or give them some other material under the same name. I chose the latter. I adjusted schedules until I was able to bring all of these pupils together in this group. I told them that I knew they did not want to study Latin and that it would be of little value to them. But they must remain in the class for the year. I asked them what we could study together that they would like and that I knew something about. We agreed on Mussolini and modern Italy. And you saw that they are greatly interested in this subject." "Yes," I replied, "but what will you do at the end of the year? Aren't they still enrolled in Latin I?" "Yes," she answered, "But that is no problem. I shall give them credit for Latin I since they are all now too intelligent to allow any counselor to enroll them in Latin II." And thus did Latin I taught by a human teacher meet the needs of the pupils.

Many teachers and students believe that pupils must learn to take outside pressures as preparation for adult life and should not be encouraged or aided in circumventing them. Everyone has pressures, demands, expectations from others in his environment. He should learn not to take them but to deal with them intelligently by a cooperative process. So I give parents and teachers this illustration. The superintendent in a city noted for its excellent schools obtained a position in a larger community. For a year his successor studied the educational program and became deeply upset over what to him was lack of organization. Each school operated as a unit within certain principles formulated by the entire educational staff with the help of parents, and each teacher in each school developed cooperatively with the children their program of living. He was especially concerned over informal teaching of the three R's, even though standardized test scores compiled during the regime of his predecessor showed pupil achievement to be much above the test norms. On the opening day of his second year, the superintendent presented to elementary school teachers and principals a long letter stating that, during the coming year, the three R's must be taught according to his time allotment and fixed content for each grade. Aided by his elementary supervisor, who came with him, he prepared the syllabi during the summer without consulting teachers or principals. Thus he injected authoritarian pressure into cooperative groups. And now for the heart of the story.

The schools were organized so that each teacher had the same group of children for three years, this being the second year of the three-year cycle. In early December while evaluating their work together, a fifth-grade teacher told the children there was something new which they must think about in their planning for the year. The superintendent had asked them to give a definite amount of time in order to cover certain materials in each of the three R's. After discussing the request, she gave them his letter and the subject outlines to read. The group decided to place this item on the agenda to consider later. After New Year's Day they again examined it, and decided that at the end of the year, by their present way of working, everyone would be better in most of the three R's than the superintendent expected. Their chief difficulty lay in meeting the fixed grade requirement and the time schedule in arithmetic. They studied their activities up to that time that year to see what content could be legitimately called arithmetic. They took the time spent on it, added the amount used in making the analysis, deducted the sum from the superintendent's total, thus obtaining their remaining time requirement for the year. They agreed that each person should find out from the superintendent's outline what subject matter he knew and did not know. They studied workbooks, textbooks, and other materials until each had his own list of what he had to learn.

The children now made two big decisions. First, they assigned the remaining arithmetic time in equal weekly amounts to Thursday afternoons, as they did not want arithmetic to interfere with other activities which they liked better. Second, they decided that during this weekly period the teacher should help each pupil understand what he did not know. He would take responsibility for developing whatever skill he desired by his own methods. At the end of the year *every pupil* was above the norm for the fifth grade in the arithmetic tests given by the superintendent. Their mean nearly equaled the sixth-grade norm and many of them were as good as the average seventh-grade pupil.

Thus did pupils who knew cooperative planning creatively convert the requirements of the superintendent to meet their needs. Much credit should be given the teacher who absorbed the demands until pupils were ready to deal with them intelligently. She had confidence in their ability and judgment; they in turn respected her friendly, humane leadership. No person, not even a parent, superintendent, or college professor, has freedom to teach or demand of others anything that he wants. The freedom for pupils to learn by a normal growth process must be preserved at all costs, and subjects must be modified to promote it.

HOW IS NEED-EXPERIENCE PROCESS APPLIED IN A SCHOOL?

Many persons who accept the need-experience or cooperative group process apply it effectively with single groups, but fail to see how it can be used with large units, such as schools or school systems. I have had the same criticism from business executives. They admit that the cooperative process works very well in small organizations with few employees and a simple structure. They assert that it is exceedingly difficult to use in large organizations with thousands of employees, especially in many plants with highly differentiated activities and a complicated overhead structure.

There is no answer to such problems within the cooperative process. There are only guides toward obtaining the most intelligent judgment at the time of action. I offer here some suggestions for applying the process in individual schools or in school systems as a whole. The underlying principles, however, hold for any organized unit, large or small.

1. The school staff must have a felt need in the area of revising the curriculum or of improving teaching and learning or of studying the behavior of pupils or of anything that offers opportunity to explore the total school experience of teachers and pupils. The need must be strong enough to encompass all members of the staff but not necessarily to the same degree. Each person must be willing to study the area realistically and allow future direction to be determined by consensus evolving from such study. But students ask, "How strong must this need be with all staff members at the outset? Can only a few persons have the original need? Can they

develop it so as to arouse a similar need in other staff members?" That depends on how the original need is studied or how well the few originators understand and use the cooperative process. From my experience, I conclude that whenever the original need is widespread, successful results may be expected. Whenever the original need is held by a few staff members, the results are generally unsatisfactory.

2. There must be at least one person within the staff or available from the outside who understands the need-experience approach to improving education. He believes in it, accepts it, conceptualizes it, and knows how to use it in school and other group situations. When the staff includes no such members, someone with this experience should be called in from the outside, as a consultant, to give continuous guidance until leaders emerge from within. I have worked in schools both as internal group member and as outside consultant. There is little choice between the two. While every school will invite outside help, it is absolutely necessary that someone be expert in the need process, otherwise the staff will merely apply ointment to the educational sore spots.

3. The need of the staff in the disturbing area, whatever it may be called, is now or can become focused on improving the quality of learning of pupils. The purpose of education or the function of the school is to provide each pupil with an opportunity for better learning toward self-enhancement. When a staff holds that subjects are of first importance or when the high self-involvement of members in their particular fields gives them tunnel vision of education as a whole, progress in exploring an area is slow, few new meanings are created, and the results are generally unsatisfactory to pupils. The real center of the area is overlooked or kept in the ground, as staff members are unable to face such polarization of experience upon themselves as persons. And yet they must see and accept their work from the point of view of the learner if they wish to improve education.

4. The outside authorities in the school system must allow the school to operate through the need-experience approach to education. The superintendent or chairman of the board of education cannot enter the situation at his pleasure to modify by authority group decisions which he does not approve. He must respect and accept the decisions as the group's best thinking. He can help by showing the staff how to improve the process, but not by vetoing their actions. Furthermore, the central office must allow the school to modify both its internal organization and its external administrative relationships. Without these releases the situation is hopeless at the outset.

If these four conditions hold to a reasonable degree there are three general ways in which a leader may approach the need area with staff members.

1. The leader may work with the staff as a whole until all members are ready and willing to move forward in the disturbing area by the need process. He tries to hold the staff together, he avoids issues or discussions that tend to polarize it, he strives always for consensus, and accepts the relatively insignificant matters on which it is reached. The results of such attempts at leadership, either in elementary school or college, have been inadequate in clearing perceptions, in creating new meanings, and in changing existing educational conditions. Only a few administrative rearrangements follow, since basic internal and external antecedents in the area are never studied.

2. The leader may work with innovators only, leaving to themselves the staff members who will make little change in their educational meanings or practices. At the outset the innovators, or persons willing to improve their practice through the need process, comprise approximately twenty-five per cent of a school staff unless selective factors operate. To work more with them and less with the noninnovators is to bifurcate the staff, which, of course, the leader wants to

prevent. This approach has generally been a failure, for reasons which will be explained later. Working too long with the staff as a whole or supporting the few innovators to the exclusion of others leads into educational blind alleys.

3. A third and more fruitful approach is a dynamic use of the two mentioned. The leader works with the group as a whole until innovators are ready to modify practice. Thereafter, he encourages both the innovators and the group as a whole, until every person becomes an innovator in his own way and to his own degree, but always in the direction of using the need process in his classes. Since every person is biologically an innovator, the leader can help each activate his creativeness by keeping the discussion process centered, through examining its meaning and use in their situation. He must not become involved in or encourage others to engage in arguments over the merits of their respective results of the process. He must assume creativeness in everyone and develop a group atmosphere in which each to his own degree may exemplify it in his professional behavior.

The staff leader performs a variety of activities all of which are variable and functionally interrelated. They follow the initial warming-up period in which the leader gets acquainted with group members or in which each takes the psychological measure of the other.

1. The leader must help the entire staff develop more and better meanings about the need-experience process, which is the operating center for improvement. I shall not summarize here those already discussed or anticipate those to be developed later. Two points, however, are crucial.

First, the essence of life is change. A static situation among living organisms is a figment of an imagination that has not yet attained accurate perceptions of reality. To improve education in the school somebody must change it. But staff members will ask, "How do you know that the change is for the better? Can't it be worse? How can you tell that it is right?" Changes are neither right nor wrong. They can be better or worse, depending upon the process which produces them. Since no one can prevent change, a group should use all available means to direct it in the best interest of everyone. The biological process is a more desirable means for directing it than are the metaphysical assumptions now controlling it.

Second, change takes place in every living organism by the same biological process, even though many diverse factors cause the results to vary. When a school changes to need-experiences, no two teachers are expected to do the same things in the same way with the same results. To require fixed ends is to admit change but deny the normal process of producing it. When accepting and directing change through the need process, uniformity and conformity become variability and creativeness. Thus each teacher can view every other as a friendly, creative, variable innovator who poses no threat to his personal or professional behavior.

2. The leader should help innovators plan to work with pupils cooperatively on some new need-experiences. I reserve the term "innovators" for teachers moving from aggregate to organic groups to distinguish them from educational experimenters who conduct their investigations within aggregate groups. There are many forms of such aggregate investigations. They differ from traditional practice in that the experimenter designates a single control factor and attempts to rule out or account for all others. Two classes are equated and pretested. One is taught the experimental factor while the other, called a control class, is taught traditional material by the usual methods. At the close of the experimental period each class is given the same final test to eliminate learning which would normally be expected. The difference in test performance of the two classes is due to the experimental factor. In most investigations in teaching and learning the experimental class is more aggregate than the control class following traditional methods. Results are evaluated by the

end-product divorced from the method of teaching or other field conditions within which the results were achieved. Such experiments have been of little value in improving the school curriculum. In the need-experience approach, innovators change the learning atmosphere so that aggregates may become organic groups. They preplan how to do this prior to working with the pupils. But such preplanning has almost the opposite purpose of that of an experimenter.

3. The leader must continuously build with all staff members a favorable attitude toward innovators, so that non-innovators will not sabotage their work. In many schools and in most school systems, conservative and reactionary individuals conduct a quiet campaign to sabotage the work of innovators or even experimenters. Sometimes the underminers claim to be supporters of the three R's, the basic subjects, general education, or the democratic way of life, which to them is their controlled education in authoritarian groups. Frequently they conduct whispering campaigns with parents at the bridge tables or over the teacups. An arched eyebrow, a shrugged shoulder, a limp hand gesture describes what they think of Miss Jones who is developing an organic group with her pupils. But these actions to belittle the work of others are not confined to conservatives. Frequently the innovators point their educational finger at the conservatives before parents or other community groups in such a way that the inferred meaning is clear to everyone. Curious labels may be attached to people and groups, such as liberal or conservative, progressive or reactionary, including the usual color patterns.

The leader prevents such cleavages by anticipating their appearance. First, he helps each teacher improve his practices within his perception of the group process. All will be moving in the same direction but at different points on the scale. Teachers can share experiences emphasizing their common process and how to improve it. They will be so busy helping and respecting each other that they will have neither time nor desire to undermine anyone. Second, the leader removes threat by helping each teacher see that the practices of one person will not be imposed upon another. All accept a common direction with variability of performance for each. Where one teacher is located at a given moment on a progress scale is of slight importance. When the direction is clear and the process of attaining it is understood, the distance between strides of each person will always be a function of his changing perception. To increase the speed and length of steps, the leader reviews at appropriate times, with the staff as a whole as well as with individuals, the basic meanings developed at the outset. As the perception clears the practice improves.

4. Continuous guidance should be given innovators by experts in the cooperative group process. Regardless of how enthusiastic and secure they are at the outset, innovators always find disturbing operational problems. Their meanings are inadequately refined for action in emergencies. In their frustration they revert to the more tangible security of textbook or workbook assignments. At these times, innovators want a competent person to help them rethink and clarify their meanings in the light of the existing experience so that they may move forward with greater security. How soon an innovator will reach this point cannot be foreseen. Some have grave difficulties within a month. Others may not have them for three months. But the remedy in each case is to help the teacher re-examine the entire process, including the meanings being applied, until he sees how to move forward with confidence.

In one consolidated school of twelve grades, I led a total staff workshop for four weeks in June, and then for two weeks teachers planned their innovations for the fall. Under the guidance of a local supervisor all worked smoothly until November, when I was asked to return promptly for a three-day conference during which the school was closed. I listened to their various difficulties and then led them in rethinking the process meanings developed in June. Almost three months of experience had revealed that their original perceptions were inadequate. Creative insight on a higher level emerged through such remarks as "I see now what to do," "That is a point which I missed," "This is where I became afraid and stepped in to control things my way," "I see now that I am as much the cause of the trouble as the pupils," "The remedy for my difficulty is more process." And so they went back to their respective rooms with keener perceptions and renewed confidence both in themselves and in the pupils.

During the Christmas holidays, the last week in February, and their Easter vacation, I returned for similar conferences. At each visit I helped them as a group to clarify the process until each creatively resolved his own difficulties. In June we began another total staff workshop for six weeks, re-examining basic concepts, evaluating the work of the year, and laying plans for new innovations. This procedure was followed for four years, after which leadership was furnished by the school system.

Innovators must learn how to improve the quality of their meanings through the aid of persons skilled in nondirective group techniques. Eventually such process guidance should replace the traditional supervision now in operation in all schools.

5. Innovators must be given professional recognition and security in the particular school, in the system as a whole, and throughout the entire teaching profession. Every educator knows that the innovating teacher is now the professional isolate. He is shunned by fellow teachers and is suspected by the profession as a whole. Because his behavior challenges the traditional control, he is called a troublemaker, a crackpot, a theorist, an impractical dreamer, or he is given some other name endemic to the particular community. Yet the experimenter who operates within the au-

thoritarian framework with aggregate groups has the confidence of and is given top professional status by the highest authorities. Innovators are rarely selected for promotion to supervisory or administrative positions. Advancement comes to persons who are safe, who cause no trouble for their superiors, who do as they are told to do, who will not develop any new and embarrassing ideas.

Thus do professional recognition, promotion, and status go to conformers who have power beyond their capacity to use it intelligently. Such status controllers fear change because they are unwilling and unable to guide it intelligently. They reject the principle of modifiability of all factors within or without the pupil-teacher learning field. They sincerely believe that their external demands must be injected into every classroom in order for them to be sure that the direction of effort and behavior is acceptable. They have and act upon a very low opinion of the intention and ability of pupils and teachers to create intelligent behaviors in their need-experiences. Thus do they reduce thinking to the level of aggregate groups reacting to conditioned-response teaching toward additive concepts of education.

Even the most exacting status controller is benevolent enough to allow innovators to make changes—within certain limitations. (a) The change is so insignificant that it will have neither harmful nor favorable consequences. Thousands of such variations from standard practices go on continuously from nursery school to university without the approval of higher authorities. (b) The change does not challenge existing basic principles or practices, and thus will not upset conservative teachers or parents and bring criticism upon higher officials. (c) The change is approved in writing in advance by the person in the central office holding such responsibility as a supervisor, research specialist, or director of instruction. (d) The results of the change will be evaluated by some conforming top officials, and the teacher must accept their judgment. These conditions are such that no person can truly innovate inasmuch as he cannot release the restrictions promoting aggregate classes.

Thus do creative teachers experience with top officials the same low quality of human relations that creative pupils obtain with status leaders in their aggregate classes. Better learning can be expected only as professional recognition is given to innovators who are the source of genuine progress. Since very institution has more conformers than innovators, special efforts must be made by the group as a whole to see that organic membership is accorded to everyone.

6. Innovating practices must be evaluated on the basis of the purposes of the innovators, not the conditions and demands of the old authoritarian education. Since innovating teachers help a class become a group so that each member may resolve his need by the need-experience process, the results should be evaluated on two kinds of evidence. These are: (a) how well the group understands and uses the process in new need-experiences, and (b) how well individual behavior indicates tendencies to action leading toward self-enhancement. Yet the favorite method of evaluating the work of innovators by an authoritarian conformer is to give pupils objective tests constructed from the subject matter taught to traditional classes. Rarely does one find the work of a regular class evaluated by the purposes of an innovating group. On many occasions in schools throughout this and other countries I have asked authorities why they did not test children in regular classes on the purposes and process of children in innovating groups. The uniform answer is that it would be unfair to the traditional children since they were not taught what the innovators learn. The unfairness of the reverse practice is almost always overlooked.

One day I visited schools with a city supervisor. In the late afternoon in an old building in an underprivileged section, she remarked that I might like to visit the room of a first-grade teacher who was trying an experiment. Here I discovered the most thrilling experience of the whole day. This teacher knew that many entering children were so immature that the usual subjects damaged them as growing selves. To remedy this condition, she asked for and obtained permission in writing from the director of research to conduct an experiment in which (a) she would remain with the children for three years, (b) she would be released from the usual grade requirements for those years, (c) she would emphasize the all-round growth or what the research director called the emotional, social, and personality development of the children, (d) she would be free to manage her program with the children in any way she wished, subject to the advice of principal and supervisor. The teacher moved her children from a regular classroom to a double room once occupied as a manual training shop and storeroom. The children arranged this for carrying on their varied activities of normal living in many ingenious ways. They were now in the spring of their third year together.

On the behavioral evidence, I concluded that these children were better adjusted emotionally, were more socially minded, had better interpersonal relations, were higher on a maturity scale, than any elementary school class I had observed that day. As a further check I examined the excellent developmental record of each child kept by the teacher for three years. I then chatted with Marie, who was the most immature at entrance. She was now an emotionally stable, friendly, outgoing, socially sensitive person. I found Walter to be an interesting, energetic, purposeful boy. And so it was with all the others. But what of the three R's? I asked Marie if she would be willing to read something to me. "What would you like?" she asked. "What do you have?" "We have animal stories, fairy stories, science stories, history stories, and our reading books." When I chose an animal story she consulted the card index, found the Dewey decimal number of a book, located it on the library shelves, sat beside me, and read with real feeling and understanding of the content. The same was true of Walter and a number of other children selected at random. As school closed I expressed to the teacher my enthusiasm with what these children had accomplished in three years, while the supervisor was silent.

When we were back in the car, the supervisor opened the conversation, "Our director of research is now preparing the tests by which to evaluate this experiment." "What kinds of tests will he give?" "A battery of achievement tests and others made especially for this group in reading, arithmetic, spelling, and language." "Does he plan to evaluate growth in emotional or social adjustment or personality maturity?" "Oh no, you cannot measure those by achievement tests." "What about the evidence the teacher has in her cumulative record of each pupil?" "That is not objective and besides it cannot be used to compare results with other third-grade pupils who take the same test."

So I went to the director of research, who confirmed the report. I tried to help him see that it was unfair to evaluate the experimental group on outcomes ancillary to the original purpose. In the end I was given the friendly advice that the purpose of elementary schools was to teach the three R's and that he was interested in the experiment only as a method of teaching them. While these children were better than the average third-grade class on the tests, the research director did not believe the statistical margin was great enough to warrant extending the experiment, especially when so many administrative releases were involved. That evening I left the city knowing that the research director would give the educational *coup de grâce* to the only bright spot the supervisor showed me in a very traditional school system. And all because his evidence was invalid to the purposes of the innovating experience.

7. The staff must continue to work as a committee of the

whole (a) to understand better all aspects of its own group process, (b) to aid teachers using such process in the various subgroups which compose the school. At times the emphasis may be placed upon one or the other of these activities. But the organic relationship between the whole and the parts must always be maintained in a healthy, functional condition.

8. The scope of wholeness must be extended to include pupils, parents, and others intimately connected with the school. Opinions differ as to how large the operating unit should be at the outset. Some hold that prior to the inclusion of parents in the over-all decisions, the staff should become an organic group, and each member should develop reasonable security in working organically with children. Others believe that children and parents should at the outset be a part of the original whole which redirects itself. All are functioning in some relationship, whether the school be a class or a group. How to proceed in a school must be determined by the field factors, for there usually are so many local forces operating that one cannot describe a policy from a distance. Eventually the result should be that all persons—staff, children, and parents—participate cooperatively in making the decisions that determine the directional guides for the school as a whole. Each individual in each subgroup therein should find working conditions where his capacities can best be discovered, released, and focused toward need-fulfillment.

9. The leader must encourage administrators outside the school to allow the staff to make the changes necessary for organic groups to function. The old aggregate administrative procedures designed to prevent cooperative interaction which is the life blood of the need-experience process, must evolve into a more flexible, dynamic organization. The centralized authoritarian controls of a few must become the decentralized emergent intelligence of everyone.

10. Finally, the leader must encourage more teachers to do more innovating toward better organic groups through the

need-experiences of pupils. He works on all fronts simultaneously, ever mindful that soundness of direction is more important than a specific act or a momentary position in a moving experience.

To many educators the difficulties involved in changing a school from aggregate to organic operation are profound. While I admit they are serious, I believe they are surmountable. Four universal yet penetrable obstacles are stated positively below.

1. *The school must find its operating unity or dynamic integrity or organic wholeness.* A school usually exists as an aggregate or summation of parts held together by some order imposed on it from without. Yet each individual in it began life as a unified whole. He differentiated all his parts and entered the outer world functioning as an integrated unit in maintaining his wholeness under internal and external pressures. To achieve this unity he is endowed internally with an intricate, balanced, and effective process of cooperative interaction. When it is impaired, wholeness of action is weak. When it is high, unity of action is strong. The aggregate school has to discover and use in interpersonal relations the individual's inner way of life. The whole did not evolve as a whole, because wholeness was never there. The parts that compose the aggregate were never differentiated. The function of each in relation to the whole was never defined, as there was no whole to differentiate it. No authoritarian structure ever gives creative autonomy to the parts. They receive from the authority only conditioned control. Creative functioning within their aggregate status is exceedingly difficult. The principles basic to a dynamic organism may appear, but in inadequate strength. The leader helps individuals create the conditions out of which the dynamic unity of the school is born, for only through such wholeness can real improvement be expected.

2. *In order to maintain the wholeness of the school, the staff must see that its own unity, which is the process, permeates the lives of all members.* To find and develop its own wholeness by a group process is not enough. The school is a learning institution in which work goes on, or energy is expended, in activities by the pupils and teachers who compose it. The cooperative process, the unity of the school, must be used in all relations in all working or learning units. At this point students ask many questions. "Can there be wholeness in a school without the cooperative group process?" The answer is *No.* There can be organization but not wholeness or unity. Frequently such a school is so well managed from the top that staff members or outside observers may erroneously assume that organic unity exists. "Can there be wholeness in the staff without application in the classrooms which are the unit parts?" Here the answer is also *No.* The staff of any school or college may by group discussion arrive at certain policies or guides which everyone academically accepts and feels emotionally in accord with. But each may act in his classroom as he did prior to the unifying agreements or as if such discussion had never taken place. An aggregate-minded individual may agree or give assent to principles developed by the group as a whole, but never accept them to act on. Yet it is the action rather than the academic assent which indicates the existence and quality of the wholeness.

Many people ask me how to change teachers so that they will accept and practice the process which is the unifying wholeness. Here I will review some points, previously discussed, since they can now be better interpreted.

First, the leader and the group furnish the environment in which each individual can remove the personal threat which every aggregate self feels when a process wholeness is being developed. Aggregate individuals find security in fixed ends, procedures, controls. Their perceptions in their field are so narrowed, they have tunnel vision directed to or on the threatening conditions. Their self-concept is so undifferentiated that any attempt to polarize or redefine it causes tremendous upheaval. Thus adoption of a cooperative process with directional guides and basic operational principles is a major upset. They fear group interaction in which the emerging climate frees normal drives which have long been suppressed. Encouraging them to innovate with adequate guidance helps them develop the positive assurance on which the normal self is built.

Second, the leader and the group help each individual find and study better his needs which he is satisfying by his behavior. A threatened person acts on the lower level of need-satisfaction rather than on the higher level of need-fulfillment. To change his direction he must have a clearer perception of what constitutes his need and what behaviors he uses to satisfy it. To clarify his need is frequently more menacing to him than the original threat of changing from fixed ends to process direction. But he must change himself in order to use, or as he uses, the need process in the classroom.

Third, the leader and the group help each member clarify by differentiation the personal and professional meanings which constitute himself. They help him symbolize or conceptualize what he thinks or believes; they recognize and accept how he feels about events under consideration; they encourage him gradually to release and take into account more ground factors in his phenomenal field, thus broadening and differentiating his self-structure. Since these changes take place with nondirective leadership or self-directive action, those with more differentiated meanings work sympathetically with others less favored. The permissive atmosphere, in which each can express, recognize, and accept his feelings as well as those of others, helps each examine the hitherto untouched aspects of his phenomenal field.

Fourth, every person helps others continuously examine and reconstruct their real selves. This statement is a summary of all preceding suggestions. The old self may verbalize all aspects of the need-experience process, but it cannot practice them with children. The new self uses the new process. Every person must view himself as he really is, not through his idealized image of himself. He must recognize his professional actions as they really affect the lives of others, not as he perceives them from his egocentric outlook. He must raise the quality of himself in order to have greater resources to contribute in all human relations. For group quality is interaction among members with stable selves and highly differentiated meanings. Free interaction among unadjusted personalities produces group quality only by accident.

3. *In changing from aggregate to organic groups, the leader and staff members must help conformers become innovators.* Conformers are more numerous in high schools, colleges, universities, and teachers colleges than in elementary schools. But other professions have their quota of traditionalists also. Sociologists say that an institution tends to attract persons whose personalities fit its demands. The existing authoritarian school tends to recruit those who find peace and security in being told what to do, or those who are unable creatively to face the realities of life.

4. *The final difficulty is that the leader and school staff must help parents and other adults release and clarify their autonomic belief that authoritarian schools offer desirable opportunities for pupils to develop into adequate selves.* They demand aggregate practices as being in the best interest of their children and all others. They mistake authoritarian education for democratic education which is developed through the cooperative process of organic groups. When such parents bring their first-born to school, it is difficult but not too late to help them differentiate better enducational meanings. A more favorable period is during the senior year in high school, for surveys show that one of the greatest expressed needs of pupils is to get married and have a better

home than the one in which they were reared. If authoritarian schools eliminated some less valuable subjects and included this area of need, pupils could develop more adequate perceptions of home life and gain better insight into the normal growth and learning of children. As parents, they would have a better differentiated field from which to view the education offered in school.

HOW IS THE NEED PROCESS APPLIED IN HOME LIFE?

Whenever I discuss the growth-learning process with parent-teacher or other community groups, someone always offers an illustration of how he uses it in his family life. He claims to be unfamiliar with the process which I have described, but believes in cooperative management as the best way of having an adequate family life for everyone. I shall present two such illustrations.

After a lecture to parents, the chairman introduced a friend who gave me this story. With her two daughters, Helen, aged five, and Claire, three, at the time of the incident, she went each summer for three months to the seashore. One day Helen rushed into the cottage as the mother was preparing lunch and said, "Mummy, we are going to have a party this afternoon at Joan's house and I told them I would bring a cake." "That's fine. And why are you having this party?" "This morning we found a new girl who has come to the beach and we thought we would give her a party." "That is a wonderful thing to do," replied the mother. "It is always nice to welcome new children, so they will feel that others who have been on the beach for many years really want them. Older people do the same thing. But, what kind of a cake do *you* plan to make? There are many different kinds. Perhaps you should look over some of these while I finish getting lunch." The mother gave Helen numerous pictures of cakes in very attractive shapes and colors cut from magazines.

After some study, Helen selected one of three layers in two

colors with a deep chocolate frosting topped with cocoanut. While they were eating lunch the mother said, "You did not tell me how many children there would be at the party." Helen counted the names and said there were eight. The mother replied, "Did you think about taking cookies instead of a cake? When a cake is cut into eight pieces each person gets only a small part like this," showing Helen in one of the pictures of a cake. "And besides a cake is sometimes difficult to make. You know that mine do not always come out well. If you took cookies you could make about seventy, or eight each in the same amount of time. Why don't you look over some cookies while I do the dishes?" The mother gave Helen pictures of cookies to examine.

Finally Helen said that she would like cookies if they could have nuts or raisins or other dainties on top as illustrated. The mother replied, "Are you really sure you prefer cookies to cake? If you are, you should telephone your friends that you would like to make the change and get their approval. They might be more surprised than pleased if you took cookies when they expected cake." Helen got most of the other children on the party line where they held a multiple-way conversation leading to a consensus for cookies. And so the mother helped Helen make, bake, and decorate the cookies, using a prepared cookie mix. Helen left in ample time for the party with eight cookies for each and some dividends. Other children brought lemonade and ice cream while Joan took care of the physical arrangements. And a good time was had by all.

This is an excellent illustration of the relationship between an adult and a child in the need-experience process. Helen had a need growing out of a group area of need. She decided how to satisfy it within the direction of action determined by the group. The mother respected Helen's right to define the need and to make the action decision. She helped Helen test the proposed action by polarizing the experience through the introduction of the new factor of cookies. When Helen modified her original decision, the mother asked her to consult the group out of which it emerged. But she left the final judgment to Helen. Furthermore, the mother expected Helen to assume responsibility for carrying out her decision. She had to make her cake or cookies with the help of mother. And so I asked, "If Helen and her friends had finally decided upon a cake would you have bought one?" "Certainly not. I would have helped Helen make it and she would have had to accept the judgment of the children as to its quality."

I told the mother that her behavior represented an excellent illustration of a desirable learning process, and asked where she had studied it. She replied, "I have never studied it. Before I married I was head nurse in the children's ward of a hospital. There I discovered that most behavior problems of children were due to the bad behaviors of their mothers. My husband and I decided to rear our children in the opposite relationship from that which I observed with these mothers. And we have. And it works. We respect each other's judgment, yet we help each improve his decisions. Each expects to and does accept the consequences of his actions in a constructive friendly way. This mutual respect is the center of our family life and makes it richer for everyone."

And so I draw two conclusions as I watch these children grow into *real maturity* in family life. The first is that the group furnishes the environment wherein each can meet his needs so as to enhance himself. The second is that one generation of children educated by this process, in home and school, can reshape the world toward better living for everyone. I salute all mothers everywhere who have and use such vision with their children.

One evening after a public lecture in a city auditorium a man approached me and said, "I am Dr. Miner, a local surgeon. I believe I have an excellent illustration of the process of human relations you described tonight. If you have time and care to accompany me to my home, I shall be pleased to share it with you." And so I learned that Dr. and Mrs. Miner had three children, two boys and a girl, the oldest of which, a boy, was in college, the others being in high school. After finishing medical school, the doctor became a general practitioner in a rural area of another state. Here the calls were many, the distances were great, the hours of service were long, the moments of relaxation and rest were few. The first year the boy was born and the other children followed rapidly. When the boy was approaching seven, the father realized that drastic changes should be made in their pattern of living. His few moments for relaxing were spent in considering disputes among the children or between them and their mother. Finally, one Sunday afternoon when calls were infrequent, he brought the group together and suggested that they try a new plan for settling their differences. Whenever difficulties arose among the children, each would state his side to the mother who would write it on a card and drop it in a letter-box which he had provided. Disagreements between mother and children or mother and father would also be written and filed. Each Sunday afternoon they would hold a family council when all reports would be read, examined, and acted upon by the group as a whole.

The first break came during one of the early meetings when the boy's complaint about his sister was read. He said, "That's all over now. We fixed it up. It wasn't my fault and it wasn't hers. It just happened." By the end of the second year there was consensus on the following points as determined by verbal expression and overt behavior. (1) When there is trouble no one person is to blame, each is partly responsible. (2) Writing down the report helps everyone see better where the difficulty lies, or as the boy said, "It doesn't look the same to you after you write it down." (3) More and more difficulties were being resolved satisfactorily and without emotional outbursts, prior to the family council.

When the oldest boy was ten, the father laid before the

council a deeper problem. He wanted to return to medical school to take the additional work necessary to become a surgeon. Many aspects of this change were considered together, such as where the family would live, what arrangement was best for the father, how the costs could be met. The consensus was that the father live in the city near the medical school, that the family remain in the country until he had finished, and that each contribute to meeting the cost by keeping all expenses at a minimum.

Immediately upon graduation, the father became the associate of an elder surgeon in the city of our chat. The family was reunited and the weekly councils continued. The whole financial problem was now opened for discussion since the earnings of a young surgeon are meager for a growing family. Everyone knew the income and expenses, passed on the family budget, and kept within his appropriate share. When the boy entered college, readjustments were willingly and simply made. Already they were developing plans for the fall when the daughter would enter the university.

I could write at length about the details of this family plan which fascinated me for hours that evening. But I shall give only the conclusions drawn by the doctor himself. First, it is remarkable the way children increase their insight into problems of living when the environment frees and encourages them to do so. Second, each individual learns to have a deep respect for the judgments of others, even though he does not always agree with them. Third, the group always makes decisions in the best interests of everyone as it views the situation at that time. Fourth, not once did anyone fail to carry out a decision cooperatively made. Frequently the group modified action by rethinking and reinterpreting a decision better to understand its meaning, but never decided to abandon, reject, or regret it. Everyone learned to accept past judgments as the best which the group could make at that time and went forward to make better ones in a moving

present. The valuable mental hygiene of such cooperative
living cannot be overestimated. Fifth, the psychology of the
family life was changed from an irritating reaction to an an-
noying authoritarian control which satisfied no one, to a mutual, cooperative sharing of feelings, thinking, and decisions
which benefited everyone. Said the father, "Progress was slow
and the going was sometimes tough in the early years, but
we persisted and no one will ever forget the benefits he derived from the experience. It is remarkable how a family
council commands the respect of and releases the creative
ability of everyone. Frequently we surprised each other by
the keenness of our insight and the quality of our judgment."
He concluded by saying, "I believe this is an illustration of
the cooperative process which you explained tonight." I
agreed that it was. I also agree that this brief account in no
way does justice to the keen insight of the surgeon into the
growth process, neither does it describe the high maturity
level of his children.

A BACKWARD AND FORWARD LOOK

At the beginning of this chapter I listed four questions
frequently asked by professional and lay groups on how to
apply the need-experience process. I have discussed three of
them. The fourth, on how a person should be educated to
use the process effectively in all life situations, will be considered in the last chapter after other meanings have been
developed. Here I will discuss three questions which generally arise when groups explore school and home practices.

1. "Is the direction of improvement in subjects always
toward meeting better the needs of pupils as they see them?
Do you improve the behavior of children in the home by helping them meet their needs?" I offer an affirmative reply to
both of these questions. Every action is always in the direction
of satisfying a need as the behaver sees it. To improve his
action, he must obtain a clearer perception of his need in his

field conditions. But this is not enough. He must learn how to select and use his environment better to meet it. Therefore each teacher should help pupils, and each parent should aid his children, to locate, define, and resolve intelligently his disturbances. Every normal child is eager to obtain outside guidance appropriate to his age and experience, if it is given on the process.

Subjects in school or demands in the home have always been and are now evaluated by children according to their needs. College students report that only a few topics in a course are valuable to them except for obtaining degrees. Improvement in subjects wherever taught comes as students select and adapt subject matter into need matter. Siblings evaluate family life according to their different needs. The treatment for maladjusted children or adults is to help them find their needs, learn a deliberative process of meeting them, and accept the consequences of their own decisions. The illustrations in this chapter show how parents and teachers worked with others in different life situations toward that end.

2. "Can this country develop specialists in various areas of knowledge, if education is centered in the need process?" Yes, and better specialists than it has developed in the past. A brighter future for the country and for the world rests not with a specialist but with a whole man: a man with a mature personality capable of interacting inelligently with every part of his environment; a man able to treat all kinds of experiences in dynamic relationship to the wholeness which is life. Specialists will emerge from creatively balanced persons whose continued wholeness of vision, through inner change and direction, precedes every outer transformation of the external environment. This denies the theory that an artist has to be temperamental, a surgeon scientifically austere, a professor absent-minded, a plumber forgetful of his tools, or that every specialist is a little queer. It accepts the premise that

existing specialists are creative in their area but generally
noncreative in other aspects of life. They should be creatively
intelligent in living as whole people to become really creative
in their specialized fields.

It is difficult through written illustrations to express the
dynamics of a moving process so that readers feel people in
interaction managing life activities in the interest of all. It
is much simpler before a live audience. When the reader finds
empathy with the people in the illustrations noted—the
mother with the child and the cake, the doctor with his family
around the council table—he has increased meaning and confidence in himself for innovating action.

Persons who apply the need process are always called upon
to explain the basic concepts underlying their actions. I have
developed the biological background of learning and have
referred to the changed viewpoint concerning it, but have
not specifically analyzed it. Since authors of books on psychology rarely discuss the wide differences in the theory of
learning underlying biological process and teaching method,
I shall in the next chapter emphasize some meanings which
are helpful to innovators in interpreting their creative efforts
to others.

Chapter **IX**

WHAT IS QUALITATIVE LEARNING?

Educators and laymen tend to use interchangeably such words as growing, developing, behaving, maturing, and learning. Rarely do they use them to indicate how they became who they are. Rather these terms express their value judgments of the overt actions of others, based upon their perceptions and what present behaviors imply for future action. Such judgments involve two interrelated aspects of the actions of others. One is the kind of life situations which an individual usually enters or those which he selects or rejects; the other is the direction, overt or implied, of his movement within these life situations. Sometimes adults use these terms to describe the total action or life process of another, whereas on other occasions they may use them to refer to one aspect of such wholeness, such as physical growth, emotional maturity, or academic learning.

In earlier chapters I have considered the meaning and use of such terms from the point of view of the behaver growing up in his environment rather than from that of the observer evaluating the behaver's actions. A person will grow in some way or learn something in any environment. But if he is to grow toward self-realization, the learning must have a quality

257

which insures more and better or broader, deeper, and higher maturity. Each individual must experience this qualitative learning in himself in order to observe it in the actions of others. Every individual who directly influences behavior, especially parents with their children and teachers in schools, must conceptualize the theory of learning which underlies his practices. A sound theory is his best basis for improving himself and for helping others to improve their behavior.

In every qualitative learning experience each individual broadens and deepens his perceptions of himself. The self is both the subject and the object or the source and the end of all experience. Under normal conditions the individual widens his outgoing and intaking relationships with his environment. Through these he obtains the need for creatively differentiating his psychological field and the materials with which to do so. He searches for the deeper meanings, the sharper insights, the clearer values, which underlie his actions. In probing for and conceptualizing these profound aspects he finds a surer, more consistent yet flexible unity than he can achieve by a superficial explanation of his life problems. He brings the covert and overt aspects of his behavior into closer relationship, or he raises the degree of correspondence between his self needs and his actions. Since everyone is normally realistic and pragmatic, he searches for a philosophy of life which will encompass all his activities, is internally consistent, directionally sound, universally applicable, and can constantly be refined in the matrix of his merging need process. He must have a theory of learning which makes such qualitative living possible. And he must see how his theory differs from others which emphasize the natural order of objects in the environment rather than their value to him in improving the quality of himself.

The innovator has little past or present practice with which to justify his actions. Only the conservative or reactionary has that doubtful asset. The innovator is creatively reconstructing practice in a new direction, which he has to justify both to himself and to others, by the soundness of his theory. He must expect conservatives to challenge him and he must be ready to meet their criticisms by a more reasonable, inclusive, and qualitative theory of learning than that which underlies their practices.

An innovating elementary school principal encountered opposition from parents, teachers in other schools, and members of the central office staff. She asked me to address an open meeting of parents and teachers on newer trends in education, during which I explained the need-experience process. The superintendent asked the first question, "Can you give us a list of school systems where such a program has been operating for twenty-five years?" He knew that I could not do so, and his smile at the audience as he asked me carried more meaning than the words. I replied that I could give no such list. "But," I said to the audience, "I would like to point out to you the reasons back of such a question and their implication for your schools." Whereupon I analyzed the theory of learning underlying a traditional program and that implied in the innovating practices of their school. The responses from laymen now came rapidly. "Tell us more about this." "It sounds reasonable to me." "How can we have more of it in our school?" The parents wanted assurance that changes were based upon a sound theory of learning which the school staff had accepted but had inadequately explained. The innovation was to help each child creatively reconstruct himself toward higher total maturity through an environment selected and organized for that purpose. Parents and superintendent were examining this new practice on the basis of inadequate and traditional learning theories. Yet they accepted and improved the innovations when they understood the reasonableness of the new theory.

Since every parent or educator is searching for better

theory to support his practices, I shall present some material, organized around a few important questions, which he can use to check his findings.

WHAT IS THE CONCEPT OF HUMAN RELATIONS?

Every theory of learning is based upon a theory of human relations, explicit or implied. Since there is a relationship among individuals during learning activities, an underlying theory of human relations is inescapable. The first question to ask about any theory of learning is, "What concept of human relations operates in the face-to-face relations among the individuals?"

I have already pointed out that the two major theories of interpersonal relations are the authoritarian or reactive and the cooperative or interactive. The corresponding theories of learning are the *association* theories for the authoritarian and the *field* theories for the cooperative human relations. Educators and laymen are generally unfamiliar with these terms, but they do know the theories by other names and can identify some of the individual types. The association group are called stimulus-response theories, such as behaviorism, connectionism, conditioned response, or trial-and-error learning. The field group are called *gestalt* or organismic theories, which include purposeful, depth, self, or personality psychology, psychiatry, and psychotherapy. Some educators, parents, and psychologists take an eclectic position composed of the best ideas from the two theories. Generally they practice an association theory, based upon their individual brand of authoritarian human relations, whose effects they have inadequately examined. Most homes and schools are authoritarian, and promote association theories of learning. Only a few schools operate on field theories of learning. Chart XIII shows these learning relationships.

Authoritarian human relations, the subject curriculum, and association theories of learning grew up together as educational companions. Each is used as evidence to support the other. Early learning experiments with animals and people, based upon authoritarian relations, supported association theories since no other result was possible. Conditions were so controlled that neither the rat in the maze nor the child in the school could use his normal creative inherited capacity. When psychologists announced that animals and chil-

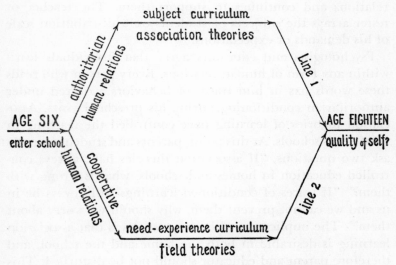

Chart XIII.   Learning Theories in Schools

dren learned by trial and error or conditioned response or connectionism, educators were joyful. The theory upheld the subject curriculum to which they were irrevocably committed. Neither group recognized the underlying human relations or perhaps each deliberately ignored them as of little value in learning.

The scientific movement in education was founded upon and still promotes association learning theories and authoritarian human relations. Early educational research, both theoretical and practical, as one aspect of this scientific movement, assumed external control over the teaching situation by the experimenter. The modern streamlined version called action research still operates under authoritarian relationships since some structured nonmodifiable factors usually shape the action. Objective teaching, another aspect of scientific education, widely promoted by association psychologists and subject educators, originated in authoritarian human relations and continues to support them. The teacher or tester arrays the subjects or students on a distribution scale of his demands or expectations.

Psychologists and educators agree that individuals learn within any form of human relations. Every person who reads these words has in him traces of behaviors acquired under authoritarian conditioning during his preschool years. Association theories of learning have controlled the teaching in most of his schools. At this point, parents and students usually ask two questions, "If association theories have always controlled education in homes and schools, what is wrong with them?" "If traces of conditioned learnings will always be in us and we cannot prevent them, why should we worry about them?" The implication of both questions is that association learning is desirable in both the home and the school, and therefore parent and educator should not be disturbed. This inference is inadequate for a number of reasons.

1. Association theories are too low on a qualitative scale of self-enhancement to become the basic learning process in schools. If all theories are placed on an immaturity-maturity scale the various association theories will fall closer to the immaturity than to the maturity end. They are found in and are promoted by other social groups or institutions, such as the family, churches, business organizations, gangs, clubs, and the like. There is no valid reason why the public should support schools offering the same low quality of learning theory that can be picked up elsewhere in the culture.

2. Association theories antedate modern knowledge of people, which began about a century ago and has developed at an increasing rate since 1900. Their experimental support comes from the older concepts of physical science, whereas the evidence for field theories is derived from the more recent physical, biological, and social sciences.

3. Association learnings have little transfer or spread value. They are conditioned as specific responses in particular situations. The individual may use them in similar situations, if he recognizes the similarity, if he recalls the original conditioned learnings, and if they show promise of effective results in the new situation. Rarely do these conditions exist, as experiments on transfer and intelligent observation of life activities tend to show. Analysts of the component factors of intelligence report that ability spreads through a learned general or process factor rather than through specific responses to elements of situations. Thus association learnings have limited value to any individual in meeting intelligently his novel life activities.

4. Association theories reverse the normal biological growth process. They assume that control of growth and learning is outside the individual and in his phenomenal environment, whereas the biological evidence indicates that control of growth and learning is inside the individual. These growth factors have been discussed in earlier chapters.

5. Association theories are basic in all cultures organized through authoritarian institutions. The evidence to support this statement is the recorded history of civilizations or the living cultures of today. From the Patricians of Athens to the Politburo of Russia, conditioned-response learning has been and is used by the top group to maintain its power. It is a weapon by which immature people dominate others so as to cover up their defective selves. Association theories are inadequate for the education of children and youth to become the leaders of or members in a democratic society.

WHAT PSYCHOLOGICAL FIELD DOES EACH THEORY IMPLY?

All theories of learning assume a psychological field in which the individual behaves. The fact that one group is called association theories and the other field theories does not mean that one has *no field* and the other has *a field*. Rather, the terms refer to two different meanings of field. The older association theories were organized prior to present concepts of psychological fields. The younger field theories are built on modern knowledge of behavior. The terms "authoritarian" and "cooperative" designate more or less adequately the existing field differences. Before discussing them, I shall present the few points of field agreement so as to sharpen disagreements which are more important.

The fields assumed under the two theories are similar in these respects. (1) The field is the area of experience taken into account by the individual at the moment of his action. This includes himself as well as his external environment. (2) The field is composed of learning objects, nonlearning objects, and the way in which they affect each other. More specifically it is made up of people, other living organisms, the physical universe, events, customs, and a process of their relationship. (3) All behavior takes place in, is determined by, and is relevant to the psychological field of the individual. He has no behaviors which originate or are consummated outside of it. (4) The field is active at all times because it is partly composed of living organisms. A field without activity would be devoid of life and would therefore cease to exist. (5) Learning in some way remakes or reshapes the field including the learner. (6) Experts study fields in order to predict the movement of all things within them. Each individual studies his field so as to predict as accurately as possible his behavior and that of others within it. Psychologists and educators must anticipate with some accuracy the behavior of individuals in their various relationships. The associationist and the field theorist each assume the field which to them has the highest predictive value. Each explores it with a similar purpose, although he begins with different perceptions and arrives at different conclusions.

The points of disagreement between association theories and field theories are many and have significant educational implications. I shall discuss only those of greatest concern to innovators who are attempting to move practice from aggregate to organic groups or from association to field theory concepts.

1. *As to the point of view from which the field is examined.* Since the field in general is composed of persons and things, there are three possible relationships—things to things, persons to things, and persons to persons. The associationist concentrates upon that between persons and things. He observes how a person acts toward external objects, such as a pupil toward a school subject. He tends to accept aspects of situations which he can quantify or measure in objective units. The field theorist centers his attention upon relations between persons and persons. He sees the actions of a pupil toward external things, such as subjects, as the relation between pupil and teacher. He looks for the personal, subjective conditions rather than those which he can objectively determine.

The associationist takes the external objective approach to behavior. He evaluates the observed actions of others against his stimuli or demands. As he changes them he expects the behavior to change. The action of the behaver is a function of the externally controlled stimulus. The field theorist takes the internal self approach to behavior. He accepts the actions of another as being the most pertinent, reasonable, and effective or the best that the behaver knows at that time. He helps him see why he acted that way, so that he may clarify his perceptions. To a field theorist the behavior of an individual is a function of the individual's perceptions or meanings of a situation at the moment of action.

2. *As to the unit of learning.* The associationist assumes
that the unit of learning is a pupil facing the situation set for
him by the observer, who controls it through stimuli related
to common things in their environment. The observer assumes
that these objective things have in and of themselves an
orderly, regular, and predictable relationship. He wishes
the pupil to accept this order so that his behavior may be predictable, for otherwise it would be erratic, irregular, and
relatively inconsistent. What he really wants is that the pupil
accept his perceptions of the things, for in them the observer
finds the order and predictability which enhances him. He
restricts interaction to stimulus responses which he approves,
hoping thereby to insure the result which he wants.

The field theorist holds that the unit of learning is a pupil
facing his own situation growing out of his own needs. He
selects, converts, and organizes the things from his environment which promote his self-enhancement according to his
perceptions which govern his actions. His behavior in relation
to these external things is always orderly, regular, and predictable to him. It differs from the internal arrangement of
the things themselves or their relationship to each other.
Knowledge of the internal structure of inanimate energy
systems offers him little clue to the behavior of people who are
energy systems that perceive, feel, understand, and reconstruct
themselves. Inanimate objects cannot reconstruct themselves.
Changes in their internal order by inside or outside forces
is toward disintegration rather than enhancement. Their
predictability, whatever it may be, is not desirable for persons.
The field theorist helps the pupil locate, explore, and act
deliberatively in his own need situations, and to improve
the organization of his field wherever possible.

3. *As to the center of the field.* The associationist asserts
that the center of the field is outside the pupil and in those
things in his environment which can be measured quantitatively and objectively. In reality, the center is in the persons

in authority who want to shape the behavior of the learner to their fixed and predictable ends.

The field theorist holds that each learner is the center of his own field, regardless of what external persons or things he may recognize within it. When many people work together, each is the center of his field, each perceives the field conditions differently, and each acts according to his perceptions. Through free and open interchange of points of view each may understand the others better, experiences may be clarified, individual organizations may be improved, and needs may be realistically met.

4. *As to the field process.* The associationist holds that field movement is controlled by forces outside the individual, but within his environment. They are never clearly defined, but are referred to in very general terms as being removed in time and space from the existing situations which the individual faces. They are customs, traditions, cultures, the public, natural laws, all of which are demands placed upon the many by the few who want the field, including the individuals therein, shaped toward their ends. The field process is reaction to the demands of those in authority, however it may be stated. They curb, restrict, or circumscribe the movements of people by devious means to keep them in a groove. Potential capacity is undeveloped because of conformity with the party line. Only the resisters save themselves as persons.

The field theorist assumes that movement in the field is controlled by the emerging intelligence of the members operating as an organic group in their areas of need. Such intelligence is unlimited, if inherited capacity is released and focused in life situations by a normal learning process. While each self is the center of his field, the quality of the psychosocial process of interaction is the most important single factor in determining what he becomes.

5. *As to the modifiability of the field.* The associationist holds that some field factors are permanent, unchanging, non-

modifiable, even extrasensory or revealed truths which must govern the amount and direction of movement. All other factors and conditions must be modified only in relation to these fixed truths. Any alteration of these permanent controls will bring serious consequences to the individual now or in the life hereafter. Every authoritarian field—home, school, church, total culture—is structured through fixed truths and unchanging values by those in authority to prevent social process innovations by behavers.

The field theorist holds that all factors in the field are modifiable. No person or group has immutable perceptions, meanings, or values which are superior in quality to those of any other person. They are valuable to the extent that others recognize and accept them, through interaction, as the best direction for releasing need tension. All feelings and thoughts, visceral and conceptual responses, of everyone are data for intelligent inquiry to be critically appraised. This holds even of the relationship of a person to inanimate objects, such as the force of gravity. Such realistic change in all field factors is necessary, if biological learning through mutual interaction is to function.

6. *As to how the individual will learn to deal with the dynamic field forces.* The associationist holds that the individual learns how to manage dynamic field forces through the accumulating of knowledge about the internal structure and relationships of the fixed exact objects, events, things in the field. He spends almost his entire educational life, whatever the number of years, in increasing his quantity of those inanimate materials. The dynamic forces are merely new combinations or rearrangements of old fixed objects and patterns of action.

The field theorist holds that dynamic energy is in people and that field dynamics emerge through interaction as they creatively assimilate selected external objects toward self-realization. Since all use the same basic process, the result is a fluid wholeness or unity in the ongoing life. Each individual learns how to manage these dynamic forces by managing them each year in the realities of his experiences. They are more than or superior to any aggregate rearrangement or synthesis of inanimate materials. They are the essence of the life of each person. From the earliest years, field theorists help children to recognize and manage their experiences by making and evaluating the major process decisions which govern their actions.

7. *As to what causes the changes in the behavior of individuals.* The associationist believes that change in or improvement of behavior is caused by the many discrete objects, things, or stimuli in the environment which exist independently of either behaver or observer. These objects are static, unchanging, immutable, and without personal reference to them or any other individual. Improvement comes from learning (a) more about these independent objects separately, (b) more about their many connections and interrelations. The greater the number of independent objects and the larger the total number of interrelations known by the individual, the higher the quality of his learning. Since all objects and interrelations existed prior to the learner, he must acquire them from a better educated person under his stimulus control. So the teacher presses into the learner these inherent relationships or natural associations of unchanging parts of objects which constitute subjects. Thus throughout his entire educational career the learner collects these prior combinations or syntheses and exhibits them at the proper time.

The field theorist asserts that behavior is the perception of the total situation held by the individual at the moment of action. This perception is the meaning which all persons or things have in his movement to achieve need-fulfillment. No person, object, or event exists in a psychological field independent of the individual. His perception of relationship to himself as the dynamic center is the existence of the person, object, or event. His behavior improves as he creates new meanings which never existed before in his field. These come by differentiating the various parts in relation to his needs. Thus he never *adds* anything as such to his field. The presence of a person or an object is the occasion for him to clarify or reorganize certain aspects of it, by modifying figure–ground relations better to focus upon the pressing situation. He tries to maintain interpersonal relations which not only allow but help him create the new meanings necessary to reconstruct his field. Improvement in learning or behavior comes through increasing the quality of the differentiations which the individual creates in his need-experiences.

8. *As to the direction of movement in the field.* The associationist holds that movement in the field of an individual or a group is directed by the fixed, unchanging, immutable objects and relations which have prior existence in the field. These are grouped under such general headings as facts, objective knowledge, or the cultural inheritance. More specifically they are ideas, meanings, attitudes, or values inserted into the field at the outset by the authorities to control behavior. The direction is within the field, but outside the individuals who compose it. They learn to be managed by and to accept the outside authority, giving back in behavior when necessary the desired knowledges.

The field theorist holds that every situation which individuals face singly or together is a disturbing configuration of behaviors unsolved in their interaction. It is merely a segment of the total ongoing life process which occurs under these conditions and under these only. Direction grows out of the creative, purposeful management of the conditions by those mutually oriented and actively engaged therein. The field movement is toward the need-fulfillment of members, the specific direction of which emerges from existing conditions, all of which are fluid and modifiable. Each field has direction but from vastly different points of view and with dissimilar effects upon the self.

9. *As to how the field as a whole is improved.* The associationist holds that the field is improved by the discovery of new and irreducible elements, together with their heretofore unknown combinations and associations. A few people with inherent drives use the laws of associative spread and similarity to push continuously into the unknown. They produce the new materials, ideas, arrangements, which are added to and organized in the environment by a small group of their associates, to be taught to and learned by the many at appropriate stages of their development. Novel phenomena, such as the discovery and isolation of new mental elements, are merely a combination of simpler earlier existing units. A new learning act is a synthesis in the present of a sequence of previously existing units. To prepare a person to discover new elements to enrich the field, more of the existing irreducible elements and their relations are taught him in the early years of his life. Since most people have neither the drive nor the specific ability to achieve such results, a few persons create the new mental elements while the majority become followers, absorbing what they can of the wisdom of their superiors by authoritarian methods.

The field theorist believes that the field as a whole is improved by qualitative interaction. Each member converts the environment to meet his needs intelligently, returning to it creative insights and meanings which never existed before for him or anyone else. Every person is born with the capacity for such creative field improvement, for without it he could not exist. The field is always emerging or becoming, since it is managed as a fluid whole by creative individuals. The field theorist helps them experience and conceptualize to the limits of their expanding abilities the creative management of their fluid fields every year of their lives.

10. *As to the educational emphasis.* The associationist assumes elementarism, which is that all behavior starts with irreducible, fixed, and unchanging mental elements which in their various combinations, associations, and syntheses form

the essence of and the basic preparation for adulthood. He divides life into large areas which are analyzed for smaller subdivision, until eventually these unit elements with their corresponding stimuli and appropriate responses are isolated. Since these atomistic units are the basis for complete living for everyone, he insists that they be taught as fixed responses to all children in schools. They can be identified, described, and objectively measured, so they become the materials for the scientific study of education. Through his past achievement in learning such essences, each pupil is given a position on a quantitative scale, which is used by his teachers to predict his future educational behaviors. A student high on the scale will have greater success in learning more of the same kind of things than one with a low position. Teaching method is analyzed into a series of steps or a sequence of operations compatible with the particular unit, such as methods of teaching reading, languages, algebra, history, and the like. How an individual learns or develops is frequently studied, but only to help him improve his conformity to the essences. Variability or nonconformity is educational heresy. Anyone who examines practices from first grade to graduate university will see this basic point of view in increasing operational control as he ascends the educational ladder.

The field theorist assumes holism, which is that all behavior emerges from the dynamics of the living whole at all times in its development. Parts are differentiated by and from the whole, discrete elements do not and cannot exist, the essence of life is creative change or modifiability of the whole in purposeful operation. The common essential in all living organisms is the process by which they carry on their differentiative development while maturing their integrative unity. Growing, behaving, learning, educating are all synonyms for whole living. The field-theory school helps everyone to understand and accept through use a critically appraised meaning of his creative life process. It begins with the life experiences of its members and develops them toward self-enhancement, recognizing that this is a variable outcome. In simplified form, the educational distinction is that field theorists emphasize developmental process while associationists strive for their fixed ends. This is probably the quickest way to observe in action the chief difference between the two concepts of psychological fields.

11. *As to the adequacy of the theory.* Every theory is a general statement of fundamental principles designed to explain and hold together in some common unity events or experiences which are known concretely. Every person develops theories in order to accept and organize into himself more of the selected fruits of everyday living. They help him understand and explain to himself his inner life, his overt behavior, his interpersonal process, his relationship to inanimate things in his environment, his actions toward or within existing social institutions, his behavior in all other roles of life. All students of behavior require some theoretical frame of reference in order to make plans for its improvement. Therefore, a pertinent question is how valid are the two theories in describing a psychological field which squares with the known conceptual and visceral experiences of growing people.

Both theories assume that learning is behaving or that learning changes behavior. To the associationist all behavior is composed of a few irreducible prior existing elements or fixed and immutable truths. Learning is acquiring these elements and truths in correct form under external controls by some form of conditioning. Improvement in learning is a change in the response system by deliberate or unconscious linkage or association of a new stimulus with old or new responses. This binding or linking of the new stimulus and response is always in the direction of some perfect achievement inherent in an anticipated goal. Thus increasing quality of behavior is a function of the quantity of responses and their probability of producing the perfect result. Novel response is merely a new and more complicated combination of prior existing simple elements. It can be produced by only a few individuals who are especially educated for this purpose. The masses are followers of the handed-down wisdom of the few.

To the field theorist behavior is the responding of the whole organism to the total confronting situation in order to control it or reduce need tension in the direction of life-fulfillment. Behavior is the organism in active interaction with the environment, during which process both are modifying or changing each other. A situation can be defined operationally only in relation to a specific organism. The organism can be defined operationally to obtain predictive power for behavior only in reference to the situation which it faces. Thus each serves to define the other, for each exists only in an organism–situation field. Learning is the product of living in mutual interaction with others so that everyone can fulfill his inherent biological promise. Each person learns what he selects and accepts to live by. He learns it to the degree to which he accepts it or to the extent to which he acts on it as he acquires it. He learns it as he creates it in the ongoing life process. By supporting an organic interpersonal group, field theory develops mature people who believe in it and continue it.

Some students state frankly that they see no differences between the two psychological fields. To them, the contrasts are just another way of saying the same thing. Each field is based upon approximately the same concepts. They derive their support from three sources. (1) Psychologists and philosophers, especially associationists, have attempted in recent years to show that they hold field theory beliefs. (2) The long period of time during which associationism has dominated the social institutions of every culture gives it a validity which no mere upstart can claim. (3) Their own successful experience is founded upon association theories of learning.

But there are two aspects of their situation which they may

have inadequately examined. First, their success may be due to learnings derived by the field theory process in uncontrolled experiences. Every person has a few of these even in a tight culture. These few may have had a marked effect upon the development of an individual with a receptive genetic pattern or a high energy potential. He may have lived in an authoritarian field loose enough to allow him to grow by a developmental process, even though he could not recognize or conceptualize it. Second, individuals may be rationalizing their association methods to protect themselves. They are unwilling to differentiate their learnings to new and different meanings which they cannot face. I try to help them by surveying briefly the historical background of each theory and suggesting that they study it further.

The association psychology with its accompanying philosophy originated in the a priori thinking which came down to us from Plato and Aristotle. Plato was deeply opposed to change. He lived in a world that was always in quest of certainty. To prevent the chaos which follows change and to insure the evenness of life which accompanies certainty, he sought a concept of man in his universe which permitted no change, but was grounded in universal immutable elements and their relationships. He reduced life to the same timeless, changeless, absolute principles which he found in mathematics. And since there were only a few men who could be educated so as to recollect and contemplate upon these timeless principles, which existed with them in their spirit world prior to their earthly existence, it followed that such persons should be the rulers of the state. Thus began the basic theory of aggregate fields which has been used continuously by all authoritarian personalities down to the present time.

Field theory psychology with its accompanying philosophy originated in the study of life as people know it, of experience as self-conscious activity, of man as a biological whole integrating his thinking and bodily movements into one continuous action, of persons examining together the life they have thus far lived in order to understand its process, of individuals interacting as groups so as to enhance the selves of all. Thus field theory grew out of a respect for people, for the process that is life, for the change that is growth, for the emerging intelligence that is direction, for the action that is the test of meanings, for the self that is the center of his universe.

The movement from the a priori philosophy of authority to the common-sense philosophy of experience had many aspects and was furthered by many people. Galileo (1564–1642) questioned the Aristotelian concept of nature and Charles Darwin (1809–1822) expanded man's outlook in relation to it. Many philosophers from Thomas Hobbes (1588–1679) to Herbert Spencer (1820–1903) supported the philosophy of experience but retained many of the atomistic controls. William Harvey (1578–1657), Claude Bernard (1813–1878), H. S. Jennings (1868–1947), Sir Charles Sherrington (1857–1952), and many others laid the biological foundations. The earlier experimental psychologists in Europe, beginning with Ernest Weber (1795–1878) and Wilhelm Wundt (1832–1920), continued the fixed element analysis of behavior in an authoritarian field. Their techniques became the basis of psychological research and educational experimentation throughout the world. In this country, Charles Peirce (1839–1914), William James (1842–1910), John Dewey (1859–1952), and William H. Kilpatrick (1871–) developed the meaning of experience into a philosophy and psychology based upon organic-field force and energy concepts. Many others in all modern life sciences have contributed their creative thinking to the interpretation of cooperative interaction of organism with environment.

Thus the underlying question is whether man shall continue to allow the a priori reasoning of Plato and Aristotle to govern and restrict his concept of himself in an aggregate field, or whether he shall use the more recent experiential evidence to release and develop his capacities through a normal biological process in a cooperative field. There seems to be no middle ground, no eclectic position which is adequate. A favored philosophical and educational movement is to use the organism-in-environment concept to promote a priori ends. This is supported deliberately by those who disparage modern evidence of how man develops self-maturity in a culture. It is promoted autonomically by others who have not yet differentiated the meanings underlying their actions. Everyone takes a position through his behavior, whether or not he recognizes it. And someday the cooperative field will prevail, for man cannot continue indefinitely to reverse his biological process through his accumulated culture and keep intact as an integrating self.

HOW DO THE TWO FIELDS OPERATE IN PRACTICE?

The curiosity of parents and educators about the two concepts of psychological fields does not end with a discussion of theoretical bases. They raise many other pertinent questions. They want to know why the associationist and field theorist use many of the same terms, and how they differ on school practices. I am selecting, therefore, a few principles of learning generally accepted in both fields to show how meanings and practices under them differ.

1. *All children are born with a capacity to learn.* To an associationist this means book learning or teaching pupils in schools the knowledge which he has selected from the culture and written in appropriate form for them to learn. His whole scheme of education or system of schools is so organized. The direction is toward selecting and encouraging the small number of pupils with high ability to think with abstract symbols. He offers no such opportunity for the majority with low abstract ability to develop their inherited capacities. Continuity is developed by ever-increasing academic requirements from

one grade to another, from one division to another, or from a bachelor's to a doctor's degree. The chief function of such an educational ladder in practice is to eliminate (although an associationist hesitates to admit this) pupils who in the judgment of observers show little promise of academic achievement. The educator who accepts this point of view refers to the few with academic ability as gifted and to the many as slow learners, or he may say that one group has high and the other low intelligence as measured by his academic scales. While admitting the capacity of everyone to learn, he prepares required courses of study, supplies uniform textbooks, gives standardized achievement tests, and uses other methods to control the scope and direction of teaching in the interests of the few.

The field theorist believes that every child is born with a capacity to learn, but that children cannot learn the same things at the same time in the same way with the same results. He assumes that no individual under existing life experiences ever discovers and develops his inherited capacity. The authoritarian cultural institutions in which he is reared will not allow him to do so. He believes that every individual learns by reconstructing his own experiences, which are his only educational capital. The secondhand materials from books or the firsthand interactions with people must be creatively assimilated. Intelligence is the functional ability to profit by or to improve or to creatively remake in action one's own experiences, whatever they are.

The field theorist strives constantly to spread the functional thinking developed by groups as they cooperatively resolve their needs. He believes that all individuals can develop better selves through their biological learning process, even though many may never achieve abstract reasoning. He organizes the school system around the conditions now known to be best for enabling children to release and develop their capacities toward becoming mature selves. He abolishes the academic hierarchy which denies to so many pupils the opportunity to improve the quality of their experiences. To him, a program which develops and spreads the functional thinking of everyone will enable the majority to evaluate better the academic thinking of the few, thus giving stability to cultural change. He eliminates subjects, uniform courses of study, promotions, degrees, and other accumulated devices of authoritarian fields and replaces them with pupils studying their own experiences in organic groups by a biological learning process. Each person assimilates necessary social skills to the degree desirable for his need-fulfillment, through cooperation with others to make life best for all.

Thus the same basic principle leads the two groups—associationists and field theorists—into directions as far apart educationally as the poles are geographically.

2. *All individuals are unique.* They differ from each other from conception to death upon almost any characteristics one wishes to name from genetic pattern through physical height to social morality. While the principle of uniqueness is now generally accepted, what to do about it is still a moot question. The associationist studies individual differences better to mold pupils toward or to eliminate them from the academic learnings which he believes are the educational essentials. If his knowledge of individual differences were functional, he would see that this practice is both humanly impossible and socially undesirable. The academic man has always been so far removed from the realities of biological growth and learning that the nonacademic masses have originated and supported many movements for cooperative interaction as a way of life. Yet pupils who fall below designated grade or subject standards are given remedial treatment designed to bring them into acceptable relation with external academic norms. Deviations from the essentials of subjects must be corrected, for conformity and uniformity are good, creativeness and variability are evil.

The field theorist accepts, respects, and enhances individual differences since they are the basis of individuality, which is both a personal asset and a social contribution. But these variable capacities to learn or private and individual ways of thinking or personal perceptions of self and others must be developed in life experiences by a process which socializes everyone to eliminate oddities, peculiarities, or idiosyncrasies from their lives. The better each develops his unique individuality, the more he can contribute positively to others and the more he is capable of receiving from them. The field theorist studies, promotes, and improves the conditions favorable to the development of mature persons whose uniqueness is grounded in social interaction. Unique behaviors derived outside this process lead individuals eventually to deny or reverse it, thus promoting authoritarian fields.

While both groups recognize individual differences, one grooves them while the other releases and develops them. Each believes that his practice is in the best interests of all.

3. *Learning is a tendency to action in the nerve cells.* The biological evidence indicates that learning does not increase the size of the brain, neither does it add one cell to the organism, as some psychologists at one time believed. Each normal child is born a complete operating energy unit, with the nervous system acting as the unifying integrating force. He has two brains and two nervous systems. One is the autonomic brain or thalamic region at the upper reaches of the autonomic nervous system. The other is a larger and more complex structure at the upper end of the central cerebrospinal nervous system. While these two systems are complete units in themselves, they work together cooperatively for interactive action, but on the principle of integrative dominance. This means that one is the integrative center which controls action, while energy from the other system is draining or being released into it.

Evidence available at the moment shows that readiness to

act in certain ways or some tendencies to action are centered more in one system than in the other. All emotional, impulsive, compulsive behavior, sometimes referred to as feelings, attitudes, beliefs, or values, is centered more in the autonomic than in the cerebrospinal system. All thoughtful, deliberative, reasonable actions are centered more in the cerebrospinal than in the autonomic system. While both function in every act, one tends to spearhead the motion, while the other gives it an energy boost. Each individual must resolve his conflicts promptly or the impulsive tendency of the autonomic system will prevail, since it is a part of the biological life system with deeper roots in physiological maintenance than the central deliberative system. Some feeling enters into every deliberative act, and some thinking is involved in every impulsive behavior. Psychologists refer to visceral and cortical thinking and feeling. When the individual thinks with the autonomic visceral system, the result is stomach ulcers or a similar structural impairment. When he feels with the cortex, it is usually a hard, cold, calculating expression of sympathy devoid of sincerity, warmth, and friendliness.

The autonomic or visceral system is the basic or life system. It controls the smooth, involuntary muscles and their functions. This system is ready for action at birth, having been activated in part during embryonic life. The cerebrospinal system controlling the voluntary muscles has to mature after birth before it begins to function on any conceptual level recognized by outside persons. While the child matures physically, both systems are building into their very structure as tendencies to action the behaviors accepted by the child for dealing successfully with his growing self and his changing environment. Since most parents are authoritarian, their interest is centered on specific responses rather than the process by which the child derives them. All such behavior involves both feeling and thinking. And each child learns as a tendency to action what he feels and thinks, not the specific outward action which the parent requires. So the child really learns his inner response to the external demands.

Since the cerebrospinal system is less developed at birth than the autonomic and since the child has limited experience and even less process for thoughtful action, his early tendencies are a feeling tone in his autonomic or life system. For his future self-development, it is imperative that these early feelings be an acceptance rather than a rejection of the environmental demands. An early favorable autonomic response makes it easier for the two systems later to function cooperatively to achieve the normal, wholesome, mature self toward which everyone strives. The test of learning is not found in the number of years in school or their accompanying degrees, but in the tendencies to action which each individual builds into the nervous system as a result of such exposure. If he receives his higher degree with his old adolescent tendencies to action, as many people do, both he and the public are the losers. And the institution should promptly be examined for its fitness to award such degrees.

The differences between the action of an associationist and that of a field theorist can now be briefly stated. The former believes: (a) What takes place in the cortex of the brain is superior to what goes on in the viscera, or how a pupil feels about what he is taught is relatively unimportant. (b) Behavior is controlled by cerebral response or by linkages among objective facts, information, knowledge. (c) Changes in feelings, attitudes, values come through more and better academic information, or inadequate feelings and attitudes are due to a lack of pertinent knowledge. (d) When pupils are given the right cortical response by appropriate conditioning, the correct or desired behavior follows. To improve his citizenship a pupil studies more United States history, to develop thoughtful action he is taught mathematics, to change his moral behavior he is indoctrinated with the fixed truths of ethics or religion. The educational slogan is: Find the facts, face the facts, follow the facts. Learn the truth so that you will always be controlled by and act on it.

The associationist becomes concerned about the feeling and attitude concomitants of cortical learnings only when they resist, retard, or conflict with the desired cortical responses. He makes case studies of the resisting individuals to determine the appropriate measures for facilitating their outward acceptance of his desired ends. Rarely does he change the outside demands upon a normal person or one with sufficient capacity to learn what he expects of him. For those with less ability he reduces the demand for cortical responses to the minimum essentials, arranged in their simplest unit relationships. Sometimes such pupils are placed in special classes or eliminated from school. Usually they are designated as slow learners, to be given an unequal chance in school, to be harassed by parents under the guise of promoting their best interests, to be treated as inferiors by their peers. Thus do associationists operate on the theory that visceral responses are controlled by cortical information. If a pupil is given the right knowledge the right behavior results.

The field theorist takes a different point of view regarding this principle that all learning is a tendency to action in the nerve cells. (a) He accepts, as does the associationist, the basic assumption that pupils learn all over in every experience, or the whole organism operates in every learning act. (b) He holds that feeling and thinking or visceral and cortical activity are but two aspects of the same internal and external behavior. They are unified in action by the individual through his purposes for resolving his needs. (c) The field theorist furnishes the environment in which he can help the pupil discover and resolve his needs with others through deliberative action so as to maintain unitary wholeness, with the autonomic system furnishing the physiological energy to support continued thoughtful endeavor. The pupil releases his earlier autonomic tendencies so that others can help him reorganize them on higher and more integrative levels.

The field theorist realizes that changes in the self are more a visceral response than an intellectual response. He is concerned over what a pupil accepts into himself or incorporates through his visceral system, or how and what he feels when he is conceptualizing his actions. Cortical knowledge changes overt action only when it is accepted into and released by the autonomic system. This is true whether the release be for or against such knowledge. If academic belief in facts brings action to improve existing conditions, all racial discrimination and inequality can be eliminated immediately. But people do not follow the facts. They follow their tendencies to action built into the autonomic system prior to the cortical teaching. And the academic knowledge does not change their old responses into more favorable action. Since the field theorist is concerned with the whole individual, including his early behavior tendencies, he accepts the biological learning process as being more favorable for continued self-development than are the reverse teaching methods. Through it the individual can facilitate action on even higher integrative levels.

4. *Need or interest, set or readiness, is the most important single factor in determining quality of learning.* One hundred years ago associationists believed effort to be the single factor in qualitative learning. Then came the Herbartians, who defined learning as the process by which the old apperceptive mass assimilated the new external materials taught. The readiness or willingness of the old to take in the new they called interest. This aroused internal controversy with champions for the older effort and vigorous advocates for the newer interest theory. In 1895, John Dewey cleared the atmosphere by stating that both sides accepted the same basic educational position, namely, that what is to be learned is selected and organized by adults without reference to the self of the

learner. The difference was merely one of method. Should the subject matter be taught by coercion or through interest? He pointed out further that interest and effort were not opposed to each other, but were merely the inner and outer aspects of a normal individual-in-environment action.

About thirty years ago, the intelligence testers asserted that the best single factor in determining quality of learning was the intelligence quotient or mental age or some other norm of academic predictability. Now this has passed from the psychological and educational scene. Both the associationist and the field theorist agree that there is some internal need or interest, set or readiness, which governs the amount and direction of the energy released, the nature of the materials taken in, and the area and depth of the internal reconstruction of the experience. These internal factors determine the quality of learning. So each group utilizes needs of pupils in its educational program but in a different way.

Associationists think of need or interest, set or readiness, as external motivation or stimulation of the pupil to show by his outward behavior that he is accepting the subject matter which they intend to teach him regardless of whether he is or is not interested. Their experimental evidence shows that if they interest him in the material by various approaches, he learns more subject matter, which is their primary objective. Therefore, they get him in readiness for or they prepare him to receive without too much internal resistance what they are about to give him. While the practice varies between the elementary school and university, the basic theory is the same. The associationist uses many devices through which to make his subject matter palatable. He divides it into units, with approaches, activities, culminating suggestions, and essentials. Frequently he uses a pseudo-cooperative approach, called pupil-teacher planning or group discussion techniques, which are only means to his preconceived ends.

The field theorist thinks of need as the internal disturbance

which releases energy for its resolution to achieve a new
equilibrium. He helps the individual to locate, conceptualize,
clarify, and focus his disturbance. He then helps him to resolve it by taking in from the surrounding environment the
best objects he can find and converting them to his best use.
The field theorist knows that each person must learn this
need process through his own experiences. He does not think
of need as a motivating force for teaching preconceived ends,
since he promotes a fluid dynamic process for upbuilding the
self within its inherited capacity. This is not an end in the
association sense, but a direction of growth or learning. He
concentrates on helping pupils understand the process and he
lets the ends fall where they may, knowing that if the process
is sound the individual variations in common experiences will
be socially acceptable. Each person learns specific knowledges
or facts or moral principles when they have value to him in
resolving his need intelligently. Thus the field theorist begins
with the existing need of the pupil and shows him how to
develop it as broadly, deeply, and thoughtfully as possible.

5. *Emotions are necessary for and vital to learning.* I have
greater difficulty in stating this principle than any of the
others, if I am to include the area of agreement and difference. The reason is that recognition of emotions and definition of their relation to learning is of recent origin both for
psychologists and educators. The association school, in which
the pronouncements of others were learned from books by
conditioned-response methods, provided a largely intellectual
education or learning through the mind only. Since 1900 the
gradually developing concepts of self and personality, of
normal and abnormal people, and of mature and immature
individuals have caused both psychologists and educators to
take into account the emotions of pupils as a learned aspect of
behavior. To different writers emotion means a movement
of or stirring up of activities of the flesh, an increasing state
of tension in the organism, some strong agitated inner dis-

turbance, a sudden acute change in energy level. A more careful study indicates that the tension within the organism has at least three important aspects: (a) a private, consciously felt, internal personal effect due to interaction; (b) a complex internal biochemical process set off by the visceral brain and integrated through the autonomic nervous system; (c) some overt behavior expressing the feeling effect of the internal changes according to previously learned tendencies to action under such conditions. While psychologists and educators are primarily concerned with the third aspect, or the overt behavior, they cannot and do not overlook the effect of the other two upon it. But they disagree as to the meaning of all three.

Internal tension is correlative with life. Through it single-celled organisms carry on their life process. With it multiple-celled, highly complex organisms called people maintain internal balance while facing external situations. This tension is never static, is constantly changing. Some internal tensions can be quantitatively measured, such as the heart beat, respiration, blood pressure, blood sugar, muscle tone, and the like. The effect of varied external conditions on these internal responses has also been carefully studied. The degree of tension in any individual at any time is due to how the self perceives the existing situation. This may be placed roughly on a scale beginning at the bottom with just enough tension to maintain the life processes and rising to the point where the individual becomes so tense that he "blows his top" for organic protection. Between these two points are various degrees, sometimes indicated as mild, deep, and disruptive.

The relations between these degrees of tension and learning are extremely important. (a) Tension must be raised from that characteristic of a minimum life process to higher levels to facilitate learning. (b) Each individual has an optimum tension range within which his resources are best mobilized for thoughtful, deliberative action. (c) Beyond this range integrative dominance shifts from the cerebrospinal to the autonomic system or from deliberative to impulsive action. (d) Every individual must locate for himself the limits of this optimum range, the internal and external conditions that raise or lower it, and the symptoms accompanying such movement. (e) The emotion is the readiness for action, but it is not the cause of the particular action. (f) The particular action is a function of the individual's perception of the relation of field conditions to his self.

The psychological aspects of any emotion for every individual are always the same in kind, though they may differ in degree. His meaning of field conditions determines the degree of emotion, the amount of energy available, the direction and nature of or adequacy of the action in releasing the tension. When the threat to the self is great, the tension is high, the perception is narrow, the meanings are cloudy, and control of the protective action is autonomic rather than deliberative. When the perceptions offer no threat, the vision is broad, experience is released, meanings are clarified, and the action is thoughtful. When emotion is dissipated under threat, tension tends to remain high long after the original situation disappears. When it is converted without threat, tension tends to remain within the range for optimum learning. It may ascend briefly but it returns to normal without damaging effects. The degree of emotion and the direction of action to release it are learned. Each affects the other. Both are of great educational significance.

The differences in practice between the two theories may now be better located. The associationist increases the emotion of a pupil as a driving force to motivate learning of the knowledge which he has organized to teach. He applies this in different ways or to different degrees at various times in the life of the learner. From birth to postadolescence, in home and school, the associationist raises the emotions of the child to seal in him specific behaviors so that he will never be able to unseal them, or will feel guilty if later he does so, to examine their value intelligently. These behaviors fall in the life areas of human relations, sex, and religion. In the compulsory school years the associationist raises the emotional level of a pupil or gets him in readiness through motivating activities to expect a certain direction of action, but teaches him subject matter quite unrelated to it. His purpose is to teach the subject matter, not to fulfill the needs or interests aroused. He attaches the biologically inadequate subject matter to an adequate need, so that later the pupil disgorges it on demand without the original need, in the same way that a trained dog salivates when his master rings a bell. This is a carry-over into human learning of the conditioning of primary or basic hunger drives of animals in mazes or authoritarian fields from which the concept of trial-and-error learning was derived.

In colleges and universities the associationist presents his organized subject knowledge objectively, leaving each student to his own resources to develop his emotional energy for such learning or accept failure as the consequence. He feels that the student should have adequate internal self drive for his work, or should change to another field, or should be dropped from college even though he lacked previous opportunity to develop the internal emotional maturity for accepting such responsibility. The professor believes that his teaching increases in quality as it becomes more objective and impersonal.

The associationist measures objectively the knowledge which he has taught the pupil without regard for his emotions. Sometimes he attempts to find the feelings of students after the test has been scored so that they will not affect the final mark in the course. His measuring instruments eliminate all reference to the process or field conditions affecting his learning or opportunity for the pupil to indicate them. He infers the validity of his objective results in predicting behavior in similar and frequently in all future situations, regardless of the field forces. He always operates under a psychological dichotomy, for he teaches and measures in an authoritarian field, while he expects the student to show the mature emotional readiness developed in a cooperative field. The associationist becomes concerned over the degree of internal tensions on all levels from elementary to graduate school only when his unrelenting pressure for his specific ends by reverse teaching methods forces the learner to overt behavior deviating widely or consistently from his accepted norms. If the overt behavior deviates slightly or widely in a direction of conformity or submissiveness, the degree of tension is not examined since the submissive action is wholly desirable.

The field theorist takes a different viewpoint of emotions, which he applies consistently throughout the life of the individual. In home, school, or life anywhere the field theorist helps a child or a college student to interact so that tension does not rise above the optimum level for deliberative action. When it does become disruptive, he helps him to understand and accept this as just an incident in normal growth. He never deliberately raises the emotional level by controlled external means to seal specific accepted behaviors from future change, since he has no such absolutes and rejects such emotional indoctrination.

The field theorist accepts the need tension indicated by the learner and works with him within it to improve the quality of his need process. He accepts the feeling and thinking of the pupil at any given moment as representing his best use of self-selected learnings under the total situational conditions including himself. The field theorist begins where normal self or personal energy is already high enough for desirable learning. He does not stimulate it by artificial means toward his own ends.

The field theorist accepts the evidence that all knowledge behavior or learning is emotionally colored by the individual who creates and integrates it within himself. Since it is a part of him, it must be subjective. Knowledge does not reside in any external inanimate object or thing or product of the efforts of deceased humans, whatever their cultural status. Each individual knows only what he invents, modifies, and supports by visceral and conceptual evidence in overt actions. Objective knowledge does not and cannot exist and consequently cannot be taught to pupils in schools. A person teaches as objective knowledge his need-satisfactions approved by others in the same cultural area with a similar degree of differentiation in their respective fields. He insists that they be taught to others as if they had an independent, immutable existence and a universal value for all.

The field theorist maintains that since emotion enters into all behavior, teachers, leaders, or parents should help younger people accept their emotional tensions, see them as one aspect of total self-development, recognize them as the source of self or personal energy, and bring them under the control of thinking to guide action in the particular experience. By accepting, understanding, and guiding his feelings through thinking, the developing learner has few occasions to fear, reject, suppress, or divert their energy into self-arresting behavior.

The field theorist is concerned over the tensions of each individual at all times as they rise or fall internally and as they are expressed in overt action. But he gives little weight to group norms and individual deviations therefrom, derived through objective instruments. Central tendencies or normative principles are extremely inaccurate in predicting individual behavior, for they do not locate what constitutes the self, which is the guiding factor in energy release. He is most concerned that field conditions help each individual recognize and bring his tensions, whatever they may be, gradually and consistently under the control of thinking.

The field theorist believes that expressing emotion is a vital contribution to normal and wholesome interaction, that each individual must feel free to release his inner feelings, and that others must accept and respect them, even though they disagree with them. He also believes that only through interaction in organic groups can each person obtain a realistic view of what his feelings are, how they affect others, and how he can better integrate them into his developing self. Since each is always in interaction with his environment, his emotions are always being modified in some way in every experience.

The field theorist holds that adequate evaluation of behavior, by behaver or observer, must include the field conditions out of which it emerged according to the perceptions of the behaver. Evaluating is an integral and continuous aspect of learning how to improve the quality of judgments and decisions made in action situations. When behaviors of learners are abstracted from their field conditions and given comparative numerical ratings by others on scales in their field and with their perceptions, such judgments contribute little toward improving the actions of behaver or rater and are therefore of slight educational significance.

Since overt behavior is but one aspect of a whole life, the field theorist holds that the best comparable basis for examining and understanding tendencies to action is the total process by which such observed behavior emerged. Whether the field be authoritarian or cooperative, the behavior of an individual is always a function of the quality of the operating process. The most significant difference, therefore, between an associationist and a field theorist, psychologist or educator, is that the former examines the product and ignores the process, while the latter improves the process and accepts the product.

A BACKWARD AND FORWARD LOOK

This discussion of qualitative learning always brings many questions from students, since the point of view is in sharp contrast with what they have learned in psychology courses, most of which are based upon aggregate or authoritarian fields. They have difficulty in accepting the fact that a psychological field is present in all behavior. I stress the differences in theory and practice between aggregate and organic fields because these, rather than the agreements, define the field conditions. But some student will invariably say, "Why not take a middle of the road position?" Usually he has two reasons: to select and synthesize the good in each, and to avoid the possible conflict involved in taking sides. No such position exists in theory or practice. Persons advocating it are associationists who have borrowed some field theory concepts to attract superficial observers, or verbal field theorists facile with academic symbols, while their old autonomic selves guide their authoritarian actions with superficial humaneness. A hybrid field does not at the moment exist, for the basic assumptions of each are as far apart as normal biological growth is from externally controlled teaching. The eclectic person operates in one field, verbally borrowing from the other such concepts as will protect his self under changing external conditions.

Many persons and educators ask, "Where is the control in the cooperative field?" The control is in the field process or the process of interpersonal relations, as it is in the aggregate field. Objections colored with high emotional tension arise immediately. They believe that control comes from some external source representing superior authority, higher power, or infinite wisdom. They fail to recognize that external wisdom must be introduced into the field by some person through some interpersonal process which shapes, organizes, or directs the action of the persons therein. Any meaning presented affects the area of inquiry, the concept each person has of himself, the freedom for selecting and accepting learnings, the over-all climate which modifies field dynamics, and all other aspects of interaction. This holds regardless of what any individual believes is the source of his meanings. If he

asserts that they are derived from a superior source, if he is
sure of their infinite validity and power, he always introduces
them in such a way as to limit the field of inquiry, thereby
proscribing the process. He is unwilling to allow others to
challenge and discuss his sources by cooperative interaction,
eventually rejecting his interpretation and attempts to manipulate their action. So the control in any field is in the
process. And the action results in authoritarian or cooperative
fields are not the same in kind or quality.

Students with successful achievement in the usual courses
in association psychologies ask two questions which have general value. One is, "Is it true that everyone learns by trial
and error?" No such learning ever exists even with animals
in authoritarian fields, where it was formulated. The error is
in the experimenter who believes that desirable learning represents the shortest line between a fixed beginning point and
a fixed end point known only to him. The behavior of an
animal is always purposive, while that of a child begins on a
purposive level and rises to a purposeful level. Whether an
animal, a child, or an adult, the behaver is always as purposive
or purposeful as he can be under the circumstances. His behavior represents his best judgment, autonomic or conceptual, under existing conditions as he perceives them. To
say that either animal or child has errors in his actions,
because they are not accepted by the adult with his perceptions based upon evidence withheld from the behaver, is
an inadequate if not a naive interpretation of behavior. Recent experiments with animals who were allowed to use their
intelligence deny earlier conclusions of trial-and-error learning. In any event it does not square with the biological
growth process and is therefore an inadequate basis for improving learning.

The second question of students is, "I have been taught
that all learning is painful. Where is the pain in this process?
Can a person learn anything important without pain?" Quali-

tative learning means changing the concept of the self toward self-enhancement on higher operating levels. To change the self is just as normal from a biological point of view as it is to grow in physical size from birth to adolescence. But students assert that it hurts to change the self, whereas it does not hurt to grow from three to six feet in height. And it really does hurt a self to change its self-concept derived by an abnormal process in an authoritarian field. Physical growth would be equally hurtful if the process were tampered with or restricted by outside forces. If the normal process of physical growth were reversed at birth, as is the self process, most babies would not survive and the few that did would be hopelessly deformed. While developing the self to its existing level may have been painful and will probably continue to be so as it matures, the causes are the abnormal conditions under which it grows. Pain or hurt are not characteristics of desirable learning. They are behavior symptoms of an inadequate process.

Many students who believe that progress comes through research ask, "Does field theory eliminate research?" That depends upon how one defines research. Most research in psychology and education is diligent systematic inquiry or investigation of a problem or hypothesis, in an authoritarian field under association theories of learning, by a small group of persons, in order to discover new facts, principles, or truth. The product or new truth discovered by the researcher to meet his needs is detached from the process and given to educators as objective truth, to be used by them in revising the purposes, materials, or expected outcomes of their teaching. This is known as scientific subject matter to distinguish it from that existing prior to the development of such research techniques. The value given it is due largely to the position of the researcher in the educational hierarchy, since the mysticism which surrounds or pervades his actions tends to make others believe that his process is above or beyond the reach of the common man. Thus the need-satisfaction of a few persons becomes the educational demands of the many. No one denies the right of the researcher to locate and meet his needs by appropriate means, but his results are merely data for the child or adult to accept or reject according to their value to him in meeting his own needs intelligently.

The field theorist has a different meaning for the word research. To him it means purposeful, systematic, thoughtful inquiry by anyone to create the new meanings necessary to raise the quality of his experiences so as to resolve his need tensions on a higher level of self-fulfillment. He does not have to discover any unusual, fixed, or universal truth unknown to others. He knows his need actions are not objective knowledge to be given to others as such. He is merely using a dynamic process of inquiry through which to extend, refine, and enrich his meanings necessary to reconstruct himself creatively. This concept of research is as old as the *Republic* of Plato or the *Dialogues* of Aristotle. It has always been and still is inherent in all creative effort by everyone to improve the quality of himself as an ongoing organized whole. The field theorist accepts this concept of research and wants to make it available to everyone.

I always summarize this discussion on qualitative learning by again reminding students that all behavior is an attempt to satisfy need. Every act of any living individual—every recorded act of history—is the result of the efforts of someone to satisfy his need as he perceived it under the existing conditions. Every demand that a parent makes upon a school is a direction of action to meet his need. Every curriculum, however defined, offered to pupils satisfies the needs of the educators. What I write in this book gives me need-fulfillment at the moment better than any other point of view or position I can express. Everyone who reads what I write will accept or reject, select or eliminate, according to his perception of his needs. The educational program in every school or the organized living in every family is now and always has been based upon the need of someone. Usually it is that of an adult or group of adults, which is not the best center for qualitative learning for children. What adults accept and expect for themselves, they reject for children or learners. Their direction of action to meet their needs becomes a demand which denies younger people the right to develop their needs by deliberative inquiry. Adults are so sure they are right that they are willing to exploit their own children or commit each younger generation to successively greater inability to face their ever more complex life situations. The potential capacity of their own children for constructive deliberative action is rarely developed because their needs are ignored, their life process is thwarted, their respect for their own experiences is depreciated, their creative meanings are unrecognized, their self-selections are rejected as being inadequate or unsatisfactory.

The life area where adult demands are greatest and the exploitation of children is highest is in moral values, which I shall discuss in the next chapter. Yet in spite of association teachings in authoritarian fields, the will to live creatively, constructively, and socially continues to survive in all newborn infants—the wealth of the world.

Chapter **X**

DO SCHOOLS PROMOTE MORAL VALUES?

Everywhere people are examining, rethinking, and revising their values. Usually they do this slowly and continuously, with only slight changes in a few values over many years. But there have been times in recorded history like the present when conditions were such that people made sweeping revisions in many values simultaneously. Such action occurs when life activities change rapidly, when these changes cut deeply into the security of the self, when individuals feel inadequate to deal with such deep-seated disturbances, and when the continued use of existing values fails to give them the release from tension or satisfaction in the outcome which they desire. Three different directions of action have been proposed in the past and are advocated in the present to alleviate these disrupting conditions. One is to return to the good old values of ancient days, applying them without change but more rigidly and rigorously in present situations. Another is to make only the slightest modification necessary in old values better to use them under existing conditions. The third is to create new values within, through, and around the novel factors in present life situations, using whatever aspects of old values seem pertinent.

In view of such sharp differences, it seems appropriate to examine the proposals for action to see their relationship to the promotion of a democratic culture to which the people of the United States of America are committed. I do not propose to review the history of moral values or to weigh the arguments of advocates of the different positions. Neither do I intend to analyze the various beliefs held by different social, educational, and religious groups. Rather I shall discuss the psychology of moral values, how each individual obtains and develops them, how they affect his self concept and those of others with whom he associates. And I shall follow the point of view developed in earlier chapters. It is in a spirit of exploration, search, and inquiry that the following reflections are presented.

WHAT ARE VALUES?

In field theory psychology, values are *tendencies to action* or *directions in action* or the *actual behavior* of individuals in active interaction with their environment, as they perceive themselves operating in their life situations. Every action of every individual represents a preference for one behavior over another. The one selected is the best, the most desirable, the most important the individual is capable of at the moment, as he views all the conditions involved. But the overt behavior is only one aspect of the value. The other is the internal perception and judgment which operate from the beginning and continue in modified form until changes in the situation cause the value action to cease. So every observed direction of action is merely the externalization of the internal value judgments created simultaneously with the overt behavior. And every instance of action involves value judgment, whether it be autonomic or conceptual, for some form of purposeful, preferential, value action exists in every human organism.

These tendencies to action or directions in action are held

by individuals either as specific patterns or as general principles. Some have more of one than the other, for there is no standard desirable ratio between them. Recently I watched Guido Cantelli conduct the NBC Symphony Orchestra. The specific patterns of action of every player and the leader were clear, visible, distinguishable, yet they all blended together in a larger whole which gave a continuous flow of rhythmic organization or harmony of movement or melodious action. The applause indicated audience approval of these specific values which the members of the orchestra externalized. Children learn arithmetic or history facts or spelling or other fixed-in-advance responses as specific patterns. They are slightly modifiable ways of behaving which operate only under specific circumstances and do not spread to other life activities. The general principle of action is well illustrated by a junior high school boy who said, "You have to watch all teachers because they hurt you." His external behavior indicated his internal acceptance of his value built a number of years before in relation to a subject for which he saw no need, taught by a teacher who had little sensitivity to him as a growing boy. He spread his self-created value to all teachers in and out of school and even to nonteachers who assumed an authoritarian relationship to him. Yet he modified his general value judgment when we worked together to find the original conditions under which it was formed. Of the two, the general value offers more opportunity for growth, since specific patterns should be more refined aspects of the broader principle or general direction of action.

DOES EVERY INDIVIDUAL HAVE VALUES?

Every individual must have values to exist as a self or to maintain his integrity as a striving, integrating, developing organism. No individual can aggregate his experiences up to any given moment in any year of his life. He is not a mere collector of experiences; he is a selector, evaluator, and reorganizer of them. He merges one into another, selecting from each those learnings which he believes will better help him to meet his needs in the future. He judges pragmatically or operationally the effect of his selections in new experiences, thereby evaluating the value of the original selections. Thus the initial situations recede, the selections are modified, new and better clarified value judgments are made, the affected area of experience is reconstructed, and the self achieves greater unity and integrity. So values are means of holding in the self large areas of prior experience whose original identification is now lost. And the values held as general principles are more important for subsequent action than the specific responses, since they hold together more past and present experience and have a wider spread to new experiences. Yet each is constantly being modified slightly or radically in every new life activity.

But the statement that each individual must have values to maintain the integrity of himself is not a judgment of their quality as viewed by the observer of his behavior. To the behaver values always represent quality, for they are his best action judgments in moving life situations. Psychoneurotics believe their values are right in spite of the objections of other people who live with them. So every individual has values regardless of how much or how little disagreement there may be between him and others as to their merits.

Many students are concerned and frequently shocked to know that every individual lives by and with values, even though others may or may not accept them. Immediately they ask, "What does the individual do with his values or how does he use them?" He uses them wherever he has a choice of action or whenever he makes a decision between or among possibilities of behavior. This means that he uses them all of the time, for choices, judgments, weighing of possibilities, and decisions for action are going on every moment in every life experience. I am making value judgments as I select the sentences and words which make up this paragraph. And the sentence selections are made in the light of broader values which I hold about education, children, learning, culture, and their relationship to each other. So value judgments are made in both the broadest and the narrowest parts of any experience: the former in determining which of the many possible life experiences the individual will engage in and the latter in differentiative refinement of the various parts of such experience. And that students may better see how values function, I participate with them in analyzing their current individual and group experiences to locate decision points and to see what and how values determine their actions.

Since all individuals have values, all cultures or culture groups have values, as they are people satisfying their needs. All institutions within culture groups have values, as they are people performing certain services for the benefit of all. And since every modern culture has schools, the schools must have and must operate by values. Yet values are not the same from culture to culture or among institutions within a culture. Thus there arise conflicts among cultures as well as stresses and strains within cultures. Honesty or dishonesty toward people may or may not be the best policy, depending upon where one lives. Cooperative, interactive behavior may be desirable within a tribe or a subculture but not with other tribes or with all parts of the same culture. All schools have values even though they seem to differ widely from culture to culture. And all schools within a culture have values even though there may be sharp disagreement as to their meanings and practices.

When this point is established students ask another question, "If every individual, culture, institution, or school has values, why should there be so much argument about values of schools?" The argument is not one of values versus no values, because the latter condition does not and cannot exist. The argument arises because some individuals or groups believe they have superior values and therefore should impose them upon all other individuals and groups. They are not willing to give others freedom to accept or reject such values, for this would deny their superiority. They try to impose them by association methods in an authoritarian field in order to keep their preferences intact. So the problem is not whether the school promotes values. It has to in order to exist. And every adult should know that the real struggle now, as it always has been, is over whose values and what psychological field shall control it.

HOW DO INDIVIDUALS OBTAIN VALUES?

There is a sharp distinction between the way individuals obtain and the way they build values.

These will be considered.

Children obtain values by psychic, emotional, or social contagion, usually as specific patterns of action in particular situations. These are the dominant or controlling tendencies in the immediate and general family environment in which they are reared. Such specific patterns are introduced by adults into their experiences at the outset in order to limit the area of activity and control the action toward their individual or group preferences. Adults deliberately groove the experiences of children into the patterns of behavior which meet their value judgments.

Every child is born and reared in an environment organized around values. Since he is dependent upon adults for his very life, he has to adjust, adapt, conform to their demands. He begins and maintains his postuterine existence by absorbing autonomically those values which the family accepts and imposes for better or worse. Physically this is not too difficult. Adults offer him food, rest, shelter, and warmth, usually in amount, quality, and rhythm that he can reasonably assimilate. But his needs go beyond mere satisfaction of physical wants. He has self needs. He is striving to adjust to his environment so as to develop the internal purposing, creativeness, and unity with which he was conceived, by which he has grown, and through which he will emerge as a consciously behaving self.

These self needs are relatively more important to the infant or child at the moment than are his physical wants, since they have a greater total effect upon who he is to become. So he barters the specific behaviors which adults demand for the affection and security so necessary to his growing self. He barters to the limit of his endurance his normal biological growth process for their emotionally charged conditioned-response values. Both the adult values and the method of obtaining them have less autonomic use to him at that moment than the security and belongingness which only his parents can give.

Yet normal living for a child or an adult should exude affection, security, and belongingness as field conditions forever present, emotionally felt, and intellectually understood. No individual should be constrained to barter his normal growth for behaviors which give or deny him these necessities. Too late he discovers that in return he received authoritarian affection, aggregate belongingness, dependent emotional security, and arrested self-development. Parents maintain authoritarian fields because they do not understand how their children grow. They are immature in parent–child relationships as a result of the inadequacy of their own early life. Many believe they have the legal and moral right to shape the self of their child in their own image, such as it may be. They have never pondered the remark of Emerson that one of them is enough for any culture to survive.

That children obtain values by unconscious methods cannot be denied, neither can it be prevented. But there are three characteristics of such methods which should be noted. First, the value comes from outside sources and is introduced at the beginning of the child's experience in order to control his behavior in a direction desired by the outside persons. Second, restricting his experience causes his emotional tension to rise, since the method more than the value denies his normal growth process. Third, parents deliberately produce and manipulate such tension through abnormal field conditions in order to place around the value an intense emotional seal which the child will never dare or know how to break. Thus he will be unable to interpret the value on a higher conscious level. They believe their imposed values are so right that they never should be changed. And as I have stated previously the three life areas in which such values are generally and deliberately sealed are those of sex, religion, and interpersonal relations. Every child begins school operating according to unconsciously accepted conditioned-response values emotionally sealed in an authoritarian field by adults who assume these values are right and good for him now and for all future time. Many adults really believe this in spite of the pyramiding evidence to the contrary. They had such beliefs sealed into them and are afraid to face realistically the effects upon their own lives.

HOW DO INDIVIDUALS BUILD VALUES?

Each individual builds his own values by thoughtful deliberative action in all life situations which he really faces. He begins with his needs, since they are basic self drives in all conscious behavior. He resolves them in interaction with his environment, internal and external, in which both are changed. He operates in a cooperative field in which all field factors, including his self and the cultural heritage, are modifiable. He self-controls the experience by critically appraising all resources, by thoughtfully selecting and converting all factors that shape covert and overt responses. He is consciously aware of his value process, which includes an identifiable need, a series of developing situations within it, a purposeful direction of responses toward deliberative action, a recognition, appraisal, and acceptance of the improved quality of his behavior. The functional level of the process rises as purposeful, creative thinking consistently permeates it. The quality of the total experiences is a function of his maturing capacities in his learning environment, assisted by understanding and helpful adults.

Values operate continuously within each need-experience, for they are brought into it in some way by every person associated with it. They emerge as purposes to implement action, they are modified as the experience moves toward its own elimination, they are criteria for making choices, they supply drive toward higher self-realization, they carry over into later behavior. Values, then, function in experience by constantly shaping it, being modified by it, emerging from it in critically appraised maturity, and again being remade in subsequent situations. But values are not fixed responses put into experience at the outset as a ready-made, unmodifiable truth to control it. They are variable approaches to life situations or mutable tendencies to action, critically appraised and creatively assimilated by the behaver. Built values begin in experience, are improved through experience, are learned creatively in the process of enriching experience, and are a product of experience consciously accepted into the self.

The educational problem involved in the method of obtaining or the process of building values is easy to locate, but it is difficult to resolve, because its roots are deeply imbedded in individual and cultural philosophies, even in metaphysical allegiances. Yet parents and educators must realistically face the two questions: (1) Should values be derived outside the experience of the learner from some remote and perhaps supernatural source to be used as fixed truth to control his behavior in a preconceived direction by conditioned-response teaching in an authoritarian field? (2) Should values be consciously built by the learner in the functional management of his own experience, growing out of it, re-entering into it as factors in determining direction, being used as criteria for judgments, supplying internal motivation, becoming modified in the process, reshaping it in retrospect, and reaching their highest relative formulation and clearest differentiation at the culmination of the experience?

Whether a person takes one or the other position is in itself a value judgment, however it may be derived. Regardless of position every person should face the fact that he is an operating system of values derived by both of these processes. What he really is to himself and how his behavior is perceived by others depends partly upon which source dominates him and the observer, and partly upon how aware each is of the nature of such dominance upon himself and others. For the sources are not of equal strength, neither do they maintain neutrality, armed or unarmed. Rather they form a unity, which is the self, around one or the other as the operating center. Whether values unconsciously obtained or consciously built control behavior is important in locating the existing level of maturity and the future possibilities for growth of every individual regardless of his chronological age.

The process of building values is in sharp contrast to the method of obtaining values. To lay the best foundation for continuing self-maturity each child in his early years should obtain a minimum of fixed values necessary for his existence, without emotional seals, in a phenomenal field emphasizing the process of building values. He will then have the stability of some fixed responses at a time when they are necessary for his growth, but without their damaging after-effects. He will be encouraged and guided by adults in making decisions, recognizing his value judgments, and assuming the consequences of his actions. Eventually he will integrate these early fixed responses into his consciously formulated general principles of action. Since they are thoughtfully and purposely developed by a normal process, he will spread them to all aspects of living, thus becoming a wholesome, balanced, integrated self. To achieve this the home and the school must have unity of purpose and cooperative action. Thus the educational conflict is not one of value versus no value, but one of what or whose values shall prevail and how they shall enter the lives of learners—children and adults.

WHAT IS A MORAL VALUE?

Individuals and groups have wide and deep differences in belief as to what is a moral value. Those in authoritarian fields disagree among themselves over the particular value, but not over the method by which it is derived and taught to others. All agree that values are exemplified or tested in overt behaviors in life situations. They also agree that moral means a certain quality or standard appropriate to the situation in the judgment of observers who are teachers rather than learners, parents rather than children, adults rather than young people.

These status persons expect those less favored to meet their requirements, which are founded upon demands made upon them by persons in higher positions or by the inherited traditions of the culture group. They judge the behavior of young people in such categories as what one does or does not do, what one's duty is or what one ought to do, or what is acceptable or unacceptable, or what is the right or wrong action as they see the situation, the right being the good, moral behavior and the wrong being the evil, immoral action. To these top persons, the moral act implies a specific rather than a general value taught to control the life of young people within the traditional cultural patterns. While they may disagree on the particular value, they agree on the method of teaching and the right and wrong or good and evil quality of the results. Their evaluative judgment is on the overt act, the conditioning being only a means to that end. The good act brings favorable consequences to the behaver and others, whereas the evil or immoral act has dire effects, primarily on the individual who exhibits it, in present or future life. All deviations from accepted cultural standards bring punishment in proportion to the extent of such heresy. There is, therefore, little psychological disagreement over the meaning of moral value among individuals and groups in authoritarian fields. They struggle for power to condition their values into everyone.

The disagreement between members of authoritarian and cooperative fields is sharper than among advocates of the former, for there are fewer common psychological points of view for discussion. In field theory psychology the moral quality of behavior lies in the entire process by which the learner resolves his life experiences. This includes the situations which he selects to face, the needs which they stir in him, the developmental choices which he makes, the direction of action which he accepts, and the consequences of the total behavior which he assumes. The morality does not lie in the final overt action but in every aspect of the process leading up to and including such action, all of which affects his future development and that of others with whom he associates. It is exceedingly important that he learn how to make choices, what to take into account in making them, how to anticipate the results of actions prior to or concurrent with their externalization, and how to assume the consequences, whatever they may be. Thus value actions obtained in an authoritarian field have a different moral quality from those built intelligently in a cooperative field. Those learned in any field by psychic or emotional contagion are lower on a moral scale than those derived by thoughtful appraisal. Since each individual has both, the moral quality of his behavior is a function of the operating relationship of the two within the self.

Since every act regardless of its derivation affects both the behaver and others in the situation, every value used by any person to influence another, directly or indirectly, either as to ends or means, is a moral value. Thus all life situations are moral situations, the relationships are moral relationships, and the values used by each person therein are moral values. Whatever an individual selects to accept into himself to affect his tendency to action is moral, since he externalizes such self changes to affect the behavior of others. No individual can designate interpersonal situations in which he elects to use values morally and others in which he chooses to use the same or other values without moral implications. Their use modifies him and his environment, and therefore the morality is inherent in the interacting situation and cannot be introduced or eliminated at the choice of any person. Being alive as a purposing, striving, creating organism is moral since the mere maintenance of life affects others and no individual can escape from the moral consequences of living, no matter how much he may wish to do so. The value he uses in any situation is moral regardless of what it is, how he acquired it, and whether he is integrating or disintegrating as a person.

While individuals differ in the way they introduce their values into life situations or how directive or nondirective they are in promoting them, their intent is always to influence the behavior of others engaged therein. Therefore, regardless of the derivation of the value or the method of using it, the value is always a moral value.

Every school, public or private, is a moral institution. Every institution permitted to function in a culture to carry on activities of group living is a moral institution. Home, church, formal community organizations, the basic economic system, informal social groups, the political and governmental structure, all are moral undertakings. They do not have the same effect upon members, but all use values for influencing their behavior. Every social institution is moral by the choices it makes, by what it includes, by what it discards.

A school has a peculiar responsibility in this respect. It is organized to help children grow into participating adulthood within certain general agreements formulated by the people as a whole. What they include in the school, directly in the curriculum, indirectly in the organization, less formally in the general life, is based upon value, for they accept some experiences and reject many from unlimited cultural possibilities. Thus adults make moral decisions by the choices of what they include in the schools for their children. However, their high moral values may become immoral values for the growing child if they structure his environment so as to deny him the right to choose among alternatives in situations arising out of his personal and social needs in his surrounding culture. The more authoritarian the field or the more restricted the right of choice, the more immoral the value, since the child must unintelligently abide by it or outwardly conform to it.

Every aspect of the school program has in it some form of morality. How it is organized, what constitutes the curriculum, the nature of the school life, the way each teacher works with children, the decisions he makes, the requirements he imposes, the examinations he gives, what the school accepts or rejects every minute of the day, all affect children or college students ranging from high morality as seen by the adult to direct and positive immorality as seen by the learner. Degrees of morality are directly related to the quality of the interpersonal relations between adults and pupils. When creative conversion operates openly in the use of values, moral quality is high. When authoritarian teaching denies it, moral quality is low, even approaching immorality in its effects. Thus what is a high moral value under authoritarian conditioned-response teaching may be a low moral value under cooperative field theory learning.

WHAT ARE DEMOCRATIC MORAL VALUES?

We, the people of the United States, expect schools, public and private, to promote or further democratic moral values to the end that all children will accept and use them in their daily living now and in the future. We want democratic moral values to become tendencies to action of all children in all life situations at all times. And this is a reasonable expectation. Since every human relationship is moral and since every psychological, social, political, religious, or educational field promotes moral values, the word democratic must connote a certain quality of relationship among people in their various life activities. Such values must grow out of or be developed in field conditions favorable to such quality. Some educational, religious, or economic fields engender democratic moral values by emotional contagion or deliberative acceptance; others promote authoritarian values which are different if not definitely opposed to them. I have already drawn distinctions between authoritarian and democratic fields. I shall carry these further by contrasting sharply a few of the most important differences in the meaning of moral values. The emphasis will be psychological rather than political or economic, since quality of behavior in all roles of life depends upon the psychological quality of the self.

1. In a democracy all human beings are accepted and respected as ends in themselves, not as means to ends fixed by others to promote their favored institution or fixed system of life which they control and perpetuate. All individuals are respected because they have a potential creative capacity for becoming unique selves functioning with others to extend and enrich the living of all. The creative possibilities in each individual are unlimited and unexplored, owing to environmental conditions which prevent such search. Yet regardless of existing conditions the democratic concept of respect for the individual has been repeatedly stated, never better than in the words of Abraham Lincoln, "I hope I may live to see the day when an unfettered start and a fair chance in the race for life is guaranteed to every American child." Such respect for potential capacity to become a unique self is not recognized and accepted in authoritarian fields. Those in control believe that they respect the individ-

ual when they condition him to their preconceived truth or fixed systems of life, coerce his uniqueness into autonomic conformity, and give him the "opportunity" to liquidate himself for their welfare or to meet their ends "for the good of the state." The democratic psychological field operates through creative, experimental inquiry; the authoritarian field maintains itself through regimented, controlled indoctrination. Thus the affective moral values are far apart.

2. In a democracy life and education operate to help each individual discover and develop to the fullest extent the potential capacity with which he is endowed. Each is born with a capacity to be developed, not with it already developed. The ability to work with others toward deliberative action is not an original endowment. It is learned in and through life experiences in order to become operational behavior. Schools help children find and utilize their capacity, each in his own unique way through his experiences toward his maximum maturity. The program of activities is cooperatively selected and managed to facilitate such growth. An authoritarian culture permits no such respect for the potential capacity of the individual. To help him discover and functionally release his inherited ability would most certainly spell the downfall of those who control him. They suppress the capacity of the masses through followership rituals, while allowing a few to be grooved into slightly higher patterns of conforming action. Their purpose is to hold potential ability in check as dangerous to their interests. In either case there is judgment, responsibility, and action, but the moral quality is different.

3. A democratic culture releases and develops potential capacity through a biological growth or need-experience process. People recognize that learning is just an outward and upward extension of their life process into the higher realm of conscious behavior. They admit that it has to be identified, used, and accepted by each in his life experience through

conscious thinking and action. They believe that such process
is cooperative and interactive and is the basic continuity in
their lives from conception to death. Thus they are willing
to fight for the morality of the process, for without it their
democracy ceases to exist. This contrasts sharply with authoritarian fields, in which the moral quality lies in the end
behaviors while the immoral quality of the method of imposing them is overlooked. If the end is right, any method
of manipulating an individual to accept it is moral, for the
end justifies the means. Whatever the effect upon the self of
the acceptor, it is to his good whether he likes it or not, for
it is within the meaning of good held by his controller.

At this point students usually ask, "Are there some ends
that are superior to others or have greater value than others?"
To this I reply, "Yes, but the morality of the ends cannot be
separated from the process by which they were derived."
Ends achieved by a democratic process in a democracy are
always superior to ends derived by authoritarian methods regardless of the benevolence of the authority. Furthermore,
any value taught by authoritarian methods which deny critical inquiry, appraisal, and an opportunity to modify the
value to the limit of rejection cannot be justified under
democratic morality, for it cannot be creatively assimilated
by each individual. Many parents and educators hold that
the schools should teach "democratic values" as verbal, academic end-responses, but of course they are never functional.
The democratic quality of the behavior is determined by
the extent to which the individual creates his own new
meanings in its development.

4. Democratic moral values operate in the direction of
better acceptance of the self by self. Self-enhancement is not
a fixed position on a progress scale, neither is it an exact or
absolute value. It is a moving dynamic person striving for
higher operating unity within himself in an ever-expanding
relationship with his environment. It is universal in that
every individual grows in that direction regardless of his

inherited capacity or the environment in which he lives. But it is variable, creative, emergent. Each maturing self is developed by the self through integrative differentiation of his own experiences. He cannot develop through meanings derived by others in their fields and passed on to him by authoritarian methods. He can use their experiences as resources which he can modify to meet his needs. He creates his knowledge or truth as he verifies it in his experiences by his purposes in his field. He controls his behavior through the empirical procedures by which he develops and tests his meanings. He believes that ordinary events of life are so interwoven that they can be recognized, explained, and interpreted only in terms of their operations, the field conditions from which they arose, and the empirical consequences to which they lead. The inherited tendency of every individual to move toward self-enhancement has in and of itself no moral quality. But the way he interacts with other people in his culture to develop his growing self does have moral quality.

The people of every culture can rightfully hold that their culture helps its members achieve selfhood. But the meaning of self, the quality of the interaction by which it develops, the effect of past process upon future growth, and many other conditions are so very different that they may be directly opposed to each other. The people of the United States expect their schools to aid all learners to develop democratic moral selves, with the self-maturity which it implies. They study the behavior of all other moral selves within or without the country better to insure belief in and modifiable stability of their own democratic way of life.

WHAT ARE SPIRITUAL VALUES?

Adults generally use the two adjectives moral and spiritual to describe the values which they wish their children to accept. Since we as a people are committed to democratic moral values, we should be consistent and support democratic spiritual values. To many individuals moral and spiritual values are different in kind because of their origin, function, and effect. And many books have been written describing those differences. But from a democratic point of view, moral and spiritual values have the same origin, function, and effect in experience. They differ only in degree on a behavior scale, spiritual being of higher quality since it releases more potential ability to convert and refine more experience. The individual creates actions which really astound him and others. He feels lifted above his usual everyday operating self into levels of integrative vision which heretofore he did not consciously possess. These higher, though sometimes momentary, levels occur because all aspects of the need situation facilitate the relaxed self-control so necessary for spiritual creativeness. Thus all democratic values are not spiritual values since the cooperative process, internal and external, may not be operating at its best. Authoritarian values rarely have spiritual quality in this meaning, for they do not release the highest creativeness of individuals. Whatever their spiritual power may be, it must stem from other sources and be found in other aspects of behavior. From the field theory or democratic point of view a value or a behavior is spiritual when made in the widest perception of the world of reality and on the highest operating level of thinking of which the self is capable at that moment. And these two principles requires some explanation.

1. Reality is the perceptual field as it is experienced, reacted to, or interacted with by the individual. No individual can react to or interact with absolute reality, whatever that may be. He reacts only to what he perceives in the situations which he faces in everyday living. To achieve spiritual quality in behavior he must continuously increase the area of his world of reality. (a) He reaches out for many new experiences of a different kind from those which already constitute his perceptual field. He builds new interests in and

purposes with the surrounding environment on an ever wider and deeper relationship. These become the leaven through which he reconstructs his prior experiences. (b) He consciously and deliberately increases his awareness to include more factors in every situation which he faces. He is sensitive to more people and the ways in which they behave. He sees more nonhuman conditions and how they function in human action. He creates new meanings and relationships among the dynamic conditions within and outside himself. He extends his range of creative interactions with others into ever wider social and cultural relations. (c) He recognizes that his spiritual quality is in him, in his own everpresent creative biological life process. This is the "spirit that giveth life," or "the kingdom of God is within you," both simple and clear expressions of the meaning and spiritual nature of his creativeness. His potential spiritual quality is conceived in him to be achieved daily in his striving to become a better self in interaction with a facilitating environment. (d) The internal striving must be externalized in a way that promises spiritual quality in his behavior. This is his need-experience process through which he can and will raise his actions to unknown conscious levels. Through it, in a modifiable field, he releases more of his creative energy to the growth of himself and others. (e) He must constantly reconstruct himself by remaking old meanings, creating new ones, differentiating new aspects of his phenomenal field, clarifying old ones, shifting figure–ground relationships. He is at all times creatively fluid, dynamically organized, thoughtfully secure, and interactively related to his environment including himself. And no person can reach high spiritual quality when his values are emotionally sealed into him in early years, for this sealing blocks a large area of his potential creativeness from functional use.

2. The high operating level of thinking necessary for spiritual quality extends above and beyond anything which the

individual has heretofore experienced. He creatively reaches up for something better. He strives to free himself from the drag of uniformity and conformity so well expressed by Emerson in the words, "Too low they build, who build beneath these stars." Thinking is the internal aspect of the total behavior in any given situation. It is a covert symbolic action that never stops but merely changes direction with the changing field conditions. It includes everything that the individual does to study a situation so as to select the most appropriate way of dealing with it prior to overt action. It is every movement during overt action to study consequences by relating them back to the purposes desired, the means used, and the need to be fulfilled. It is all that the individual does in retrospect to draw conclusions from the whole experiences and to project them as covert symbolic data into new situations. Thinking is a unified organism creating-in-situation to control a dynamically impinging field in the direction of self-enhancement.

These two principles of the widest perception of the world of reality and the highest operating level of thinking of which the individual is capable at that moment are the basis of the spiritual quality of moral values or behavior. While every individual creates that quality for himself, he cannot achieve these highest levels alone. He must grow up in an environment that helps him reach out and up in himself and in his world. No special situations are necessary to teach children spiritual values. The psychological conditions promoting need-fulfillment and self-realization are those in which perception is widened and sharpened, thinking reaches its highest level, and moral judgments transcend the commonplace to spiritual quality. But there is one other aspect of covert behavior or symbolic thinking which must be mentioned. With the guidance of others, each individual must criticize and appraise his specific behaviors to integrate them into a few generalized values which are more dependable in revising upward his subsequent actions. Thus he becomes a self who is flexibly secure, intelligently creative, and spiritually moral in all of his value judgments.

And so there is a distinction between moral and spiritual values within a democratic field, as there is between them in an authoritarian field. But the differences between the two fields are much greater. Obtaining or building moral and spiritual values in an authoritarian field is inadequate preparation for achieving them in a democratic field. While parents, educators, and the public agree that all schools should promote moral and spiritual values, they have not yet decided whose values should be taught and in what field. If they should eventually agree upon democratic moral and spiritual values, they must have the courage to remake all of their cultural institutions. Without such a decision, authoritarian moral and spiritual values will continue to control them.

HOW DOES THE WAY VALUES ARE LEARNED AFFECT THE SELF?

Throughout this book I have used the word self in a variety of relationships within a constant frame of reference which I shall now summarize briefly in order to show how the method or process of learning values affects the self. I find difficulty in discussing the self as unitary functioning, since the vocabulary which I must employ grew out of philosophical dualism, psychological atomism, and educational authoritarianism.

Self is a shorthand word for the individual as known only to the individual, for the awareness of being, for conscious functioning as "I" or "me" with all the meanings related thereto, for the life which the individual accepts as *his* life. For there is a life known to the life, whatever people may name it, whatever they may believe about its origin or possibilities, or however it may act. This life or self begins at conception and grows, develops, matures through interaction

with its environment both internal and external, a process
held in common with every other living organism. But the
young of man have possibilities of developing selfhood on
the psychological moral spiritual level which distinguishes
them from the brutes. A man can recognize himself from
others, he can see and study how his behavior affects others,
he can separate, define, and think about past, present, and
possible future events in relation to his actions, he can focus
the selected resources of his experience toward deliberative
action in any situation he may face. No life at conception or
birth possesses this high level called selfhood. It must be
achieved, and man alone has the capacity to attain it. The
movement of life or the self from the moment of conception
is in the direction of the highest moral and spiritual level
of selfhood of which it is capable.

While every developing self shares the biological growth
process with others, perhaps the most common characteristic
of selves is that they are all different. Each is unique from
the beginning in its tailor-made genetic pattern up to any
moment of action throughout life. Psychologists describe
this unique self as being composed of two interacting aspects.
One is the *self concept*, which is what the individual considers himself to be or what he thinks he really is. It is composed of those parts of the phenomenal field which he has
selected and differentiated as a definite, relatively stable, consistent characteristic of himself. His self concept is his inner
core or real, true, genuine, and intimate self. The other aspect
of the self is the *outer sheath* surrounding the inner core
and known as the protective, seeming, acting, pseudo-self or
ego. The self concept is relatively better established and more
permanent than the protective sheath, which takes the first
shocks of interaction with the environment. This unique
self is the center of the individual's phenomenal field, which
is always organized by him around him. His field, his organization of it, and his self are not open to observation

by outside persons. They can observe what he does or how he acts, from which they infer his protective sheath, but rarely the inner core, which is seldom revealed to the critical and perhaps hostile stares of observers. Whether the self is what is known only to the self or whether it is what is inferred by the outside observer or both, everything which constitutes it is always changing, always dynamic, always becoming. The self is not the sum of anything, for it is not a quantity. Rather it is the qualitative selection and focus of learnings operating in every action situation. This unique self is not composed of body and mind, but is body-mind organism or unitary life interacting with its environment. Also there is no self and environment but only self-environment relationships or the self-in-continuous-interaction with nonself aspects of the individual's universe. And all of these relationships are so close, so necessary, and so unitary that in real life they must be considered aspects of a functional situation in order to interpret behavior adequately. To separate them is to emphasize either the individual or his environment and to neglect the interactive process which is the most important aspect of each.

The growing, developing self is the center of all behavior, for the self *is* the learning, the interacting, the maturing. It is the unified life that struggles to continue living. The predictive quality of the action lies in the self concept or the extent to which it functions in particular situations. If the field conditions are favorable, the inner self directs action promptly. If conditions are unfavorable, the outer self uses various protective mechanisms to shield the inner self from hurt. The more unwilling the individual is to modify his self concept through a critical examination of how he behaves, the less he is likely to expose it to public observation. The predictive quality of his behavior either to the individual or to an outside observer lies in an understanding of what is his self concept. And the way in which such concept is acquired, the process by which it is accepted, or the method by which it is imposed has a profound effect upon the total self—the inner, unifying, real self and the structure of the sheath which protects it.

The self differs from the a priori concepts of mind or conscience or soul of the traditional philosophy and psychology. They originated outside the individual as a superior power with which he must identify himself and to which he must give allegiance. They represent the perfect, unchanging, lasting reality of the dualistic metaphysics. The self is the organized life, ever moving, constantly regenerating itself, continuously emerging into a richer life on higher operating levels within the realities of its own experiences. It is not an entity placed in the body to shape the growth and action of the organism to its goals. It is the dynamic purposeful life unity trying to maintain and improve its integrity within its potential capacity with the nutrients available in its environment. In either case every individual has a self concept which is the center of his behavior. And anyone who can locate and understand it can better predict how the individual is likely to act in given situations under certain circumstances.

The individual interacts as a whole to his phenomenal field as the self perceives it from its internal frame of reference, regardless of the consequences. But growing and learning evolve through differentiation of the unevenly developed phenomenal field. Some meanings and values are clear, exact, criticized, and tested in experience. Others are cloudy, loose, vaguely understood, seldom brought into conceptual examination. The phenomenal field is not divided into areas called the "id," the "ego," and the "super ego," from which arise unconscious, conscious, and conscientious behavior. It is organized as a whole into one unit around the self on a figure–ground relationship, those meanings and values in the figure being highly differentiated while those in the ground trail off to a gross total mass of experience. The self is in the figure or the area relatively more differentiated than the surrounding group. Highly conscious behavior corresponds to or originates in the highly differentiated parts of the field, while vague, indefinite, fuzzy behavior comes from the vague and uncompletely differentiated aspects. While all behavior emanates from the self and is generally consistent with it, there are times when it originates in some less differentiated part of the phenomenal field to satisfy needs that are still gross total disturbances, not yet centered and symbolized. In such cases the self may reject the behavior as being inconsistent with it or the self may rationalize the behavior as belonging to it when in reality it denies the inner self concept.

Available evidence from many sources indicates that there are at least three distinguishable and clearly marked levels of differentiation of the self. On the first and highest, the meanings, values, and all other learnings are fully accepted as being in accord with the individual's concept of himself. These learnings are consciously and deliberately derived, critically appraised, and sharply defined. They are checked and rechecked with sensory, visceral, and intellectual experience. They are highly conceptualized and symbolized. They are the constant and consistent, yet fluid and dynamic growing zone through which the individual continues to increase the quality of his experience and his selfhood. He acquires these highly differentiated functional learnings by his biological growth or need-experience process in those life areas where it can operate. He affirms the validity of the learnings and the process through operational consequences in many and varied experiences. He learns to use and to trust his own physiological equipment in providing the data for making and continuously revising his value judgments. His self-differentiated learnings are the basic structure of his life, the life which to him is good to live.

On the second level, the self learnings are only partially differentiated and accepted. They are ideas and values intro-

jected into experience by an outside authority that emphasizes
their correct, perfect, enduring quality. They are parts of a
preconceived authoritarian system of ideas which adults do
not want him to question. They are so thoroughly impressed
into his experience with high emotional attitudes of threat,
fear, and guilt that he is unable to differentiate them on
higher levels. They remain inadequately symbolized and partially tested through personal organic evidence. The need-
value behavior emanating from this undifferentiated and
partially symbolized mass is antagonistic to other aspects
of the self, producing a threatening situation which must be
dealt with in some fashion. So the individual rationalizes it,
providing plausible rather than actual reasons for his behavior since they are too fanciful to acknowledge. He selects
some aspects of the situation which are self-enhancing and
ignores others which are not. He protects his self by so modifying his perceptions that what he has done or plans to do
will appear justifiable to him and others. Thus he removes
the feelings of guilt and anxiety, avoids discomfort, and makes
peace with himself. A child learns to give socially accepted
reasons for his behavior and learns to accept the reasons
which he gives. He forces himself into rationalization for social
deception which results in his own self-deception. And both
work well. He obtains social acceptance and protects his own
self-esteem by avoiding the guilt and anxiety which would arise
if he faced the real reasons for his behavior. By social deception he becomes acceptable to his parents and by self-deception
he tries to experience himself as the sort of person they think
he is. But the needs and values which instituted the action
are still only partially differentiated. Thus each individual
carries over into adult life a great mass of experience that is
partially symbolized, inadequately clarified, fearfully held,
and emotionally sealed. It is a serious threat to the more
deliberative, creative, and meaningful aspects of the self.

The third level of differentiation represents rejected learnings which are denied awareness because they are inconsistent with the self. One group represents behaviors initiated and carried on by the organism to meet physiological conditions without conscious control. Such behaviors are not regarded by the individual as a part of the self. The other group includes those visceral and sensory experiences which he disowns or rejects as impossible since the actions are contrary to his accepted self-concept.* Because of their threat to the existing self, such rejected behaviors are never brought into the orbit of even partial symbolization or meaningful recognition. The greater the threat, the tighter the individual closes the existing self structure. So all such rejected experiences are not open to differentiation on a higher level.

A tentative answer can now be given to the topic under consideration: How does the way values are learned affect the self? The way an individual learns his values determines their level of differentiation in the self at that time and profoundly affects levels of differentiation in the self throughout life. The method of learning values may promote the growth of the self to higher operating levels or it may permanently arrest the self on some lower level of development. While each self has all three levels of differentiation—the fully accepted, the partially accepted, and the rejected—each also has great variability in the proportion of total learnings falling into each level and in the quality of the differentiation within each level. Childhood values introjected by parents go into the second or partially accepted level, for they are based upon and presuppose adult experience. Children have little conceptual basis for understanding such values, parents generally do not relate them to their own needs within their experience, and children do not understand their need-experience process well enough to evaluate and clarify them on the highest level of differentiation.

Yet the child must have some values for the present good life in home and school. They can be brought into his experiences in either of two general ways: First, as fixed truth by an authoritarian method to control behavior, thereby surrounding them with emotional ties which the child dare not break; second, as temporary and reasonable guides to action in present situations, open to study and re-evaluation as experience expands, with final acceptance or rejection after the child has tested them functionally in many and varied situations. And in the difference between the two methods lies the difference in differentiation. In the former, the child is taught not to differentiate such values. In the latter, he learns values by a process which emphasizes how to differentiate them as life proceeds. While all individuals in childhood acquire some values each way, they obtain more of them by authoritarian method than by deliberative process. And the greater the area of experience obtained in either way, the more or the less can the individual integrate the self on higher levels. Adults should introduce values in the experiences of children as fluid guides to action, constantly changing as life experiences critically evolve. Therefore parents and educators should teach children how to live an evaluating process and help them build confidence in such process rather than in a rigid system of introjected responses.

The evidence to support this position may be summarized as follows. All behavior of an individual is pertinent and relevant to his phenomenal field as he sees it. The field is organized around himself as the center. He improves his behavior or learning through a clearer differentiation or perception of the field, which means himself in interaction with the non-self aspects. The field is organized on a psychological gradient from the highly differentiated figure to the less differentiated ground. In a normal field the energy flows continuously from the figure or self into the less differentiated ground, from which something is chosen to satisfy the self need. The more fluid the figure and the more flexible or available the ground, the more the entire field, including the self, can be clarified and reorganized on higher levels.

This interacting process of self with phenomenal environment takes place best when the self is free of threat from any source in the field. The individual releases more of his total energy for learning, perceives and accepts into the self structure more of his organic experiences, raises to the level of conscious criticism the introjected values of early years, accepts and consciously satisfies *all* his needs, thereby preventing the partial acceptance or rejection of those conflicting with the self. Thus a greater area of experience is available for conscious symbolization and organic self-valuing when field conditions permit the relaxed control necessary for creative assimilation of need selections into the inner self. And the individual develops to the maximum his inherited capacity to learn only when he continuously uses wider and deeper areas of the field on ever higher conceptual levels.

So the adult values of early years must enter the child's life without fear, regret, hate, or guilt in changing them later into more consciously differentiated meanings. For these feelings of regret, fear, hate, and guilt are an enormous waste of powerful organic energy. No person can ever build a better self on them. He can only wallow in their restricting and constricting slime. So the way in which an individual learns his values does affect the quality of the self. It controls the amount of potential capacity which he will release for learning, it frees or restricts the self in better differentiating more aspects of experience, it gives or denies confidence in data supplied by the individual's own sensory and visceral responses for making and continuously revising his value judgments.

HOW DOES THE PROCESS OF LEARNING AFFECT THE USE OF VALUES?

The way a value is learned determines how it will be used. Those upper level values which are built by the self consciously, deliberately, and intelligently are used intelligently. Those which are obtained by emotionally sealed introjection fall into the middle level and are used autonomically, unless the individual can raise them to the level of conceptual meaning. √Sealed values limit the release of the individual's inherited capacity, arrest his normal self-development, thereby causing him to produce a protective idealized image which eventually becomes a compulsive drive to action that depresses, depreciates, and even absorbs the real self. Thus the more important the adult value, the less it should be introjected into the child's experience. To preserve the value and mature the child, the value should be introduced into his activities with his fullest understanding and his highest emotional acceptance. There should be the closest validation through experience and the least possible preference or domination by adults. Values should be considered as any other cultural aspect—a way of effecting good living—to be changed as situations and circumstances evolve. They are developed in a phenomenal environment of warmth and protection, in an atmosphere of confidence, mutual trust and security, in friendly encouragement to test them in expanding experiences, and in a psychological climate of constructive discipline. Thus the child develops confidence in himself and others which is the basic confidence necessary to enhance his real self.

At this point students usually raise some objections. The first is that the self has to be organized. The child is too young to do it. Adults must place values in his experience at the outset to control it toward a desirable organization which he cannot achieve. So I tell them the story of my observations of the teaching of art in many schools in Europe. In the early grades children draw or paint everything in the greatest detail as to form and color, never missing the veins of a leaf, the parts of a flower, or a single blade of grass. The principal of one school, insisting upon the exactness in every detail, told me that the purpose was to organize the unorganized self, to unify the scattered pieces of the self, to furnish the self an ordered structure without which it would be lost, except that in each case he used the word soul where I have written the word self. His belief in the rightness of his actions was so compulsive that he would not even entertain suggestions for other ways by which the self could become organized or the unity of the soul could be preserved. Since the self is organized by the self, there is no issue as to who shall organize it. The issue is one of direction. Shall the self move upward toward maturity or regress toward earlier behaviors? The adult can either help or hinder the child in becoming a normal self. The principal who could not face himself impressed his limitations upon children, while telling them he was saving their souls.

But some student always says, "I cannot see the serious difficulties which you believe exist in introjective teaching of values." A survey of a group shows that others hold the same doubts. So I summarize these difficulties. First, each individual develops his real self through his need-experience process within his inherited capacity to learn. Others merely facilitate, frustrate, or deny him the opportunity to use this normal process. Especially do adults try to deny a child self-selection, creative assimilation, and differentiation of experience in the early years when he should be given the greatest sympathy, encouragement, and opportunity to find security in his own learning process. He organizes himself as best he can under difficult circumstances. Because of lack of experience with his process and the environment in which he must function, his efforts to enhance himself are not always satisfactory to him or to others. The remedy is not to introject adult values to control his behavior but to help him use better his life process on his level of experience so as to increase his insight into the real self which he is developing.

Second, the introduction of right values to control experience so limits the phenomenal field that normal expanding, differentiating, and integrating of the self is difficult, if not entirely denied. The child develops a conflict between his internal drives and the external demands which are the claims or expectations of adults already insecure in their behavior. This produces the basic anxiety which causes him to divert his energies from normal channels of self-enhancement to abnormal actions of compliance, aggressiveness, or aloofness. In such small beginnings and by such continued demands is developed the neurotic self with feelings of inferiority, self-rejection, unrealistic ambitions, vindictiveness toward others, a desire always to be right, and what is more damaging, a compulsive drive to satisfy his needs by demanding from others behaviors similar to those which arrested his real self. Many parents and educators rationalize their behavior as being for the good of the child, when in reality this behavior is their normal tendency to action in their phenomenal fields controlled by their introjected and partially accepted values.

A third important factor is that many parents and educators do not want children to control the organization of themselves through a normal growth process. They fear the results. They prefer that children and adults behave through undifferentiated values sealed into them in early years. They argue that such action is for the individual's good and is the only way to preserve the cultural heritage. This is their best possible behavior as they perceive themselves in their phenomenal field. And the only way to improve it is to help them become better selves.

At this point students ask, "What are the possibilities that a child born in our culture will grow up to be a normal self?" There are now generally open to him three possibilities. First, a few children will be fortunate enough to grow up normally in their environment by a need-experience process, creatively assimilating the surrounding culture to meet their needs. Adults help them by providing sympathetic understanding, a thorough knowledge of the process, a familiarity with possibilities in the environment, and a wholehearted, intelligent support of their decisions, judgments, and directions of behavior. All aspects of the self are constantly evaluated and refined through fluid figure–ground relationships. While such children will have an area of undifferentiated experience, they gradually conceptualize, test, and refine it through action. They develop deep, abiding, intelligently constructed values with no unbroken emotional seals. Such an opportunity to develop a normal self exists only to a limited degree in our culture.

The second and most prevalent direction is toward a self with only partial opportunity for full growth. The individual has a small core or fluid zone developed by a normal, biological process. He has a large area containing many introjected sealed values which are not and cannot be conceptualized or subjected to empirical tests. Each individual develops his own mechanisms for dealing with such a dualism, which—singly or in combination—do not enhance him. With little knowledge of his real self or the process of his actions, he tends to live only in an environment where his arrested development causes him and his associates little difficulty. He moves through life considering himself normal and making a satisfactory adjustment in a limited area. Here the observer finds a majority of the people today, usually including himself. Theoretically it is possible for any individual with sufficient need to move out of this category into the first one at any age in life, but few people ever achieve such reconversion. The need must be deep enough to release the blocked emotional zone of the self, and some form of group or individual therapy must be provided. Most people feel that the treatment is desirable for someone else but is too rigorous for them. They expand and contract their environment until they stabilize it at their developmental level, usually with excuses as to why they are unable to do better. Thus it is important that, during the years of physical growth, schools offer children opportunities to keep their whole personalities fluid, by helping them to use the process of their self-development.

The third and rapidly increasing group of people is moving toward the extinction of the real self, a state in which behavior is dominated by an idealized image, with all the compulsive neurotic claims, demands, expectations, and tendencies which such self-rejection implies. These persons have a deep but irrational belief in some cause. They know they are right, while those who disagree are wrong. They promote their neurotic ambitions at the expense of others by proclaiming that competitive human relations are based upon natural law. They are endlessly searching for, and mistaking a mirage for, the realities of life. And yet, regardless of direction of movement, the self, whatever it may be, is always organized by the self within the possibilities of the environment. The neurotic self is the result of attempts by a normal individual to live in a diseased environment.

But how is the process of differentiation of the self related to moral values and action? All behavior is moral, every action is moral, every deed, covert or overt, is moral, all life is moral. Thus everyone has moral behavior, but not everyone has the democratic moral behavior which the schools of the United States are organized to promote. Democratic morality is acting with others so as to discover, release, and develop the potential capacity of everyone. Only then can an individual become an end in himself instead of a means to the end of someone else. Democratic morality is based upon biological growth extended upward into conceptual behavior as a need-experience process permeating all levels of the self and all degrees of differentiation of the phenomenal field. It moves toward a thoughtful, deliberative, total self that creates and refines values through emergent experiences in the realities of life. The entire phenomenal field is open to conversion through interaction. The only constant is the modifiable life process. The real self, the inner core of reality or highly differentiated meanings called the self concept, is always bringing forward new constructs with other aspects of the self and phenomenal environment on one continuous direction of intelligent refinement through new figure–ground relationships. As new values arise, they are critically appraised and applied in emergent experience. Behavior is moral, values are democratic, action both internal and external is spiritual, since it emanates from a released self creatively remaking the internal and external environment to his own better development. Thus democratic morality is the action of a self which has intelligently built its own values in childhood years. And such morality is spiritual when the total organism is so relaxed and the external climate is so favorable that the self can extend beyond existing limits his creative insight into and thoughtful management of the experience. For democratic spiritual quality is always associated with constructive maturity, never with regressive adaptation.

But students ask, "What is the morality in an authoritarian field?" It is authoritarian morality but it is not democratic morality. If there be a spiritual quality in it, it is authoritarian spirituality, which comes from allegiance to or self-identification with the external force either individually or through a surrogate. Fixed values are introduced from without to control experience, normal learning becomes reverse teaching, child behaviors are sealed by immature adults, parents and teachers promote compulsive dependency or good actions, sensory and visceral experiences are the appearances of life, not to be trusted in evaluative action, and creativeness is so curbed into cultural patterns as to warp or deny its very existence. In such a field, action stems from restricted ability, undeveloped capacity, and compulsive dependence, and becomes autonomic morality. People do what they are told to do to satisfy the demands of their controllers, yet are taught to verbalize a hollow justification for their actions.

The authoritarian field can never become a source of democratic morality so long as it operates through introjected values. It is moral but not democratically moral. It is autonomically spiritual but not creatively spiritual, for it denies the creative process which it claims to foster. The inherited ability of man becomes the brain-washed dogmatism of those who would control others to their own ends. Democratic moral and spiritual values emerge and are incorporated into the self only under democratic field conditions. To perpetuate itself, every democratic society must expect all children to learn a need-experience process through living together in free public schools where such field conditions can operate. For private schools, with few exceptions, maintain authoritarian psychological fields through which to promote their own brand of autonomic morality.

A BACKWARD AND FORWARD LOOK

The question raised at the beginning of this chapter, "Do the schools promote moral values?" can now be examined in retrospect. Every school promotes both moral and spiritual values. But not all schools promote democratic moral and spiritual values. People giving allegiance to schools organized as authoritarian fields to promote authoritarian morality fear the release of capacity, the development of intelligence, the internally controlled selves, the spiritual quality of the interaction, which free democratic schools can and do promote. Rather than change their own institutions into democratic fields they use totalitarian techniques to disparage such democratic efforts. Since they cannot or will not have democratic morality, they assert that others do not have it, and thus attempt to distract the attention of the public from their own shortcomings and true intentions.

So the forward step must be taken if democracy is to survive. The children of all the people must attend a free public democratic process school during the period of compulsory education, so that they may mature themselves through the cooperative interaction in which resides the moral and spiritual quality for their continued development. Anyone who can read the behaviors of people in authoritarian cultural fields in any part of the world realizes that the time is not far distant when we the people of the United States of America must make such a major decision if we are to develop our humane authoritarian human relations into genuine democratic action.

Chapter XI

A FORWARD LOOK

I must now do what everyone does throughout life—evaluate my experiences in retrospect, either autonomically or conceptually or both, and select the learnings which I believe are most valuable in shaping my subsequent experiences toward better need-fulfillment. Every person takes up and carries on something from each life activity. He has somewhere within him traces of every experience from conception to this very moment of action. Each self has a little of every other self with which it has come in close association. But retrospective evaluation is made by a changed self in a different phenomenal field, a self different from the one making the process decisions by which the experience was developed to its consummation. And the forward look is always an integrative extension into future behavior of the retrospective selections, within the process used in making present decisions. A person who meets experiences through values introjected by authoritarian methods will make different selections from common past experiences than will the person who faces situations through criticized values of his own making. Thus the forward look is relative to the quality of the backward look, but both are dependent upon the method or process of meeting present experiences, or the ability of the individual consciously to define and constructively to translate his traces into predictive behavior.

The quality of the backward or forward look depends upon how well the individual has learned to create new meaningful relations between various things, objects, and persons or among all aspects of his phenomenal field, within himself as the center of his universe. The ability and drive to create are inherited, but the quality of the created meanings is learned. Under normal conditions, each person gradually builds his meanings into general principles by which he directs his own conduct and judges the behavior of others. He holds them as beliefs in which he has faith, trust, and confidence, for they are the integrating center of the self and are therefore coeval with his very life. Such meanings are not dogmas or fixed truth prescribed for him from without as specific codes of conduct. Rather they are personally derived by him, are based upon his perception of his experiences, are his immanent, dynamic, unique differentiations in his phenomenal field. These generalized values are flexible enough to be verified, modified, and recreated in subsequent experience. They are permanent enough to define broadly his life tendencies to an outside observer. They are inclusive enough to allow others the same freedom to develop their creative meanings into those differentiations which are their unique selves. Thus they are personalized creations, verified through behavior in social situations by their consequences to the individual and to others.

Every individual begins every new experience guided by previous meanings held as general principles of action, to be extended, enriched, clarified as the experience develops. I am no exception. I began writing this book with certain meanings, hypotheses, or generalizations about people to guide my actions. I shall now select some of them in retrospect, reformulate or recreate them in the present, and propose a few future trends which seem reasonable and valid inferences to me in my psychological field within the existing organization of myself or within the logic of my experience.

1. *Every individual creates himself*. Who he is now, who he was in the past, and who he expects to become in the future are all a product of the creativeness of the fertilized egg interacting with the external environment to become the normal baby, the growing child, the maturing adult.

2. *Every individual uses little of his potential capacity for creative growth*. He does not understand or is unable to interpret his biological growth process well enough to release and constructively employ such capacity to achieve his self-maturity. His development is restricted by the reverse cultural teaching methods of adults, who impose upon him their fixed ends or the products of the behavior of others which meet their needs.

3. *Every individual represents some form of arrested development on a maturity scale which has no known limits*. The cultural influences tend to stay the development and standardize the behavior of the masses of the people on some maintenance level of dependent relationship. A few individuals rebel against or circumvent such controls, thus moving to higher maturity than the culture group generally accepts. Many persons never rise even to the permitted levels. So adults form a skewed distribution toward the lower end of a maturity scale, since cultural pressure tends to produce such a result. The few near the top of the scale are relatively immature in relation to their potential capacity. They are only relatively mature in relation to the greater degree of arrested development of others.

4. *The biological drive or the life purpose for self fulfillment is always toward the highest possible maturity within the internal and external conditions*. Each individual has the physiological energy, the creative biological process, the life purpose, and the self-enhancement direction to reach a ma-

turity level way beyond any now extant. He lacks the field ✓
conditions in which to attain it.

5. *The great need of each individual is for a criticized, functional process of living which releases his capacity to create the new meanings necessary for differentiating his self on ever higher operating levels.* With this as his life continuity, he can so continuously and qualitatively reconstruct the environment that the atmosphere for normal growth and learning of all will be greatly improved.

6. *The better life which people everywhere in the world struggle to achieve can be realized only as they become more mature selves by a biological growth or need-experience process.* They have the inherited capacity to remake the external environment to that end. They lack the process necessary to convert this capacity into creative functional intelligence. With it, the possibilities for better living for everyone are unlimited. Without it, the struggle for mere existence will continue. For the better life can be achieved by man only through the release and development of more of his inherited creativeness in organic groups through deliberative social action. It will never be provided for him by any power outside himself.

7. *The home and school are the two most strategic institutions affecting the maturity of the individual.* They shape the beginning of the self. What a growing child feels, how he thinks, the values he acts by, his belief in himself and his experience, his attitudes toward people, how he approaches his life situations, are all shaped in some way by these two forms of group life. The adults carry in themselves and transmit to children their selections from the cultural heritage. If children are to grow to higher maturity, they must have more opportunity to make better selections in a richer environment in their years from birth to young adulthood. Their parents and teachers must become more mature selves, with confidence in young people and the courage to allow

them to develop by a normal process in a more flexible psychological field. Herein lies the core of the problem of creating a better life for all.

8. *The unity in a culture comes through the need-experience process.* All existing culture groups maintain their organization by a dual process. One is the need-experience process, by which a few people make the new additions, and the other is the reverse teaching method by which selected aspects are transmitted to the younger generation. Neither is adequate. Those who make the additions lack the insight into their need process to see the effect of their creative efforts upon themselves and others. Those who receive the indoctrinated and sealed responses become autonomic followers of tradition. Both groups are unwilling to face change and are unable to release their energy to guide it intelligently. The result is an aggregate cultural stability—based upon internal and external struggles for power—which characterizes authoritaritarian organizations. Unity is the interpersonal quality which emerges as people resolve their needs by cooperative interaction. To have it within or among culture groups, everyone must know how to use his need-experience process intelligently in all life situations. He can release his creative energy simultaneously to improve the quality of his experience and to help others—children or adults— grow through their needs. Wide differences in individual and group differentiations are expected and accepted. They offer no threat to anyone, for they are always open for modification by the biological process through which they were derived. So unified, but differentiated, culture groups can resolve disturbances arising among them and thus promote harmonious living for all.

9. *The professional competence of educators lies in the need-experience process.* In traditional aggregate education the professional competence of every educator at any level or in any type of position lies in his knowledge of the es-

sential subject matter, together with the approved methods of teaching it, within the framework of the authoritarian system. Educators spend years acquiring the designated knowledge, but only a brief period to obtain a superficial understanding of how they or their pupils grow, learn, or behave. Exposure to this quantity of knowledge, with appropriate responses at the right times to the right people, gives the credits necessary for entering the profession. Thereafter the individual keeps his certificate "alive" through alertness courses, most of which follow his preservice patterns. And the many attempts to improve such professional education are usually within aggregate groups by association psychologies.

If educators are to meet their responsibilities of educating all the people to become more mature selves, they must shift the operating center of professional education from subject matter to the need-experience process. Every person at every level, from kindergarten to graduate university, must be competent in the process, both in keeping himself maturing as a whole person in all aspects of life and in helping others— children and adults—use it to develop themselves. But this is not enough. Educators should take the lead in studying the process in order better to understand its meaning and application in every life situation in or out of school. Teacher-education institutions should be the center for educating men and women to become the process experts not only to serve in the schools but to act as consultants to every type of community institution. Every businessman should be able to call on the schools for help in dealing with human problems in his industry, for only by such cooperative, interactive process can private enterprise be maintained. Much of the difficulty between educators and parents or the public would disappear if all used such process in their deliberations instead of arguing about accepting results derived by noncooperative efforts. The school would then become the central integrating institution in American life and educators should

become the leaders in moving such life forward. Since direction is a function of the process rather than an end-product
manipulated by method, arguments over differentiated cultural aspects would be greatly reduced. Our plural culture
would be held together, as is the physical organism, by cooperative interaction among differentiated parts operating
for the benefit and perpetuation of the integrity of the whole.
Thus the schools would render the expected service to our
democratic society, and education would become a profession.

I have examined these meanings or generalized values from
a number of different points of view. I have discussed the
nature of the biological growth process and the concepts of
learning which facilitate or thwart it. I have concluded that
life never was constituted to function normally as two opposed growth systems, one for the body and one for the mind.
The person or self develops as a unit by one basic process in
which it selects something from the outside environment to
convert into new materials or forms of energy to satisfy its
inner disturbances. On the conscious learning level, this is
called the need-experience process. The self changes its
selected materials into its creative meanings, which become
tendencies to action in the nerve cells or the overt behavior
observed by outside individuals.

I have discussed the reasons why and the ways in which
individuals use the need-experience process to become better
selves, examining particularly the three related aspects. First
is the growing individual and the need which prompts his
actions; second is the nature of the external environment, or
what is sometimes called the culture; third is the way the two
get together, frequently referred to as the method or process
of their relationship. To the growing individual the order
of importance of these three is himself and his need, the
process of his relationship with the outside environment, and
the way this affects what he selects and converts to his use.
To the outside adult, the order is what he thinks is valuable

for younger people to learn in the outside environment, the method of teaching it to them, and the way it affects the growing self.

Various studies beginning during World War I show a number of important findings on the relationship of this need-experience process to the development of people. First, each individual must know all three aspects of it to reach normal maturity. Second, the most important and the most neglected of the three aspects for the growing child is an understanding of himself. Third, children constantly grope to find themselves because adults with whom they live do not know themselves, and therefore can furnish young people little help in self-understanding. Fourth, adults lead children to hunt for solutions to their problems or the answers to their needs in the nonhuman objects or fixed values existing in their environment. Fifth, when people seem to be the disturbing factor in a situation, adults never look to or in themselves to find contributing causes, but always place the blame upon other persons. Sixth, rarely do parents or educators see behavior as interaction toward need-fulfillment, for they are unwilling to locate and face the need which lies behind their actions. Seventh, adults organize themselves into groups and institutions to maintain their point of view about life and culture, with little knowledge of or regard for the normal biological process by which the young must grow to become the mature people which they expect. The result is a neurotic paradox, since adults expect a quality of behavior which they will not allow children to develop. So everyone is or becomes an arrested self.

I have discussed the nature of the groups in which children are born and reared, in which they learn a meaning of living and learning, upon which they found their own homes in later years, and which they transmit to or perpetuate in their children. In such intimate groups, interacting individuals absorb a way of life which has a deep emotional effect upon their growing selves. And the nature of or the quality of such interpersonal relations tends to persist in behavior long after the particular life situations with their specific events have been forgotten.

Externalized by culture groups in institutions, these human relations form the operating climate or the psychological fields in which children are reared. Since, for centuries, they have been designated as either authoritarian or cooperative, I have used the former to indicate an external adult-controlled field, a reverse cultural teaching method, an association concept of learning, and an autonomic morality. I have used the latter to direct attention to an internal self-controlled field, a normal biological or cooperative need-experience process, a field theory concept of learning, and a conscious deliberative social morality. Existing cultures are organized in authoritarian fields and produce authoritarian personalities who compete for power, thus promoting in others the arrested development from which they suffer. To raise the maturity level of people, field conditions must change from authoritarian to cooperative, which means a profound reorganization of home, school, and religious life as well as all other major social institutions.

I have discussed in theory and practice in homes and schools the conditions necessary to change authoritarian into cooperative fields, or the environment favorable for discovering, releasing, and guiding the inherited abilities of children toward more mature selves. They must be helped to locate, define, and study their own needs in their own fields with others in organic groups by a cooperative interactive process, where each evaluates his self-selections through group interaction and where quality of learning is determined by the enhancement of the self as revealed by the individual and inferred by others from his behavior.

But adults expect children to grow up exhibiting and outwardly accepting certain specific and general behaviors which

they believe are right and refer to as moral, ethical, or spiritual actions. So I have examined the psychology of the values
which underlies such actions, better to locate differences
between authoritarian and cooperative fields in their origin,
in the method of their transmission to the young, in the way
in which the method of learning affects their use, and in the
probable results of the learning process of each field upon
the maturity of the self. I have concluded that authoritarian
fields tend to produce people with dependent selves, conditioned values, and autonomic morality, while cooperative
fields tend to develop people with independent selves, critically appraised values, and socially intelligent morally. To
mature people, both the values and the process of their transmission to the young must be changed so as to free the
potential self-energy now blocked by conditioned teaching.
And adults must re-examine critically their whole cultural
system of moral and spiritual values in order to approve such
maturing experiences for their children.

I come now to the prognosis—the future look. Near the
close of each year, students invariably ask three questions:
What is the probability that enough individuals will become
the better selves who, by cooperative interaction, release the
functional intelligence necessary to build a better life in a
more favorable world? What is the possibility that enough
individuals have a need to, and can, activate their arrested
inherited creativeness so as to raise their maturity levels?
What is the guarantee that better selves will use their increased maturity to make a better life for everyone, rather
than destroy the culture that produced them?

Obviously, I am unable to answer these questions. But
there seem to be three possible directions of action for the
future. The first is to muddle along meeting life situations
with uncertainty, fear, and anxiety, as people did prior to the
sixteenth century when they first began to catch a faint glim-
mer of the idea of progress and to believe that man could by

thinking direct his culture toward a better life for everyone on this earth. The second is to make minor changes in existing authoritarian fields under the erroneous belief that such fields furnish the conditions for developing the mature people who will create the better world. The third is to change the whole cultural direction, structure, institutional organization, and interpersonal field according to known principles of biological growth, on the assumption that this direction offers the best opportunity for developing the more mature people to make the better world. These three possibilities will now be discussed.

1. By muddling along or failing to manage existing life situations thoughtfully toward constructive social ends, people in some form of culture will survive even though many individuals and some culture groups may be sacrificed. Any form of illness or sickness of individuals, whether it be called mental or organic, always arises out of a diseased environment. To maintain a normal self an individual must live in a healthy environment, even though he may sometimes overcome his illness temporarily under the old diseased conditions. He mobilizes all of his individual energy to pass the crises. The outside forces for a time direct their energy on his behalf. He gathers strength, begins to convalesce, and moves about again with increased optimism, confidence, and courage. But when the energy mobilized for his life preservation recedes to normal and the external environment assumes its old pressure and hurtful effect, he soon finds himself in a new illness more hopeless than the one he survived.

An individual or a culture group may endure a number of such crises until the will to survive is lost and the energy for self-continuance is either unreleased or depleted. Some hardy persons will in the future as in the past survive existing threats to themselves in their present group cultures. But they will merely adapt to new authoritarian alignments in their external environment. Shortly they will face new and more

difficult problems, both within themselves and toward the
world in which they live. Their disturbances have not yet
penetrated deeply enough into themselves to become a need
to study adequately the impinging centers, to locate the
reverse cultural causes, and to recreate in interaction the
biological learning process with which they were born.

Too many individuals and groups both in this country and
abroad are willing to take any action to ease temporarily their
internal tension, regardless of its effect upon their subsequent
behavior. They are either so inadequately disturbed as to
feel that present decisions will have slight effect upon future
behavior or they are so profoundly upset that normal deliberative action is superseded by autonomic responses. And yet
by such conforming or appeasing behavior, many individuals
and groups may survive in authoritarian fields until the
more powerful ones move in for the kill. Those who are
liquidated may not foresee their impending doom and those
who survive may not know what they have destroyed. Very
few if any Romans in the fourth century A.D. realized that
their civilization was crumbling and very few if any of the
barbarians from the North knew that they had overturned the
once mightiest civilization of their times. Few people today
realize that the policies of appeasement, stalemate, and con-
tainment are merely the modern streamlined version of the
muddling along directions of ancient and medieval times.
So the belief that existing individual and group crises will
pass and normal times will be restored is purely a relative
and temporary perception. Authoritarian fields tend to produce crises better to keep the people immature and more
amenable to external controls. At least this has been the history of western civilization up to the moment. So a muddling
direction of action for the future seems inadequate to raise
the level of group interaction so that people may become
better selves.

2. The dominant behavior of adults in all cultures in the

world today is to refine existing authoritarian controls. Individuals do this by rationalizing their autonomically sealed and partially accepted childhood behaviors. Groups do it by regimenting the behavior of individuals while struggling for supremacy against other groups. But prognosis relates to the directional trend of behavior of an individual over a period of years or to that of a culture group over many generations. This is inferred from the process used by one generation to meet its life needs and from that transmitted to the young to become their tendency to action. Adults use and transmit conditioned teaching in aggregate groups, with all of the interpersonal and other environmental concomitants which such authoritarian fields imply. And this conditioned teaching operates in all cultures of the universe, regardless of political, family, educational, or religious organizations. Whatever they name their institutions, the differences are only in degree of authoritarian pressure and the humaneness with which they are applied, or the deference which they give to the life of the individual and the nature of the active morality which they practice.

Yet over the past three thousand years enough loopholes have appeared in such tight cultures for a few people with sufficient energy to use their normal need-experience process to create the new objects, artifacts, and implements which make life more enjoyable yet more precarious, for many of these material creations are a double-edged instrument. They are used to meet the physical demands of life with greater ease and freedom, but when controlled by certain authoritarian individuals they can and almost have destroyed them and their world. So authoritarian methods in authoritarian fields have developed a few individuals who create new material objects which may eventually destroy both their creators and the authoritarian culture which nurtured them.

While these gadgets are being developed people maintain their interpersonal relations by a series of specific responses to life situations developed for an earlier world when no such gadgets were available. For authoritarian institutions always promote and demand such specific responses to keep the masses dependent. Thus the behavior field of individuals becomes bifurcated, for groups develop a cultural lag since they allow the gadgets of civilization to increase rapidly in number, diversity, and complexity, while they maintain the codes of human action relatively unchanged. And the instruments for keeping individuals and groups within accepted traditional codes and values are the emotional seals of the home, the rituals of the churches, and the subject curriculum in the schools. These represent a common purpose with an interlocking relationship of continuous pressure which is difficult for any growing child or maturing adult to combat. Thus the anticipated outcome of present methods to maintain an authoritarian field is for a wider and deeper cultural lag which produces more and greater upsets than the selves of a depressed people can endure. They will demand release of controls, changes in institutions, modifications of social structure, more liberal social values, and greater freedom for self-development. The result will be what it always has been in authoritarian fields. The group in power will be overthrown, a different one will take its place, some concessions will be made, economic conditions especially will be improved. But the old codes of values will be maintained. The same institutions will safeguard them and the same reverse methods of teaching will be used to impress them upon the young. For too few people will understand a better process of life and they will be unable to influence greatly those in power. The traditionalists will organize a new emotional drive to support the old values, when in reality they are the instruments which cause the disability. Thus do an arrested people continue their self-repressions. Making major or minor changes in authoritarian fields offers little hope for raising their maturity.

3. The third and most hopeful direction for the future is to remake the entire authoritarian culture into a cooperative, interactive field. While this is an enormous undertaking, there are many favorable conditions which facilitate such action.

First, increasing numbers of people are breaking with authoritarian tradition. Homes are becoming less dominated by either or both parents. Many individuals are giving only lip service within religious groups dominated by authoritarian creeds and rituals. Parents and educators are studying the effects of formal education upon children and requesting modification of the traditional demands. Paternalistic control of industry is giving way to joint employer-employee management. Psychiatrists are locating the conditions in existing cultures that are incipient causes of mental breakdown. Mental hygienists are making the public aware of the need for and the bases of mental health and vigor. Social psychologists are analyzing the effects of various cultures upon people, pointing out the forces that arrest individual and group development. And of course there is a strong movement to resolve differences among large culture groups through situational analyses, discussions, and deliberative actions.

Second, there are many more loopholes in tight cultures than people know how to use. These can be broadened by those who would change to a cooperative field as well as those who would overthrow existing authorities to place themselves in power. Those who believe in and know how to change field conditions must enter such breaks or accept such opportunities to guide interpersonal relations into a more normal biological process.

Third, as internal cultural and external world crises become more frequent and profound, more individuals question the old methods of dealing with these situations. In every country of the world today, an increasing number of people see the futility of continuing national and international policies based upon the economic, political, educational, and religious values of the past. They are ripe for a new outlook from those who can furnish leadership in a new process more hopeful for achieving the good life here and now.

Fourth, the biological growth process is becoming better known, despite the efforts of some groups to suppress it or to assert that man is superior to it, deriving his learning energy and direction of behavior from outside sources. More people, however, are becoming aware of the reasons why some individuals satisfy their needs by promoting cultural traditions which arose prior to modern investigations into the biology of life.

Fifth, there is an accumulating verbal communication as well as published literature of the success of the need-experience process in individual and group learning, wherever it has really been tried in homes, schools, religious groups, and industry. This wealth of information has not yet been adequately explored, analyzed, or grasped understandingly.

Sixth, the heads of authoritarian institutions or culture groups throughout the world are beginning to see the futility of their existence and the probability of their elimination at some future date. Here are enormous possibilities for those who understand the need-experience process to effect orderly changes toward sounder human relations and a more hopeful outlook for the good life.

But there are also unfavorable conditions which must be considered in any movement to change authoritarian cultural fields into cooperative interactive fields. Three of the most important will be noted.

First, there are persistent efforts of authoritarian groups to control communication better to suppress information or prevent cross-fertilization of meanings and values, thereby promoting inbreeding of autonomic behaviors.

Second, many individuals who have a powerful drive to change field conditions lack understanding of the biological growth process. They want release from hurtful cultural controls. They autonomically grope in new directions and many do develop better learning with small groups. But generally they have not conceptualized the process as a life value to guide their behavior so that they can share it intelligently with others.

Third, those who believe in and use a cooperative field process lack organization for action. To many of them cooperation is the escape from external pressure. It is laissez faire, or everyone for himself. It does not mean a cooperative organization to promote cooperative action. An individual works with others toward common purposes until a group decision for action threatens his egocentric self or goes against his usual patterns of behavior, when he withdraws, alleging infringement of his personal liberties, or, in larger groups, with national sovereignty. Such people believe in cooperative effort on minor matters as a temporary release from damaging authoritarian controls, but they do not accept it as an organized positive movement to remake social conditions for the higher self-maturity of all.

Since the hope for the better life on earth seems to lie in changing the field conditions including ourselves, the question of what can be done to promote such action arises.

As individuals. We can believe in the potential creative capacity of people regardless of their place of origin, color, creed, or economic status. We can accept our own experience and that of others as the basis for all behavior and all improvement in learning or action. We can recognize that when we disparage or reject our experience or that of others we thereby undermine our own selfhood and their integrity. We can locate the level of our arrested development and release the sealed, partially accepted values which keep us there. We can deliberately search for new and different kinds of experience to polarize our psychological field, thereby causing us to make wider and deeper differentiations on higher conceptual levels

of action. We can use the need-experience process as an
approach to and a way of studying all life situations, sharing
it with others to the end that all may benefit thereby. We
can see, feel, accept ourselves in interaction with others,
giving yet receiving, approving yet appraising, guiding yet
following, self-selecting yet reconstructing, always in the
direction of improving the quality of living for the benefit of
all.

As educators. We can believe in children as embodying
the creative potentialities of life. We can accept them as
they are, moving with their inexhaustible energy to become
better selves. We can encourage them to respect their own
experiences as the only basis for their self-development. We
can help them broaden and enrich their environmental relationships better to locate and define their needs. We can
champion the needs of children with all lay groups. We can
set a human climate which promotes a cooperative interactive
field. We can aid children in forming organic groups to see
how they operate and how in them individuals learn to respect yet improve the behavior of everyone. We can help
children understand, accept, and use a need-experience process and conceptualize it in a way appropriate to their age and
experience. We can give them freedom to make decisions yet
accept responsibility for their acts. We can encourage them
openly to self-select and evaluate learnings in relation to
their needs. We can set such an informal, friendly, empathic
atmosphere that the deep, innermost meanings of real selves
will be shared and creatively remade. We can do these things
and many more as educators, whether we work with kindergarten children or college students, for these beliefs and
actions are but aspects of our professional competence.

As citizens. We can individually or in groups help parents
remove hurtful authoritarian controls from their children.
We can advocate, explain, and use the biological process of
learning in all of our community relations. We can help mal-

adjusted children in or out of school find the environment in which to upbuild themselves and recreate their behaviors before they become emotionally fixed. We can become actively interested in and promote the practice of education in schools that exemplify cooperative field relationships. We can search out and expose the exploiters of children everywhere. We can by some of these actions realize that our life is richer and our self-fulfillment is higher. Yet the greatest compensation comes in seeing the younger generation grow to levels of maturity never open to us at their ages.

In conclusion, the prognosis for the future is favorable, even though there may be temporary discouragements. Children are still born with biological creativeness, for cultural attempts to suppress it do not affect their genes. Opportunities for them to understand and use their normal growth process are increasing. The walls of authoritarian institutions are beginning to crack. More top persons realize that their aggregate fields will eventually destroy them, so they are ready to make reasonable and realistic modifications. More parents now understand the damaging effects of their demands upon their children. More teachers are cooperatively managing with children their living together. More employers are using group process with their employees to settle differences of large or small import. More people are accepting real religion as a positive factor in releasing inherited capacity for deliberative action toward higher self-enhancement. Culture groups are beginning to recognize that interdependence in the modern world means the development and use of cooperative intelligence to settle their differences. Better than at any other age in the history of mankind are we able to see the infinite plasticity, the unlimited creativeness, the wonderful emergence, the basic cooperativeness, the common life process of people. These can be used to make the highest ideals and ambitions of man become his daily living.

Life is predicated on hope. Man will always live in hope,

despite personal tragedies, despite wars, despite how he feels
about or what he is permitted to say concerning his leaders,
even though he may believe they are guiding him to destruc-
tion. Man will always believe in the future. Whatever the
present conditions, he will always have faith that the future
will afford him a better life. And man will continue to
struggle for, to cherish, and to achieve freedom. What he has
now is inadequate. His creativeness can be satisfied only with
more opportunity to rediscover, rethink, remake, recreate his
world. But above all, he must realize that mere freedom is
not enough. The exhilaration that comes from breaking with
the old is only a temporary uplift. He must struggle to understand the process of utilizing freedom for his better selfhood
and, through interaction in organic groups, for the higher
development of all. His hope must be a *process* hope. His
freedom must be cooperative interactive freedom. His aspirations must be released energy aspirations. His future lies in
people, free to remake themselves creatively in groups, free
to discover the functional intelligence on which their life purposes rest. Man can, he must, create his better life in a friendly
world.

You and I have a contribution and a responsibility. We can
work with others in every life situation so as to

> Draw back the veil over their eyes
> Lift the curtain which covers their minds
> Break the emotional seals of their childhood years
> Release the capacity with which they are endowed
> Teach them the process of their emerging selves
>
> And thus, bring into being a better world
> Exemplifying the glory of your God, whoever He may be
> Through the human, creative intelligence of Man.

References

ALLEE, W. C., *Cooperation Among Animals,* New York: Henry Schumann, 1951.

ALVAREZ, WALTER, *The Neuroses.* Philadelphia: W. B. Saunders, 1951.

ASH, SOLOMON, *Social Psychology.* New York: Prentice-Hall, 1952.

ASHLEY, MONTAGUE, M. F., *On Being Human.* New York: Henry Schumann, 1951.

BOAS, GEORGE, *Our New Ways of Thinking.* New York: Harper & Brothers, 1930.

BODE, BOYD H., *How We Learn.* Boston: D. C. Heath, 1940.

BOGOSLOVSKY, BORIS, *The Technique of Controversy.* New York: Harcourt, Brace, 1928.

BONNER, HERBERT, *Social Psychology.* Boston: American Book, 1953.

BOWER, W. C., *Moral and Spiritual Values in Education.* Lexington: University of Kentucky Press, 1952.

BRONOSKI, J., *The Common Sense of Science.* Cambridge: Harvard University Press, 1953.

BRUBACHER, JOHN, *A History of the Problems of Education.* New York: McGraw-Hill, 1947.

BRYSON, LYMAN, *The Next America.* New York: Harper & Brothers, 1952.

BUTTS, R. FREEMAN, AND CREMIN, LAWRENCE A., *A History of Education in American Culture.* New York: Henry Holt, 1953.

CANTRIL, HADLEY, *The "Why" of Man's Experience.* New York: Macmillan, 1950.

COBB, STANLEY, *Emotions and Clinical Medicine.* New York: W. W. Norton, 1950.

COREY, STEPHEN M., *Action Research to Improve School Practices.* New York: Bureau of Publications, Teachers College, 1953.

CORNER, GEORGE W., *Ourselves Unborn.* New Haven: Yale University Press, 1944.

COUTU, WALTER, *Emergent Human Nature.* New York: Alfred A. Knopf, 1949.

DAVIS, ELMER, *But We Were Born Free.* New York: Bobbs Merrill, 1954.

DE BROGLIE, LOUIS, *The Revolution in Physics.* New York: The Noonday Press, 1953.

DEWEY, JOHN, *A Common Faith.* New Haven: Yale University Press, 1934.

——— *Logic, The Theory of Inquiry.* New York: Henry Holt, 1938.

DOLL, RONALD C. AND OTHERS, *Organizing for Curriculum Improvement.* New York: Bureau of Publications, Teachers College, 1953.

FRANK, LAWRENCE K., *Nature and Human Nature.* New Brunswick: Rutgers University Press, 1951.

FRANK, MARY AND LAURENCE, *How to Help Your Child in School.* New York: The Viking Press, 1953.

FRANK, PHILLIP, *Relativity—A Richer Truth.* Boston: The Beacon Press, 1950.

FRONDIZI, RISIERI, *The Nature of Self.* New Haven: Yale University Press, 1953.

GHISELYN, BREWSTER, *The Creative Process—A Symposium.* Los Angeles: University of California Press, 1952.

HOOKER, DAVENPORT, *The Prenatal Origin of Behavior.* Lawrence: University of Kansas Press, 1952.

HOMANS, GEORGE C., *The Human Group.* New York: Harcourt, Brace, 1950.

HORNEY, KAREN, *Self-Analysis.* New York: W. W. Norton, 1942.

——— *Neurosis and Human Growth.* W. W. Norton, 1950.

HOSKINS, R. E., *The Biology of Schizophrenia.* New York: W. W. Norton, 1946.

JERSILD, ARTHUR T., *In Search of Self.* New York: Bureau of Publications, Teachers College, 1952.

KELLEY, EARL, AND RASEY, MARIE, *Education and the Nature of Man.* New York: Harper & Brothers, 1952.

KILPATRICK, WILLIAM H., *Philosophy of Education.* New York: Macmillan, 1951.

LECKY, PRESCOTT, *Self-Consistency.* New York: The Island Press, 1945.

LILGE, FREDERICK, *The Abuse of Learning.* New York: Macmillan, 1948.

LINDGREN, HENRY C., *The Art of Human Relations.* New York: Hermitage House, 1953.

MACDONALD, JOHN, *Mind, School and Civilization.* Chicago: University of Chicago Press, 1952.

MAY, ROLLO, *Man's Search for Himself.* New York: W. W. Norton, 1953.

MOORE, RUTH, *Man, Time and Fossils.* New York: Alfred A. Knopf, 1953.

MUSIL, ROBERT, *The Man Without Qualities.* New York: McCann-Coward, 1953.

NESBITT, MARION, *A Public School for Tomorrow.* New York: Harper & Brothers, 1953.

NOAR, GERTRUDE, *Freedom to Live and Learn.* Philadelphia: Franklin Publishing Co., 1948.

OLSON, WILLARD, *Child Development.* Boston: D. C. Heath, 1949.

ORWELL, GEORGE, *Nineteen Eighty-Four.* New York: Harcourt, Brace, 1949.

OTTO, MAX, *Science and the Moral Life.* New York: Mentor Press, 1952.

OVERSTREET, HARRY, *The Mature Mind.* New York: W. W. Norton, 1949.

PLANT, JAMES, *The Envelope.* New York: Commonwealth Fund, 1950.

ROE, ANNE, *A Psychological Study of Physical Scientists.* Provincetown: Journal Press, 1951.

ROGERS, CARL, *Client-Centered Therapy.* New York: Houghton-Mifflin, 1951.

ROUSELMAN, BEULAH, *The Troubled Mind*. New York: The Ronald Press, 1953.

RUGG, HAROLD, *The Teacher of Teachers*. New York: Harper & Brothers, 1952.

SHARP, GEORGE, *Curriculum Development as Re-education of Teachers*. New York: Bureau of Publications, Teachers College, 1951.

SIMPSON, GEORGE G., *The Meaning of Evolution*. New Haven: Yale University Press, 1950.

SINNOTT, E. W., *Cell and Psyche*. Chapel Hill: University of North Carolina Press, 1950.

SNYDER, LAURENCE H., *The Principles of Heredity*. Boston: D. C. Heath, 1951.

SNYGG, DONALD AND COMBS, ARTHUR, *Individual Behavior*. New York: Harper & Brothers, 1949.

STUART, JESSE, *The Thread that Runs so True*. New York: Charles Scribners Sons, 1949.

SYMONDS, PERCIVAL, *The Dynamics of Parent-Child Relationships*. New York: Bureau of Publications, Teachers College, 1947.

TALMADGE, G. KASTEN, *Basic Biology of Man*. New York: Random House, 1952.

THOMPSON, MARY M., *Talk It Out with Your Child*. New York: McGraw-Hill, 1953.

WHYTE, LANCELOT L., *The Unitary Principle in Physics and Biology*. New York: Henry Holt, 1949.

WILLIAMS, ROGER J., *Free and Unequal*. Austin: University of Texas Press, 1953.

Index